Managing Teacher Appraisal an Performance

D0143268

This book deals with the biggest single issue currently facing school managers, how they should appraise the performance of their staff and the implications of this process. Recent government initiatives have brought this matter to the fore and headteachers are now required by law to implement appraisal. This book brings together the latest thinking on the subject and places it directly in the context of school management.

Managing Teacher Appraisal and Performance examines the ways in which various countries have tackled the issue, ranging from the 'hire and fire' approach, to concentrating on professional development. The book includes sections on school leadership, the professional development of teachers and the implications for the future of teacher appraisal and performance. The chapters are written by distinguished international academics, writers and researchers, who report and analyse the significance of their work in the UK, Australia, New Zealand, Canada, South Africa, Singapore and the USA.

This timely and authoritative book is essential reading for headteachers and school managers seeking guidance on the appraisal process.

David Middlewood is Director of School-based Programmes at the University of Leicester's Educational Management Development Unit.

Carol Cardno is Professor of Educational Management and Head of the School of Education at UNITEC Institute of Technology, New Zealand.

Managing Teacher Appraisal and Performance

A Comparative Approach

Edited by David Middlewood
and Carol Cardno

London and New York

First published 2001
by RoutledgeFalmer
11 New Fetter Lane, London EC4P 4EE

Simultaneously published in the USA and Canada
by RoutledgeFalmer
29 West 35th Street, New York, NY 10001

RoutledgeFalmer is an imprint of the Taylor & Francis Group

Typeset in Goudy by Keystroke, Jacaranda Lodge, Wolverhampton
Printed and bound in Great Britain by MPG Books Ltd, Bodmin

British Library Cataloguing in Publication Data
A catalogue record for this book is available from the British Library

Library of Congress Cataloging in Publication Data
Managing teacher appraisal and performance: a comparative
approach/edited by David Middlewood and Carol Cardno.
     p. cm.
   Includes bibliographical references and index.
   1. Teachers Rating of Cross-cultural studies. 2. Teaching Evaluation
Cross-cultural studies. I. Middlewood, David. II. Cardno, Carol E. M.
LB2838 .M35 2001
371.14'4 dc21   2001019244

ISBN 0–415–24221–5 (hbk)
ISBN 0–415–24222–3 (pbk)

Contents

Figures and Tables

Figures

Tables

Contributors

The editors

David Middlewood is Director of School-based Programmes in the Educational Management Development Unit of the University of Leicester, and was previously a secondary school headteacher. He has edited and contributed to volumes on topics such as strategic management, home–school links, curriculum management, recruitment and selection and staff development. He is also co-author of *Practitioner Research in Education: making a difference* (1999). He has published and researched in the field of performance appraisal, in the United Kingdom, New Zealand and South Africa and has acted as consultant to and evaluator of appraisal schemes for various organisations. His book (with Tony Bush) *Managing People in Education* (1997) is a best-selling book on Human Resources in Education and is the set text on HRM in a majority of UK University Masters courses. David is also co-editor of the national journal *Headship Matters*.

Carol Cardno is Professor of Educational Management and Head of the School of Education at UNITEC Institute of Technology, New Zealand. She has a wide experience of teaching in primary, secondary and tertiary sectors. She has also held several school management positions and was principal of a secondary school before establishing an Education Management Centre at UNITEC in 1991. Carol is the author of *Collaborative Management in New Zealand Schools* (1990, Longman Paul) and *Effective Performance Appraisal – Integrating Accountability and Development in Staff Appraisal* (1997, with Eileen Piggot-Irvine, Longman) and several papers on topics related to her research interests which are staff appraisal, organisational learning and teams, collaborative management and management development.

The contributors

Catherine F. Battaglia is Principal of City Honors School in Buffalo, New York, following a period on Special Assignment for the Niagara Falls Board of Education, Niagara Falls, New York, where she has developed and co-ordinated professional development programmes and training for district employees for twelve years. She earned her Ph.D. in Social Foundations from the State University of New York at Buffalo. She also serves as an adjunct professor at Niagara University.

Her research interests revolve around the issues of creating learning communities, promotions, job-embedded staff development using Action Research to link professional development with teacher appraisal, and fostering university and school-based partnerships, which focus on enhancing teacher performance.

Joy Chew is Associate Professor and Head of Policy and Management Studies Academic Group at the National Institute of Education, Nanyang Technological University, Singapore. Her academic background, including her doctorate, is in Sociology of Education. Her research areas are in values education, mentoring as a tool for principalship training and sociology of schooling. She has been involved in the management education of school principals and incumbent heads of departments in Singapore. She has intimate research-based knowledge of the assessment of principals' performance in Singapore and its impact upon the principals' and schools' performance.

Wayne L. Edwards is Associate Professor of Education at Massey University, Palmerston North, New Zealand, where he is responsible for the Master of Educational Administration Programme. A former classroom teacher and teachers college lecturer, his major interests lie in the leadership, culture and improvement which might enhance the work of educational places.

Wayne has held a number of fellowships and appointments for research, teaching and consultancy in different parts of the world – primarily in North America, England and Australia. In 1997, he was a member of the three-person panel appointed by the New Zealand Government to review the nature and work of New Zealand's Education Review Office, leading to the publication *Achieving Excellence*. Wayne is currently a member of the Minister of Education's Working Party charged with reviewing the length of the school year and day in New Zealand.

Professor Edwards is a Fellow of the Commonwealth Council for Educational Administration and Management and a Fellow of the New Zealand Educational Administration Society. In 1995 he received the OBE for his services to education and intercultural programmes.

Tanya Fitzgerald is Associate Professor in the School of Education at UNITEC Institute of Technology, Auckland. She has a varied background in the education sector; as a teacher and Head of Department in secondary schools and as a lecturer in the History and Education Departments at the University of Auckland. Tanya has also held management positions in the corporate sector. Her current teaching is in the area of education management and her research interests are gender issues in education, policy studies, appraisal, governance and management in self-managed schools and the history of women's education. Tanya has presented numerous papers at both national and international conferences, and has examined performance appraisal in both educational and business contexts.

Lawrence Ingvarson is Head of the Division for Teaching and Learning with the Australian Council for Educational Research. He is also a member of a Ministerial Advisory Committee to establish a professional body for teachers. Before that, he was Associate Professor in the Faculty of Education at Monash University, Melbourne, Australia. Lawrence has worked extensively in Australia and the USA on reforms to teacher career structures and pay systems. His main interest is in teachers' professional development, as well as the development of schools as learning communities. He carried out research for the introduction of the Advanced Skills Teacher in Australia and has recently edited a book based on the work of the National Board since it was established in 1987.

Stephen L. Jacobson is Professor of Educational Administration in the Department of Educational Leadership and Policy at the State University of New York at Buffalo (UB). He earned his Ph.D. in Educational Administration from Cornell University in 1986. His research interests include the reform of school leadership preparation and practice, and such matters of school finance and personnel as teacher compensation, staff development and employee absence.

Jacobson's most recent books include: *School Administration: Persistent Dilemmas in Preparation and Practice* (Praeger 1996) and *Transforming Schools and Schools of Education: A New Vision for Preparing Educators* (Corwin 1998), and he received the MCB University Press 1998 Literati Club 'Highly Commended' Award for his article 'The inclusive school: Integrating diversity and solidarity through community-based management' in the *Journal of Educational Administration*, 1997.

In 1994 he was awarded the University Council on Educational Administration's Jack Culbertson Award for outstanding contributions to the field of educational administration. He is currently Director of UB's Centre for Continuing Professional Education and President of the American Education Finance Association.

Kenneth Leithwood is Professor of Educational Administration and Director, Centre for Leadership Development at OISE/University of Toronto. Specialising in the areas of leadership and educational change, his most recent books include *Changing Leadership for Changing Times* (Open University Press) and *Organisational Learning in Schools* (edited with K.S. Louis, published by Swets and Zeitlinger). He is the senior editor of the recent *International Handbook of Educational Leadership and Administration* (Kluwer). Kenneth Leithwood is one of the most respected writers on educational leadership in the world. His books and articles are widely published internationally and he has lectured in many countries.

Shamella Ramnarain is Head of Department in Asoka Secondary School in Durban, South Africa, and completed her Masters in Education in 1999. She has both practical and research-based experience of research into teacher appraisal.

Michael Thurlow is Professor of Educational Management at the University of Natal, Durban, South Africa, where formerly he was Dean of the Faculty of Education and Head of the Department of Education. During 1996 he served as a member of the national Minister of Education's Task Team on Education Management Development and during 1997 served as a consultant in the same Minister's Interim Unit for Education Management Development. He served during the same period as the South African liaison person for the national component of the Canada–South Africa Education Management programme and currently is strategic planning consultant to the Kwazulu Natal Department of Education and Culture. He is a co-ordinator, with Professor Tony Bush, for the Partnership for Research and Development between the University of Leicester's EMDU and the University of Natal, which has led to education management publications in South Africa, where Michael has published widely.

John West-Burnham is Professor of International Leadership at the University of Hull. He worked in secondary modern, grammar and comprehensive schools and in further and adult education for fifteen years and was Principal Lecturer in In-Service Education Crewe and Alsager College, Cheshire for five years. He then became Development Officer, Cheshire LEA for two years, responsible for appraisal and management development and followed this with two years as Director of the Distance Learning MBA in Educational Management, University of Leicester. He joined the University of Lincolnshire and Humberside in 1995 as Professor of Educational Leadership, and the University of Hull in 2000.

John is author of *Managing Quality in Schools* (1992, 1997) and co-author of *Effective Learning in Schools* (1997) and of *The Appraisal Handbook* (1994). His research and writing interests include learning and school improvement, effective leadership and quality management in education. He is currently researching the processes by which educational leaders learn to be effective and is writing *Leadership for Learning* to be published by Routledge. John has worked with a large number of schools, LEAs and professional bodies in Britain and has also worked in Australia, New Zealand, South Africa, USA and Israel.

Acknowledgements

The editors' grateful thanks go to a number of people: Justina Erculj of the National Leadership School of Slovenia for the paper submitted to us; Samantha Sarris and Michalis Benudakis for their help with research into Greek teacher appraisal practice; Philip Middlewood and Philip Harris for their help with research into non-educational sectors; Hilary Morris for her help with diagrams in Chapters 9 and 12; Christopher Bowring-Carr for compiling the index; and Jacqui Middlewood for her support throughout the work on this book.

Finally, the book probably would not have been completed without the unflinching support and expertise of Felicity Murray at Leicester University's EMDU. We owe her a great deal indeed.

Preface

The catalyst for this book was a joint research project in New Zealand (kindly funded by the British Council of New Zealand) between the Educational Management Development Unit of the University of Leicester and the School of Education of UNITEC, Auckland. This involved a visit by David Middlewood to Auckland in September/October 1998, during which he and Carol Cardno worked together on research and teaching. We had both had an active involvement in teacher appraisal in our two countries and had published on the topic. More significantly, both of us had argued that appraisal of the performance of teachers could only be effective if:

- it addressed the issue of a balance between the need for accountability and for professional development;
- it was managed in the context of the whole process of how teachers are managed as people in the school; and
- its success depended upon the success of the leaders and managers at individual school level in ensuring that national schemes were seen as relevant, and adapted to those individual contexts.

Through conferences, visits and other contacts (with school principals, headteachers, teachers and academics), we were also aware of the significance of the issue in a number of countries. Under a variety of descriptions – teacher assessment, teacher evaluation, appraisal – the question of how teachers could be helped, persuaded, encouraged or even 'forced' to perform effectively, and to improve where that performance was below expectations, was one to which the answer was being sought in a wide variety of contexts. As we explore in Chapter 1, the cultural, historical and political contexts inevitably play significant parts in seeking any answers.

Both New Zealand and the United Kingdom have adopted the terms 'performance' and 'performance management' to apply to teachers in schools, terms taken of course from the world of business and industry, a fact which is not necessarily likely to endear them to teachers anyway!

In presenting practice in this area from a number of countries, based on practice and research by distinguished writers and workers in the field, we in no way claim this book as any kind of extensive survey. Such a survey would inevitably run the risk of being both superficial and descriptive. Rather, we have been concerned to present studies from key countries, based on the research and experience of academics and practitioners, which illustrate some of the most important aspects of teacher performance and appraisal from which school managers may learn. Certainly, in the United Kingdom, with the new emphasis on performance management for teachers, these studies have a special relevance at this time.

In our first chapter we have outlined this relevance and importance and tried to identify some of the issues faced by leaders and managers. Thereafter, the book is in three parts. Part I focuses on school headteachers and principals, both from the point of view of examining their own performance and appraisal and also something of their role in the process as far as others are concerned.

Part II presents some of the issues involved in performance appraisal of teachers in studies from four different countries. A common theme is the extent to which teacher development can or should be part of an effective management process in this field. All the studies agree that it should, but the influence of different contexts, previous experience, and political initiatives is shown clearly through the different experiences.

Part III looks at some aspects of the future of this field, including an examination of addressing the dilemmas facing leaders, a query as to whether performance appraisal is as important as assessment for career progression and, finally, an attempt to predict some future trends and identify points which will be of value to managers.

This last point is for us, and all the contributors, the ultimate purpose of a book such as this. Effective leaders and managers are those who seek to understand and clarify the concepts and issues involved in a topic such as teacher performance and appraisal, and then adapt and apply these to their individual circumstances, never losing sight of the person for whom their effective management is ultimately intended – the school learner.

The project of this book has been stimulating and demanding and we are above all extremely grateful to all the contributors for their work. All chapters were specially commissioned for this book.

David Middlewood and Carol Cardno
December 2000

Abbreviations

AJHR	Appendices to the Journals of the House of Representatives (N.Z.)
ANC	African National Congress
APR	Annual Performance Review
AR	Action Research
BARS	Behaviourally Anchored Rating System
DfEE	Department for Education and Employment
ELRC	Education Labour Relations Council
EPU	Education Policy Unit
ERO	Education Review Office
IiE	Industry into Education
ITIP	Instructional Theory into Practice
LPSH	Leadership Programme for Serving Heads
MoE	Ministry of Education
NAG	National Administrative Guideline
NBPTS	National Board for Professional Teaching Standards
NPQH	National Professional Qualification for Headship
NZ	New Zealand
NZPPTA	New Zealand Post-Primary Teachers' Association
OECD	Organisation for Economic and Cultural Development
OFSTED	Office for Standards in Education
PGP	Professional Growth Plan
PPM	Principal Performance Management
PRP	Performance Related Pay
SA	South Africa
SADTU	South African Democratic Teachers' Union
SBM	Site-Based Management
SDT	Staff Development Team
SES	Socio-Economic Status
STA	School Trustees Association
TRB	Teacher Registration Board
TTA	Teacher Training Agency

Chapter 1

The significance of teacher performance and its appraisal

David Middlewood and Carol Cardno

The context of the growing importance of education

In the last quarter of the twentieth century, an increasing consensus developed concerning the link between economic prosperity and the effectiveness of a country's education provision. As globalisation gathered pace dramatically in the 1980s and 1990s, this link became more overt as the comparison and competitiveness between nations inevitably increased. At the heart of the argument for the link is the need for an educated workforce, without which a country's economy will not keep pace. This has been equally clear in the established western countries and the emerging Asian 'tiger' economies of the 1980s and 1990s. What is meant by an 'educated workforce' will necessarily differ but central to the production of this clearly lies the quality of teaching and learning in a nation's schools, colleges and universities.

These two factors at the macro international level – the emphasis on comparisons and competitiveness and on the quality of teaching and learning – have been reflected within many countries. The concern of governments in countries whose practice is described in this book, has been increasingly with comparisons between schools. This has been accompanied by the international movement towards schools' self-governance and self-management, leading to the conflict, real or potential, between the laudable desire to raise standards for all school students and the influence of the marketisation upon schools. This latter influence has led to intense debate in countries such as New Zealand, the United Kingdom, USA, and Canada about the disadvantaging of certain students, especially in urban areas, caused by resource allocation.

All this is very familiar but the significance for teaching and learning and consequently for any assessment of teacher performance is that comparisons and competitiveness inevitably have meant that governments have placed the emphasis upon education *outcomes*, such as proficiency in literacy and numeracy, examination results, test scores, and numbers of students continuing beyond statutory schooling. The significance of these is that outcomes have to be seen to be measurable, because only in measurable outcomes can comparisons be visibly made. This emphasis on the measurable brings with it a considerable risk. As Preedy (2000: 95) suggests:

> Many of the most valuable outcomes of education are multi-dimensional, complex and long term. . . . By focusing on measuring outcomes against pre-specified objectives, the product evaluation model ignores unplanned outcomes, and fails to explore the value and worth of the prescribed objectives and purposes. There is also a tendency to de-emphasise contextual factors . . .

None of this is any argument against teachers and schools needing to be accountable. Clearly they have to be accountable in a visible way, both to the students and parents whom they serve and to the taxpayer for the considerable sums invested in education. Any system of performance and its appraisal in education must capture this essential requirement and, later in this chapter, we examine this in detail.

Preedy's comment captures the essence of a potential dilemma in the assessment of teachers' performance. If the emphasis in an educational system is on measurable outcomes and schools are deemed successes or failures according to those outcomes, then effective teaching will be seen as that which achieves those outcomes. The temptation therefore is for national bodies to promulgate a model of teaching which lends itself to this and to appraise teachers accordingly. In the UK, the model of effective teaching as presented by the OFSTED Framework of Inspection of Schools (OFSTED, 1997), and against which teachers' lessons were formally graded during one-off inspections, was widely criticised, not because it was an invalid model but because it was presented as the *only* model. It was above all an outcomes model because the inspection model of the UK in the 1990s was itself essentially one concerned with inspecting schools' attainments.

The complexity of assessment of teaching

The question of defining good teaching has concerned educationalists and academics for some considerable time. As Kyriacou (1986) postulated, perceptions of teaching depend upon philosophical premises anyway – is it a craft, an art, a science for example? The debates about the 'deskilling' of teachers (Ozga 1995) and whether teachers are professionals (Hoyle 1995) simply illustrate the complexity further. However, even if a model based upon measurable outcomes is assumed for the purposes of appraising the effectiveness or otherwise of a teacher's performance, the issue of *context* remains a complicating factor.

Much of the issue of context that is relevant here is related to the extent to which schools are held responsible for the success or otherwise of their students. Stoll and Myers (1998: 9), draw attention to the distinct difference between the majority of countries who refer to 'failure of pupils' and a few who talk in terms of 'school failure'. Where school failure is emphasised, external context has low consideration and school managers and teachers are criticised for having low expectations of pupils. The school improvement literature has come to acknowledge the significance of the context of schools. Stoll and Reynolds (1997: 31) recognise that: 'What is needed is knowledge of specific factors that will generate improvement for particular schools in particular socioeconomic and cultural contexts.'

The issue for assessing the performance of teachers who work in schools in very different contexts and situations is that it reveals the inadequacy of any single narrow model of appraisal, especially one focused upon measurable outcomes. Any list of criteria of effective teaching will be perceived as unfair when it is linked to required outcomes which can be affected so significantly by factors outside the teacher's and indeed the school's control. Thrupp (1999: 157) says that:

> A nationally consistent list of attributes of quality or competent teachers is likely to remain elusive. Rather, contextual differences related to student composition will have to be carefully considered if we are at all serious about assessing teachers fairly.

Thrupp goes on to make the important point that even if a value-added approach is able to take account of individual differences between students, teachers working in disadvantaged school contexts will 'inevitably appear inferior because of additional difficulties related to the *group* characteristics of their students' (ibid.).

For the managers of teacher performance and its appraisal, Thrupp's (1999) own study of schools in Wellington, New Zealand, illustrated some of the contextual issues beyond the manager's control. For example, a school in a prosperous area with powerful parental support attracted a good field of applicants for advertised teaching posts. In that situation, where teachers were under-performing, rigorous action could be taken. In less advantaged schools, whilst managers would not tolerate incompetence and were equally ready to start competency procedures where appropriate, there was less scope for action since:

> Not only were they limited in this time they could spend on competency procedures, but they often struggled to find good staff in any case. . . . Senior staff . . . were aware that some staff were ineffectual but consoled themselves that such teachers were valuable to the school in other ways.
>
> (Thrupp 1999: 114–15)

It can also be argued that what it means to be an effective teacher will actually be quite different in different contexts. So that, in contrasting the most successful teachers in a working-class school with those in a school in an affluent area, Thrupp (1999: 130) claimed that success was achieved in quite different ways. In the working-class school:

> the most successful teachers were those who took a highly structured role which could create controlled classroom environments. . . . In this sense they

were 'trainers'. An emphasis on motivation / discipline and structured learning tasks seemed to be necessary.

In contrast, at the advantaged school, the most successful teachers 'were those who took a low-key role by providing the necessary stimulus material or discussion starters that allowed students to learn independently' (ibid.).

Even if it is true that 'gifted teachers create excellence almost regardless of what is going on around them' (OECD 1997: 21) no system of appraising performance can rely for its basis on such a serendipitous view. If a single system based on measurable outcomes is deficient, similarly a generalised list of qualities of the 'good' teacher has only limited value. Lists such as those of Hopkins *et al.* (1994), OECD (1997), Ramsay and Oliver (1998) incorporate qualities such as intelligence, commitment, compassion, sense of humour, determination, etc. These are critically important in understanding the nature of teachers and teaching but are relatively unhelpful to managers of performance appraisal. To our knowledge, no one has ever successfully 'assessed' a sense of humour, for example!

Nevertheless, these lists of qualities draw attention to the vitally important point that a measurable outcomes only assessment model ignores, i.e. that teachers are not automatons. Teachers are persons with emotions, aspirations, and need for self-esteem; and their success in their jobs will depend upon the extent to which these are successfully channelled. This is true of most occupations, but is particularly so in jobs such as teaching where relationships with others are at the core of effectiveness (in their case with the students). The issue therefore of how teachers are personally and professionally developed is central to their performance and therefore of the appraisal of that performance.

The performance management context

If the management of performance may be seen as having at least three key ingredients for the employee:

- knowing what is required to be done;
- receiving guidance, support and challenge when required;
- receiving regular feedback about progress and achievement

then managing the professional development of those employees is crucial particularly to the second of these and forms the key part of the regular cycle of target-setting, implementing, reviewing, feeding back, and taking new action.

As various chapters in this book show, practice in different countries varies according to the emphasis placed upon accountability or upon the professional development of teachers. Thus systems of performance appraisal may be seen as existing on a simple continuum (Figure 1.1), according to where the emphasis lies.

As writers such as Day (1996) and Middlewood (1997) have argued, professional development can be as affected by individual school context as the quality of

| Emphasis on assessing performance outcomes | Emphasis on teachers' professional development |

Figure 1.1 Continuum of emphasis in systems of performance appraisal.

teaching and, similarly, no one simplistic model of professional development could provide for all teachers. Missing ingredients seen as essential to the development of certain teachers will not be met by any one recipe of training and may only be provided perhaps by school leaders and managers offering a culture within which development opportunities occur. For school headteachers/principals themselves, O'Neill (2000: 8), has drawn attention to 'The missing professional standards' of 'Ethics and social justice' in the current appraisal of principals, whilst West-Burnham in Chapter 2 of this book suggests that some elements of leadership, as opposed to management, cannot be instilled through training courses.

Any acknowledgement that teachers have personal and professional needs as well as being employees who produce outcomes has to recognise also one other factor. In common with certain other occupations (commonly and sometimes unhelpfully known as the 'caring' professions), teachers have strong beliefs and values concerned with the work they do. *Most* teachers believe not just in teaching but in the value of education itself, as a 'force for good'. This is a belief that education can have a transformational influence upon the young people in the system, and that there are many invisible elements to this, of which class lessons form one – a critically important one but not the only element. Middlewood (1997: 183) has described the tension between this 'transformational' aspect of education and the 'transactional' aspect of lessons as being necessary to acknowledge in any appraisal of teacher performance. The reason that we draw attention to this is twofold:

1   By recognising the importance of education, teachers need to accept (and there is evidence in this book that most do) the need to be accountable in the work they do.
2   Their belief in education being more than measurable results suggests that it is essential to acknowledge their worth as people by developing their self-esteem, motivation, etc. as described above.

This second point is often brought out in work done on students' perceptions of teachers who acknowledge not only efficiency (e.g. in preparing them for examinations) but fairness, ability to motivate, and similar qualities.

In reconciling any tension between the need for accountability and for professional development, any system of performance and its appraisal ideally needs to address ways of managing this tension. In the next section of this chapter, we examine the context for performance appraisal in particular and explore the notions of teacher accountability and development.

Different purposes of performance appraisal

New Zealand schools illustrate well the situation of those that have now been struggling for a decade to implement effective appraisal systems that serve several purposes simultaneously. This struggle is compounded by the fact that in an integrated system, the dual purposes of appraisal must be met at several levels as Table 1.1 shows. The multi-level purposes of appraisal are related to accountability and development at the level of the education system, the organisation, and the individual at both a professional and personal level.

Table 1.1 Multi-level purposes of appraisal systems

Levels	Purposes	
EDUCATION SYSTEM	Accountability School review and audit	Development Improving the quality of teaching
ORGANISATION	Charter goals	School improvement
INDIVIDUAL Professional	Management decisions	Performance improvement
INDIVIDUAL Personal	Professional responsibility	Self-reflection and improvement

The challenge is heightened further when these needs are expected to be met at both the organisational and the individual level. Appraisal invariably exacerbates the essential dilemma faced by leaders which, as Beare *et al.* (1989) assert, is a concern for meeting the needs of the organisation and a concern for relationships between individuals.

Attempts to separate these dimensions of appraisal and attend to them in isolation from one another have not succeeded in education in the past. It is contended here that such polarised approaches will not succeed in the future either. To manage a performance appraisal system effectively it is necessary to understand the complexity inherent in appraisal system development and in the interpersonal dynamics that dominate the implementation of these systems. What is needed is a reframing of the demands of appraisal activity in a human resource format (Bolman and Deal 1997) to highlight the particularly difficult dimensions that need to be confronted and made part of an ongoing dialogue in an integrated approach.

An integration of accountability and developmental impulses in a performance appraisal system offers considerable possibilities for the organisation to make links between strategic intent, staff performance, the achievement of effective educational outcomes for students, and the development and training staff need to meet professional and strategic objectives. However, this potential cannot be realised unless several hurdles are recognised and overcome. This is not easy because:

- there is a need to consider what the individual wants from performance and his or her appraisal and what the school wants;
- there is a need to balance accountability concerns with concern for the development of the individual;
- there is a need to examine the many and varied concepts of accountability in education settings in order to appreciate the demands of this expectation;
- there is a need to establish processes so that the appraisal of a person's performance can identify development needs and inform development outcomes; and
- there is a need to link individual development objectives to team goals and ultimately to the strategic goals of the organisation.

These prevailing tensions are examined below in relation to the accountability versus the development challenge and the individual versus organisation challenge.

The accountability versus the development challenge

In countries where self-management is well developed, schools must now make their own management decisions about the quality of teaching and learning and how this can be improved. The quality of the personnel information managers have makes a big difference to the effectiveness of the decisions they make. Whether these are decisions about the teaching, or the management of staffing, or a professional development plan, it is necessary to know how staff are performing in order to determine what might actually need to be improved. This is a matter of accountability from one particular perspective.

Kelly (1987: 215) makes this perspective of accountability clear when he says:

> Accountability, as was well appreciated by the ancient Greeks, is an essential element of democracy – an element which is too little evident in present day versions of democracy. And some form of evaluation or appraisal of performance is clearly its base. Thus, in the context of schooling, teachers along with all others responsible for educational planning and provision, must expect to be required to give an account of their attempts to meet their responsibilities, and some procedures of evaluation of appraisal must be instituted to assess the degree of their success or failure. Furthermore, without some kind of evaluation it is difficult to see what basis might exist for any real development either of the curriculum or of the teachers themselves. For a prerequisite of improvement must be some evaluation of previous performance.

In implementing this kind of accountability the view most often taken by staff in schools is that:

- they show that they are accountable by being appraised against documented expectations;
- that participation in the process (which usually involves observation of practice, feedback, self-appraisal and a formal review interview) is a commitment to being accountable;
- that the reports of this process lodged with the principal / headteacher are a record of accountability; and
- that accountability includes a commitment to agreed improvement strategies in areas identified by the appraisal process.

Another perspective of accountability is presented in the work of Timperley and Robinson (1998: 164) who have examined in their research the failure of New Zealand schools to implement appraisal policy in ways that meet both its accountability and development requirements. These authors draw a distinction between two types of accountability, democratic accountability and professional accountability. They argue that 'Performance appraisal systems in most New Zealand schools reflect professional rather than democratic forms of accountability.'

Whilst Kelly's (1987) view of accountability stems from a 'democratic' impulse, it lends itself to a 'professional' approach to accountability where members of the profession are the people who engage in the evaluation of co-professionals. The version of democratic accountability postulated by Timperley and Robinson is a much more demanding form of accountability to external stakeholders at both state and community levels. Furthermore, this version of accountability appears to widen the gap between rendering accounts of performance and the provision of professional development which, in an integrated approach to appraisal, are two sides of the same coin. Whilst not eschewing the need to achieve accountability to external stakeholders, the potential of the integrated approach rests on a close connection between those to whom one is accountable and those who resource development.

Heightening accountability

This heightened form of democratic accountability (based on Strike's (1990) descriptions of models of legitimate authority over the evaluation of teachers) makes individuals liable to a review undertaken in the nature of democratic control. One form of this is *bureaucratic democracy* which is closely identified with legislated control and is exercised, in New Zealand and the UK for example, through central curriculum controls exerted by the government ministries and by national inspection agencies against accountability standards. A second form, called *communitarian democracy*, allows for a high level of participation in decision-making by key stakeholders in education – the teachers, parents and students. New Zealand schools and UK schools are required to render accounts on two fronts: to state bureaucracies such as the Ministry and the Inspectorate and to their local community representatives – the Boards of Trustees/Governors.

Professional accountability, characterised by self-regulating, self-disciplined collective responsibility for professional practice is seen to be in conflict with democratic accountability. Timperley and Robinson (1998: 164) assert that:

> According to Strike (1990), this definition of professionalism is undemocratic because it legitimates teacher expertise rather than democracy as the source of authority for public schooling. We agree with Strike that although teachers must have sufficient operational autonomy to undertake their role, the tension between democratic control and professionalism should not be resolved by ignoring accountability to legitimate democratic authorities. School managers should exercise sufficient hierarchical control to enable them to report relevant information on the quality of teaching and learning in the school to community and state agencies.

The Timperley and Robinson (1998) research in New Zealand shows that principals are not prepared to meet this communitarian democratic obligation under the umbrella of accountability. Schools have no choice in meeting bureaucratic accountability. In addition, for many schools even professional forms of accountability are not being met.

This confirms a belief that school leaders are inordinately challenged by the tension between teacher autonomy, teacher trust of the confidentiality of performance appraisal systems and the demand that they report information to those outside and even those within the formal hierarchies that exist in schools. Schools will need a special kind of assistance to grapple with the complexities of reconciling the demands of communitarian democratic accountability with its requirements for information with the demands of staff for assurance that their performance is managed and appraised in a climate of confidentiality and trust.

This dilemma challenges the reconciliation of an organisational need to meet public accountability requirements (beyond those of internal management accountability) and a concern with meeting the needs of the individual to work in a secure developmental ethos of performance management and its appraisal.

Appraisal in a performance management framework

It could be argued that the business model of *performance management* proposed in some countries has created a managerial focus that emphasises the structural aspects of a system that integrates far more than professional accountability and professional development. Performance management, according to Rudman (1999) encompasses a wide and complex range of activity spanning entry to and exit from an organisation. The breadth of this concept, which locates appraisal and development as central elements, is shown below.

Performance management elements

- strategic personnel management;
- operational personnel management;
- the recruitment, selection and appointment of staff;
- the remuneration of staff;
- the induction and initial monitoring of staff;
- the appraisal of staff;
- the professional development of staff;
- the promotion and reward of staff;
- the discipline of staff;
- the dismissal of staff;
- the exit of staff from the organisation.

It could be argued that in many schools in New Zealand the appraisal processes intended to have a significant development aspect have been captured to meet managerial accountability purposes to the detriment of the professional account-ability that lies at the heart of effective appraisal.

Setting priorities in a staff development programme is an essential task for school managers who wish to align individual and organisational goals and to make the best use of limited resources. Staff need to know clearly what the strategic priorities for school development are and how they can contribute to them. Individual needs should be catered for in a framework of knowledge and commitment to school-wide goals. As Middlewood (1997: 176) states: 'There is a need to incorporate appraisal of individual performance much more clearly into institutional development planning and staff development policies and programmes.'

Identifying school-wide and individual professional development needs, and making planned provision to meet them, are the responsibility of schools. To introduce or to improve performance and appraisal practice puts a spotlight on current professional development practices. This is undoubtedly the case in systems that purport to meet both accountability and development goals for the organ-isation and for individuals in the organisation.

It is clear that the wheel has begun to turn in favour of accountability being the main driver of appraisal. This was not evident in the middle of the last decade when 'soft forms' of appraisal, resting mainly on selling it as non-threatening, non-judgemental activity were in evidence as the favoured approach (Cardno 1995; Peel and Inkson 1993; Middlewood in Chapter 9 of this book). Teachers were 'sold' appraisal systems on the basis that they were developmental, only to find that sometime later demands for accountability had arisen and very often overtaken the system so that development became an 'add-on' rather than the 'other side of the coin'.

Five years down the track, in both New Zealand and the UK, many schools are now advised to meet a new accountability demand that requires attestation of staff ability to demonstrate minimum competence standards at various career levels to move over salary bars by adding this purpose to appraisal policy.

Thus one can see yet another perspective of accountability as the heavy weight on the appraisal balance scale, tipping the fundamental purpose of performance appraisal towards a control and regulation focus rather than an improvement and developmental focus. This happens when the appraisal system itself is utilised to manage the promotion and reward of staff, to introduce performance pay, and to deal with minimum competency concerns.

Piggot-Irvine (2000) goes as far as to say that the emphasis on accountability in the New Zealand performance appraisal system is contributing to greater control of teachers because it leads to:

- the avoidance of assembling objective evidence;
- the stigmatising of appraisal's failure in this context as another 'Ministry failure'; and
- the marginalisation of the developmental aspect of appraisal.

Losing sight of the fundamental benefit of appraisal

Several authors argue that appraisal's most critical benefit for the individual is that it creates opportunity for dialogue about performance based on observation and reflection on practice (Cardno and Piggot-Irvine 1997; Hutchinson 1997; Middlewood 1997). Hence, the giving and receiving of feedback is fundamental and the purpose is to focus on *performance* with the aim of achieving stretch or challenge. Ideally, feedback builds a platform for launching possibilities for development. This implies that the most important appraisal activity is inter-personal and not technical. When technical purposes overtake the improvement purposes we find that the appraisal processes may be honed down to become just a mechanism for check-listing that minimum criteria have been met so that staff can be allocated a performance pay bonus or move to the next level on the pay scale.

The organisational versus individual challenge

Whilst the basic conflict that arises between human personality and the way in which organisations are constructed and managed was recognised by early human resource theorists (Argyris, 1976), the tension between meeting organisational needs and meeting the needs of individuals is no less evident in today's organisation. This fundamental dilemma for leaders, which is the need to be concerned about meeting the goals of the organisation and concern for maintaining positive collegial relationships, is exacerbated in the context of managing staff performance and its appraisal. It is this dilemma that creates the greatest challenge for those who need to manage the appraisal of professional colleagues.

When appraisal activity is intended to meet a number of purposes, the potential for conflict to emerge is exponentially greater. For example, a primary form of conflict emerges from the different sets of goals that the organisation and individuals might have for the performance appraisal process. The organisation might hold the view that staff appraisal and development is intended to link to strategic initiatives so that the work of the organisation is aligned and staff are committed to development that impacts on the achievement of organisation goals. Staff might have very different expectations of the appraisal process which could be seen as a form of positive reinforcement, affirmation and a means for identifying development needs in a supportive and constructive environment. Conversely, staff might view appraisal as a way of seeking acknowledgement directly related to reward or career progression. These disparate views of appraisal purposes are one manifestation of the organisation versus individual tension. Managers can address this conflict by being open about multiple purposes and by clarifying policy and procedure to show how various purposes that are intended to meet the needs of both the organisation and the individuals are to be met. In integrated appraisal systems, where the manager is often likely to be the evaluator and the developer of colleagues, it is essential to articulate clearly the dual purposes: the accountability demand – required of both the organisation and the individual professional – and the development intent which has to be both a school-wide strategic focus and a focus on individual staff who have to be motivated to meet growth and self-actualisation needs (Rudman 1999).

What has happened in New Zealand is that the accountability edge and thus the organisational demands of performance appraisal have insidiously been increased to a level where performance appraisal has been described in contradictory terms. The Ministry of Education (1997: 1) guidelines for performance appraisal stated that: 'Timely dialogue and feedback between teachers and principals will help ensure schools meet goals and objectives.' And also that: 'The professional growth of every teacher is a vital component of effective performance management and directly benefits all students.'

The Ministry of Education document (1999: 48) prescribing the integration of Performance Standards in appraisal, defines performance appraisal as:

> Annual assessment of an individual's performance against the professional standards and the tasks or objectives set or agreed at the beginning of the cycle in the written statement of performance expectations, including development objectives.

And at the same time confirms that the professional standards are linked to teachers' pay progression (p. 11).

Leaders in New Zealand schools are in no doubt that because appraisal is one essential component of a performance management system now required in all schools, it is the pivotal process for evaluating performance, improving performance and rewarding performance. Centrally driven policy is consistently and incrementally 'upping the ante' in relation to the accountability demands of appraisal systems. But are they making a difference?

Ultimately, if appraisal is to move from the structural level (where policy and procedural compliance are measures of implementation success) to the inter-personal effectiveness level (where the ability of appraiser and appraisee to engage in open and honest dialogue about performance becomes paramount) then interpersonal skills are critical. Managers of appraisal will be the key players in taking the challenges beyond the system establishment level to the system implementation level and beyond this to the level of institutionalising practice that could make a difference (Fullan 1991).

Managing appraisal dilemmas – issues for performance managers

The expectations now held of New Zealand principals, and other managers in the school who appraise staff, create the greatest challenge at the point where they must mesh the needs of the organisation with the needs to maintain positive collegial relationships with teachers whilst implementing change that is intended to impact upon the quality of learning and teaching. New competencies are demanded which go far beyond the administration or management of the technical aspects of personnel management such as recruitment, induction, teacher regis-tration, budgeting for professional development and the setting up of appraisal systems and procedures. It is in the realm of interpersonal effectiveness that the need for new competencies is surfacing, especially those skills associated with effective implementation and institutionalisation of norms related to practice in managing performance and its appraisal. Chapter 10 of this book explores the possibilities for training in this area.

External factors affecting the effectiveness of performance appraisal systems

Although we have argued in the preceding sections that it is essential and also possible to integrate the need for accountability and fulfil professional develop-ment needs, the reality is that actual practice in a country will be affected by a number of factors. Three of these are briefly considered here.

Culture and tradition

Under this heading, we may include aspects such as the general standing or esteem in which teachers are held in the particular society. This of course may well change over a period of time but it is undeniable that public attitudes towards how people in an occupation are assessed are influenced by the status that occupation is accorded in the first place. There is certainly an increasing demand for openness and accountability at all levels in many societies, but the issue of how trustworthy people are remains important. The relationship therefore between teachers and parents who entrust their children, as it varies according to different cultures, may affect attitudes towards ideas of a 'good' or 'poor' teacher. Denmark, for example, has a tradition of home, school and community coherence which encourages trust of teachers, whilst the USA's and UK's recent practice places parents more in the role of consumers, with consequent demands for visible evidence of competence (OECD 1997).

Another aspect worth mentioning is the relative power and influence of the teaching profession or teaching unions in particular countries. In Japan (OECD 1997) and in Israel (Yariv 2000), unions have considerable influence and in the latter object to any increase in the power of the school principal to evaluate staff for promotion purposes.

Previous history of teacher appraisal

There is no doubt that, as suggested in the continuum of Figure 1.1, a range of practice exists, and equally that this practice is affected by previous practice. In the UK (Chapter 9), current practice is affected by the previous system being seen to have been ineffective and the initial system was undoubtedly affected by the pilot schemes used. In a new country, such as the Republic of South Africa (Chapter 7), the current practice is a clear reaction against an autocratic mode of evaluation that operated during the apartheid regime. In countries such as Slovenia, a newly created independent state, or Greece (Chapter 12), the situation where teacher observation or assessment exists 'on paper' but has become little used in practice, makes it difficult for managers to change a system or indeed to attempt to implement properly the existing one. Millman and Darling-Hammond (1990) noted that considerable actions in a number of states in the USA to introduce affective teacher evaluation were affected by the lengthy preceding period during which the issue had received little or no attention.

Political imperatives

Obviously, systems will also be strongly influenced by what the political pressures are from and on the government of the day in any country. The reasons for this were described at the beginning of this chapter and will be returned to in Chapter 12.

The chapters that follow describe and reflect on key aspects of managing teachers' appraisal and performance in several countries.

References

Argyris, C. (1976) *Integrating the Individual and the Organisation*, New York: Wiley.

Beare, H., Caldwell, B.J. and Millikan, R.H. (1989) *Creating an Excellent School*, London: Routledge.

Bolman, L.G. and Deal, T.E. (1997) *Reframing Organisations: Artistry, Choice and Leadership*, San Francisco: Jossey-Bass.

Cardno, C. (1995) 'Diversity, dilemmas and defensiveness: leadership challenges in staff appraisal contexts', *School Organisation* 15(2): 117–31.

Cardno, C. and Piggot-Irvine, E. (1997) *Effective Performance Appraisal: Integrating Accountability and Development in Staff Appraisal*, Auckland: Longman.

Day, C. (1996) 'Leadership and professional development: Developing reflecting practice', in H. Busher and R. Saran (eds) *Managing Teachers as Professionals in Schools*, London: Kogan Page.

Fullan, M. (1991) *The New Meaning of Educational Change*, New York: Teachers College Press.

Hopkins, D., Ainscow, M. and West, M. (1994) *School Improvement in an Era of Change*, London: Cassell.

Hoyle, E. (1995) 'Changing conceptions of a profession', in H. Busher and R. Saran (eds) *Managing Teachers as Professionals in Schools*, London: Kogan Page.

Hutchinson, B. (1997) 'Appraising appraisal: some tensions and some possibilities', in L. Kydd, M. Crawford and C. Riches (eds) *Professional Development for Educational Management*, pp. 157–68, Buckingham: Open University Press.

Kelly, A.V. (1987) *Knowledge and Curriculum Planning*, London: Harper & Row.

Kyriacou, C. (1986) *Effective Teaching in Schools*, Oxford: Basil Blackwell.

Middlewood, D. (1997) 'Managing appraisal', in T. Bush and D. Middlewood (eds) *Managing People in Education*, London: Paul Chapman.

Millman, J. and Darling-Hammond, L. (1990) *Embracing Contraries: Implementing and Sustaining Teacher Evaluation*, Newbury Park: Sage.

Ministry of Education (1997) *Performance Management Systems: PMS 1–5*, Wellington: Learning Media (February Supplement in the *Education Gazette*).

Ministry of Education (1999) *National Education Guidelines*, the *Education Gazette*, 29 November, p. 25, Wellington: Learning Media.

OECD (1997) *Parents as Partners in Schooling*, Paris, OECD.

OFSTED (1997) *Chief Inspector Sets Out Range of Improvements for School Inspections*, London, OFSTED.

O'Neill, J. (2000) 'The missing professional standards', *Headship Matters* 1(5): 8–9.

Ozga, J. (1995) 'Deskilling a profession', in H. Busher and R. Saran (eds) *Managing Teachers as Professionals in Schools*, London: Kogan Page.

Peel, S. and Inkson, K. (1993) 'High school principals' attitudes to performance evaluation: Professional development or accountability', *New Zealand Journal of Educational Studies* 28(2): 125–41.

Piggot-Irvine, E. (2000) 'Appraisal: The impact of increased control on the "state of play" in New Zealand schools', *Journal of Educational Administration* 38(4): 331–47.

Preedy, M. (2001) 'Managing evaluation', in D. Middlewood and N. Burton (eds) *Managing the Curriculum*, London: Paul Chapman.

Ramsay, P. and Oliver, D. (1998) 'Capacities and behaviours of quality classroom teachers', *School Effectiveness and School Improvement*, 6: 332–66.

Rudman, R. (1999) (third edn) *Human Resource Management in New Zealand*, Auckland: Longman.

Stoll, L. and Myers, K. (1998) *No Quick Fixes: Perspectives on Schools in Difficulty*, London: Falmer Press.

Stoll, L. and Reynolds, D. (1997) 'Connecting school effectiveness and school improvement', in T. Townsend (ed.) *Restructuring and Quality: Issues for Tomorrow's Schools*, London: Routledge.

Strike, P. (1990) 'The ethics of teacher evaluation', in J. Millman and L. Darling-Hammond (eds) *The New Handbook of Teacher Evaluation: Assessing Elementary and Secondary Teachers*, pp. 356–73, Newbury Park: Sage.

Thrupp, M. (1999) *Schools Making a Difference. Let's be Realistic!*, Buckingham: Open University Press.

Timperley, H.S. and Robinson, V.M.J. (1998) 'The micropolitics of accountability: The case of staff appraisal', *Educational Policy* 12(1, 2): 162–76.

Yariv, E. (2000) Teacher effectiveness and its assessment. Unpublished Ed. D. thesis, University of Leicester.

Part I

Performance appraisal and school leadership

School leaders, headteachers or principals, are clearly central to the effectiveness of teacher performance, primarily through the way they themselves perform in their role. Not only are they ultimately responsible for how the performance of all the staff of the school is appraised, but their own performance has to be appraised. As writers in this part note, the way the latter is done will in itself have considerable impact upon the former. In an area as potentially sensitive as appraisal of performance, the eyes of others will be keenly focused on how the leader is assessed.

In Chapter 2, John West-Burnham considers current and proposed models in the light of a whole new shift in thinking about the role of school leaders. In the new paradigm of learning, the role of the headteacher is essentially to lead learning and indeed to be 'head learner'. The way in which appraisal of the role is carried out, he argues, must focus on or take account of this. Without it, there is the risk of the school leader being seen merely as an administrator of tasks, processes and systems.

In contrast, as Joy Chew describes in Chapter 3, Singapore has only recently moved from a process which assessed principals in a way uniform with other branches of the Civil Service. The new arrangements, in a small and therefore centralised state, acknowledge the difference of principals as a group, but recent research there queries whether sufficient attention can be given to individuality. Given Singapore's eminence in world educational standards and its commitment to a coherent state approach, questions may arise on reflection about the balance between national and individual needs.

Kenneth Leithwood also demonstrates, in the detailed study in Chapter 4, that the issue of context is complex. Whilst it is accepted that accountability is an essential component of school leaders' performance, he argues that the context for this accountability differs greatly. The demands of stakeholders may be quite different according to the school's context and therefore the criteria for assessing the leader's performance have to be flexible and sensitive enough to take account of this.

Finally in this part, Wayne Edwards argues in Chapter 5 that too much focus upon clear and efficient processes in appraising the performance of principals can lead to essential rights and ethical issues being at risk. The openness and transparency of the process, which are clearly desirable, may be necessarily limited because the principal has his or her own rights to privacy, and the possible conflict between this and the need for others to know leads Edwards to propose a set of guidelines to address these ethical issues, many of which are of course equally applicable to performance appraisal of any employee.

Chapter 2

Appraising headteachers or developing leaders?

Headteacher appraisal in the UK

John West-Burnham

There are two key issues in any discussion of headteacher appraisal: what is to be appraised and how is that appraisal to be conducted? To these central concerns have to be added a number of subsidiary issues: who is to appraise; what are the outcomes of the process; who owns the process; and when is it to be conducted? To these concerns must be added a number of fundamental conceptual issues:

- Is the process to be formative or summative?
- Should it include rewards and sanctions?
- What aspect of the work of the headteacher should it focus on?
- Who guarantees the integrity of the process?
- What is the status of evidence in harmonising any judgements to be made?
- What are the implications in terms of resources – notably time?
- How is the process related to professional development and learning?

The issue of headteacher appraisal has been a constant theme in the growth of management perspectives in the organisation of schools. As professional development grew in status and significance in schools so did the issue of appraisal, notably as the diagnostic component of any effective developmental strategy. In this context appraisal was perceived as being almost entirely formative in nature and this was reflected in the provisions for headteacher appraisal contained in the Education (School Teacher Appraisal) Regulations 1991. These Regulations required headteachers to engage in an appraisal process which largely replicated the provisions for teachers with appropriate recognition of the distinctive (and hierarchical) role of the headteacher.

The 1991 Regulations were posited on a number of fundamental assumptions:

- The importance of evidence-based diagnosis.
- The cyclical nature of development.
- The importance of collaboration and consent.
- The possibility of distilling a job into a number of targeted outcomes.

It is perhaps significant that the majority of the concerns about the 1991 Regulations were essentially bureaucratic, i.e. anxieties about the management of the system, e.g. the status of documentation. Two factors militated against the full implementation of the 1991 model. First, the lack of appropriate resourcing, notably time, to allow the process to work properly. Second, the lack of a sophisticated model of continuing professional development which had the potential to respond to the development needs identified through the appraisal process. In such a context it is hardly surprising that the scheme lacked credibility from the outset; was implemented inconsistently and failed to secure significant impact or acceptance. Most importantly the relationship between the appraisal process and changes in classroom and management practice was problematic, if it existed at all. This failure was corroborated by the lack of any regard for existing schemes that many schools had developed independently, which often operated highly successfully.

If this pessimistic diagnosis is true of teachers, it is particularly true of headteachers. The problems were exacerbated because of a range of practical differences and cultural issues. The practical difficulties centred on time, credibility of appraisals and the identification of suitable outcomes. The cultural issues were more profound. First, there was the issue of separating the review and development of the headteacher from that of the school as a whole; it was often difficult to disentangle personal and organisational needs. Second, there was the phenomenon of the altruistic behaviour of headteachers. As schools came under increasing pressure, one of the first casualties was the personal growth and development of the headteacher. Finally, the reforms introduced after 1988 provided a very explicit agenda for headteachers which was largely concerned with gathering of information about the implementation of externally imposed initiatives. What time there was for professional learning had to focus on specific and pragmatic issues, largely concerned with the implementation of policy.

For all these reasons, it is reasonable to argue that by the end of the 1990s headteacher appraisal was not a central issue. Where it existed it was the result of local provision or individual initiative.

Performance management

It was into the ambiguous situation outlined above that the Education (School Teacher Appraisal) (England) Regulations 2000 were introduced. The crucial conceptual and semantic change was a shift from the concept of appraisal to one of performance management. The concept of performance is elusive and complex; the notion of performance management is problematic, almost an oxymoron; management implies control and structure rather than motivation and inspiration. In the context of the Regulations performance management is defined as 'a shared commitment to high performance' (DfEE 2000a: 1) which seems somewhat tautological. A more elaborate definition is provided:

The outcomes of performance reviews will help set priorities for future planning and professional development and will inform governing bodies' decisions about discretionary pay awards.

(DfEE 2000a: 1)

A more sophisticated rationale is provided by Anthea Millett (DfEE 2000b: 6):

We know that, where teachers are clear about what they expect pupils to achieve, standards tend to rise. We also know that teachers who analyse their performance improve their practice. . . . This means continuous learning, which is what performance management is about.

Performance management therefore seems to be concerned with:

- Planning.
- Professional development/continuous learning.
- Pay awards.
- Sustaining high performance and school improvement.

All of these are valid components of a performance management system, but whether one system can meet such a range of outcomes is problematic. There is also a lack of clear definition as to what actually constitutes performance. Performance is a neutral concept, it has to be measured against criteria: performance is relatively excellent or average or poor; it is never just performance. The issue of determining the criteria for headteacher performance is discussed below, but it is appropriate to clarify a number of conceptual issues at this stage. The success of any appraisal or performance management system is directly related to the perceived criteria against which judgements are to be made. Such criteria need to be credible, appropriate, valid, capable of generating objective data and widely accepted. It is highly contentious to argue that one set of criteria can be used, in the same process, to identify the components of continuous learning and the extent to which a salary increment should be awarded – it could be seen as akin to trying to reconcile God and mammon.

One of the most significant developments in the management of school improvement in recent years in England has been the emergence of national criteria covering almost every facet of education. The OFSTED framework has provided, for the first time, a common structure for the review of schools through the inspection process. The work of the Teacher Training Agency (TTA) in generating national standards for headteachers and teachers has provided a comprehensive, systematic and detailed taxonomy of the components of the work of professionals in schools. Perhaps the most complex area of all – what constitutes an effective teacher – has now been addressed by the Hay McBer Consultancy which has identified sixteen professional characteristics. The sum total of these initiatives is a battery of definitions, criteria, competences, characteristics, etc.

Interestingly they are not referred to in the documentation on performance management, although in time they will presumably be assimilated.

Such a wealth of data provokes three broad responses. First, a sense of relief that historic ambiguity and uncertainty has been replaced by authoritative and largely consensual definitions to inform the full range of human resource functions in schools. Second, a degree of anxiety at any attempt to produce criteria that meet all situations and must be subject to the rationalistic fallacy, the misguided view that definition automatically produces coherence. The third response is an even more fundamental concern – are the various formulations actually appropriate? For example, in all of them there are historic assumptions about the nature of headship and the role of the teacher.

Any attempt at ostensive definitions inevitably codifies implicit values and assumptions, and the very process of codification lends an authority and status to the outcome. The danger is that what is defined may be partial or valid in a now defunct context. For example, much of the language about the role of the teacher is strangely silent on the issue of the nature of learning; discussion of headship often precludes contemporary theory and practice relating to leadership.

A further issue to be raised about the model of performance management in the 2000 Regulations is the implicit assumption about human motivation. Whilst it is reasonable and proper to assume a degree of altruism as one of the characteristics of a professional, the use of financial inducements introduces a contradictory element. Sustained high performance is the result of intrinsic commitment, not extrinsic inducement. The development of capability, the capacity to improve and sustain high performance is not a matter for incremental adjustment. Directly linked to the issue of individual motivation is the extent to which it is possible to isolate individual performance from other factors. In processes as complex as school improvement it is very difficult to isolate the contribution, or lack of contribution, of one individual. The variables influencing changes in performance are multiple and subject to wide-ranging interpretations. Undoubtedly the target-setting process will help to isolate individual contributions but this does beg the question of the skill of those who set the targets, the nature of the evidence available to consolidate the achievement of targets, and the isolation of variables which might inhibit or prevent achievement. This problem is particularly acute for headteachers for whom it might be very difficult to isolate a unique contribution and who will be judged by governors who may, or may not, have appropriate skills and knowledge to set valid targets and pass judgement on their successful achievement. At the heart of this issue is the problem of defining the role of the headteacher and this will be discussed in the next section.

Headship and leadership

This heading might appear to be a semantic distinction, but in fact it is crucial to this discussion: in essence the concern about the model of headteacher appraisal that is being introduced in England centres on this distinction. It might be possible to apply the principles of performance management to headship (with the caveats outlined above) but it is very difficult to see how they might be applied to leadership. The distinction is captured by MacBeath and Myers (1999: 2):

> 'competen*cies*' (are) qualities that people bring to their task and infuse what they do with new meaning and direction. They are different and distinct from 'competen*ces*' – the prescriptive repertoire of skills that a job requires.

Thus it might be appropriate to distinguish between the competences of headship and the competencies of leadership; MacBeath and Myers capture the essence of the distinction:

> . . . we must recognise that the more pinned down the competences and the more scripted the role the more we risk precluding the X factor – the surprise, the chemistry, the shift in perspective that may be brought by a candidate who does not fit the arithmetic but may, nonetheless, bring a magical quality to the leadership task.
>
> (MacBeath and Myers 1999: 2)

This is where those with political and administrative responsibility for educational policy and standards begin to worry – if not actually panic. It is much easier to operate a system based on the defined competences of headship than to explore 'magic' as one of the competencies of leadership.

The contribution of leadership to organisational improvement is a vast topic, beyond the scope of this discussion. However, it is worth stating a number of propositions to reinforce the conceptual distinction that needs to be drawn between the performance management of the role of the headteacher and the development of the competencies, qualities or characteristics of leadership:

- Leadership is a distinctive, higher order activity, symbiotic with management but qualitatively different.
- Leadership is essential to any notion of development, growth, change or improvement.
- Leadership cannot be taught, it has to be learnt.
- Leadership is a complex interaction of knowledge, skills, experience and qualities.
- The qualities of highly successful leaders include challenging authority, risk taking, moral confidence, creativity, the ability to cope with ambiguity.

The list is obviously incomplete but it serves to highlight the distinction that has to be drawn between the notion of being a leader and holding a post with hierachical status, be it general, bishop, minister, headteacher or teacher. The National Standards for Headteachers (TTA 1998) developed and published by the Teacher Training Agency (TTA) provide a detailed and comprehensive overview of the components of the work of headteachers. The Standards list eighty-three components of the job of headteacher as well as a number of narratives on the core purpose and key outcomes of headship. The Standards are exhaustive (and probably exhausting) and provide a systematic basis for training and preparation for headship, a detailed basis for accountability and an appropriate model for performance management. Although the Standards make several references to leadership there is no definition of leadership *per se*.

There is little doubt that the combination of these Standards with the performance management process will do much to inform and enhance the quality of headship. The extent to which they will impact on leadership is less clear. The Standards provide a detailed inventory for the appointment, development and review of headship. Their significance has already been attested to in the National Professional Qualification for Headship (NPQH) which has translated the Standards into a systematic, vigorous and comprehensive preparation for headship. Combined with the Headlamp Programme for newly appointed headteachers, NPQH represents one of the most structured preparation programmes for headship that is available and yet this combination does little to address the 'higher order' issues of leadership.

This concern has to some extent been addressed by the introduction of the Leadership Programme for Serving Heads (LPSH). Using the international standards for effective leadership developed by the Hay McBer Consultancy, NPQH is a demanding and challenging process which is intellectually and professionally rigorous and personally highly challenging. LPSH is based on rigorous criteria and is evidence based, *but* is a once in a career event – not that most people could handle the intensity on a regular basis. It is a genuine leadership appraisal and will undoubtedly come to be seen as the major milestone in leadership development. However, it needs to be buttressed by a supportive infrastructure that works to similar rigour but on a more manageable basis for regular review and reflection.

Understanding educational leadership

There can be little doubt that the battery of policy driven school reforms in England have had a significant impact on educational standards and the effectiveness of schools. It can also be stated with confidence that headship has been pivotal in this process. For example, Barber (2000: 24) states that: 'In the turnaround of failing schools . . . a change of head has been a feature in around 75 per cent of cases.' He is equally clear about the nature of the challenge:

> The systematic problem is clear. The people currently in, or on the brink of leadership positions, have been promoted expecting to administer the traditional education system, only to reach the top and find it in a process of radical transformation. Their careers have prepared them to manage a system which no longer exists. Instead of managing stability they have to lead change.

In place of an emphasis on smooth administration they find an unrelenting focus on pupil outcomes.

(Barber 2000: 24)

It is debatable as to the extent to which a performance management system is appropriate to the 'radical transformation' of the education system. Certainly there are signs that the historic models (or lack of them) of preparation for headship have failed. The pressures of policy driven reform have led to increasing numbers of headteachers seeking early retirement on health grounds, difficulty in filling a number of posts and anecdotal evidence of high levels of stress and low morale. There is hope that the performance management model will help to ameliorate the 'I will work harder' syndrome, and provide focused and regular support.

However the 'radical transformation' of schools points to a different range of qualities and characteristics from those offered in the national standards. The key challenges facing school teachers may be summarised as follows:

- The continued, unremitting, focus on raising achievement expressed through a wide range of indicators and the central factor in personal and institutional accountability.
- The impact of information and communication technology, in particular the implications for the management of information, the impact on learning and teaching strategies, and on school management and administration.
- The emergence of the 'science of learning', in particular the impact of brain-based learning, the extension of thinking skills, and the emergence of a cognitive curriculum.
- Increasing awareness of the relationship between school improvement and community involvement.
- A growing realisation of the need for schools to respond at a fundamental level to the social and economic changes that will have significant implications for the adult lives of school pupils. In particular, the changing nature of employment, the moral ambiguity of society, and changes to established patterns of social relationships.
- The growing recognition of the need to develop ecological awareness and sensitivity in a world that is under increasing environmental stress.

Of course, schools can offer only a limited contribution to some of the items on this list but all are implicit to any notion of 'transforming' schools if education is not to become increasingly marginal and irrelevant.

The issues are neatly summarised by MacBeath *et al.* (1998: 28):

How can school leaders make sense of the changing context and how can they be enabled to respond effectively to the challenge of a new world order? How can school leaders face outwards to a changing world, and inwards to the internal culture of a school struggling to assert continuity, permanence and timeless values? How can conflicting expectations be met, exceeded and challenged?

MacBeath and his colleagues respond to these challenges by arguing that: 'The primary task for leadership is to build the conditions for reflection, open dialogue, mutual respect for ideas and for both professional and institutional growth.'

This represents a significant shift in the criteria for effective leadership, away from transactional maintenance to transformation. There are numerous inventories of the components of leadership for transformation but the following list provides an indication of the sort of qualities that are relevant in this context:

- Courage – to question and challenge the status quo.
- Creativity – to lead in the formulation of new responses.
- Emotional Intelligence – to focus on relationships as the heart and soul of any organisation.
- Moral Confidence – 'to do the right things' and create moral communities.
- Strategic Thinking – to create a compelling vision of how the school should be.
- Trust – to secure maximum engagement and commitment.
- Humour and Resilience – to survive.

None of these can be taught, none are available as a result of attending short courses, none can be developed by a reading programme or a virtual network. Yet all are at the heart of leadership that will transform schools. None of these factors are amenable to a performance related target yet schools need them as much as any other component.

Developing leadership

At the heart of leadership development is learning; leaders have to be learners to improve as leaders and to model the appropriate behaviour for the leader of a learning community. Just as this discussion has offered a number of propositions about leadership so it is necessary to offer propositions about learning in the context of leadership development:

- Learning is an individual, unique and subjective process.
- Learning is the result of a complex interaction of neurological, psychological and social variables.
- Learning is most effective when the motivation is intrinsic.
- Learning requires challenge, not threat.
- Effective learning recognises different learning styles, multiple intelligences and varied teaching strategies.
- The outcomes of learning are complex, diffuse and unpredictable.

Reeves and Dempster (1998: 164) offer a model of a professional development strategy which:

- uses a voluntarist, self-help approach . . . ;
- relies on commitment from networks of colleagues;
- moves from individual experience through shared understanding to personal learning;
- expands the individual and collective skills of those who participate;
- models information based learning;
- values personal experience but exposes it to a broader perspective;
- treats practical problems as worthy of research;
- can be used to build bridges between researchers and practitioners.

Almost every one of these factors is a denial of the performance management approach. The emphasis on leadership learning being mediated through shared and collaborative strategies is particularly important. While the headteacher will retain personal, contractual accountability, her or his effectiveness as a leader will be significantly determined by collaborative working. The emergence of the leadership group is a powerful corroboration of this point. The most effective leadership learning is participative; a complex interaction of the individual and the group. The notion of open, shared and collaborative leadership requires open, shared and collaborative learning.

Headteacher appraisal

The importance and relevance of the performance management process for headteachers has already been conceded. However, as has hopefully been demonstrated, it does not address *leadership* development. The immediate danger is to introduce another, parallel system, which is the last thing that headteachers require, but in fact this is not necessary. Most effective headteachers are already engaged in a range of sophisticated and demanding developmental programmes over and above their formal, accountability based, activities. What is needed to build leadership capability and sustainability is a model which integrates the propositions about leadership and learning outlined above and extends the lessons learnt from a programme like LPSH.

Such a model of headteacher appraisal would need to include the following elements:

- Shared criteria for leadership for transformation focusing on the qualities necessary for profound and sustainable change.
- A clear model of leadership learning based on personal change and growth, the development of wisdom, intuition and the confidence to act.
- The creation of genuine learning partnerships; in particular the development of coaching relationships to enhance learning through action.

- The establishment of supportive networks, virtual and real, to allow for the benchmarking, consolidation, exchange and celebration of best practice.
- The creation of a 'reservoir of ideas' to stimulate and inform reflection and support the generation of new ideas and strategies.

Most of these elements are already available to headteachers. What is needed is a codification of the components, a contractual statement of entitlement, funding to create time (especially for the heads of small schools), and high-level endorsement of the importance of leadership learning and development, as well as the performance management of headteachers.

References

Barber, M. (2000) *High Expectations and Standards for All*, TES 7 July.

DES (1991) Education (School Teacher Appraisal) Regulations, London: HMSO.

DfEE (2000a) *Performance Management: Guidance for Governors.*

DfEE (2000b) *Performance Management: Training for Headteachers.*

MacBeath, J., Moos, L. and Riley, K. (1998) 'Time for a change', in J. MacBeath (ed.) *Effective School Leadership: Responding to Change*, London: Paul Chapman.

MacBeath, J. and Myers, K. (1999) *Effective School Leaders*, London: Pitman, *Financial Times.*

Reeves, J. and Dempster, N. (1998) 'Developing effective school leaders', in J. MacBeath (ed.) *Effective School Leadership: Responding to Change*, London: Paul Chapman.

TTA (1998) *National Standards for Headteachers*, TTA.

Chapter 3

Principal performance appraisal in Singapore

Joy Chew

The changing context for appraisal in the 1990s

The performance appraisal and promotion of principals in Singapore has undergone major alteration since 1998. Since 1996 the Singapore government has taken several far-reaching measures to enable the Ministry of Education (MOE) to become more responsive to the twin problems of a high resignation rate amongst younger education officers and the need to replenish the Education Service with newly trained teachers arising from large numbers of teachers nearing the retirement age, which is 55 or 60 years.[1] In March 1996, the Education Minister reported to a Parliament session that the resignation rate among young teachers was 5 per cent each year, higher than that for older education officers on the pension scheme (MOE: Press Release, 20 March 1996). In the same breath, he said that between 1997 and 2007, a large number of pensionable teachers were nearing retirement. It had become crucial to address the two trends decisively if the education system was to be successfully revamped for the twenty-first century.

It is important to note that ongoing developments in the Education Service are part and parcel of a concerted effort to restructure the Civil Service. In May 1995, the Civil Service launched a programme called 'Public Service for the 21st Century' or 'PS21' to reposition itself to meet the challenges of the twenty-first century. One of its objectives has been to foster a work environment that embraces continuous change for greater efficiency and effectiveness by employing modern management tools and techniques while at the same time being attentive to the morale and welfare of all public officers. Existing structures and arrangements for appraisal in each government ministry were closely scrutinised and major steps were taken to improve work procedures.

Until 1990 when the Education Service Commission was set up, the appraisal and promotion of education officers, principals included, was administered by the Public Service Commission.[2] The latter had single-handedly managed the annual appraisal exercise for 60,000 Civil Service employees in the teaching service, police force, civil defence and nursing fields. Of this figure, there are close to 24,000 teachers in the Education Service. This arrangement was seen to be most unsatisfactory for the Education Service which employs up to 40 per cent of the total Civil Service (Lee, 1996). It had contributed to serious bottlenecks in the processing of annual promotions of deserving education officers. The high resignation of younger education officers was but one manifestation of an overworked Public Service Commission. A solution was to allow it to relinquish some of its personnel management functions.

By January 1995, the Civil Service began to devolve its authority for managing key personnel functions such as appointments and promotions of Divisions I and II officers from the Public Service Commission (PSC) to the Education Service Commission. It did so by setting up a system of Personnel Boards in each of the respective Civil Service sectors. The PSC retained its authority to take charge of all Superscale officers Grade D and above and to discipline civil servants, leading to a reduction in rank or dismissal (Tay 1999: 12). For the first time, the Personnel Board at the MOE became responsible for carrying out annual promotion exercises to upgrade and promote classroom teachers and school administrators. The climate was finally right to review how education officers could be appraised more sensitively and, at the same time, to motivate younger and higher calibre teachers and administrators to work towards faster promotion.

In the Education Minister's March 1996 speech on the subject of 'Shaping up the Education Service for the 21st Century', three key problems were outlined with unusual candour. They were the remuneration and status of principals, poor promotional prospects for teachers, and the less attractive terms of employment for beginning teachers compared to their peers in other careers. Together, these problems served as the rationale for bold measures that were needed to improve the service conditions for recruiting and promoting better qualified teachers for schools. The speech was a much awaited one as the government had by then announced that the national school and tertiary education system would be revamped to prepare Singaporeans for an emerging global and knowledge-based economy. With a multi-ethnic and multi-religious population of nearly four million (in 2000) who are bilingually competent in English and at least one other language (Chinese, Malay, Tamil, among others), the island republic of Singapore was gearing itself strategically to become a high-tech entrepreneurial business environment. Hence the MOE's urgent goal of transforming the education system to produce school graduates who are IT-savvy and able to exploit new technologies for independent and self-directed learning (Tan 1998).

There are 381 schools and junior colleges in Singapore today (MOE: 2000 Directory of Schools) of which 201 are at the primary level and 163 at the secondary level. The post-secondary sector consists of fifteen junior colleges and two three-year pre-university institutes, four polytechnics and three universities. The total enrolment of students in the school system was 498,192 in June 1999 (MOE 1999). Each school has a principal and vice-principal and a team of eight to ten heads of departments who together supervise the curriculum work of fifty to ninety classroom teachers. Given the immense responsibility of each school's leadership team for implementing new national policies aimed at bringing about school reform, it became especially important for the MOE to ensure that adequate measures are taken to redress shortcomings in the existing personnel management system and to provide for human resource development.

Beginning in April 1997, the MOE launched a series of policy initiatives and mandates for overhauling the education system. They were, in sequence, the IT Masterplan for schools,[3] (MOE April 1997a), the launch of National Education (MOE, May 1997),[4] and the Prime Minister's announcement of the Thinking Schools, Learning Nation concept (Goh 1997),[5] all of which have been implemented in different degrees at the school level. Each major policy signalled the waves of change that were to be felt in the following years. It became expedient for the MOE to seek new ways of attracting and retaining larger numbers of better qualified teachers to the school system. The MOE's target since 1997 has been to recruit new teachers from the top one-third of each year's university, polytechnic and 'A' graduate pool (Wong 1999).

Redressing principals' status and remuneration

The issue of principals' appraisal and increasing their opportunities for promotion was immediately dealt with under the terms of the new service conditions announced in 1996. Reporting on the work of an Education Service Review Committee formed in 1995, the March 1996 speech listed that the key problem was the low remuneration and status of principals, and that principals' salaries had not been commensurate with their heavy workload. Thus while the 1996 revision to the salary scale and establishment grading system took into account the two-track career path for graduate and non-graduate principals, it retained the salary gap between the two categories of role incumbents. The disparity in status and remuneration continues to be a source of discontent amongst many non-graduate principals, particularly for those who have not been promoted to a higher grade.

Another factor that has contributed to the disquiet amongst many principals regarding the annual appraisal and promotional exercises arises from a radical change in recent policies on promotion in the Education Service. In response to the Education Service Review Committee's recommendation that more promotional posts should be created between the position of classroom teachers and that of Head of Department, the MOE has since 1997 added three new middle-management posts at the primary and the secondary school levels: Level Heads, Subject Heads, and Senior Teachers. These posts were created to provide additional ways of recognising and rewarding outstanding classroom teachers who have demonstrated their potential as teacher leaders but are not prepared to take up administrative posts.

By increasing promotional opportunities from one in three posts at the SEO level in the post-1996 period, compared to the one in twenty posts at the SEO level before that watershed year, the prospect for earlier promotion has increased tremendously for younger education officers judged by their reporting officers to be promising. However, what is seen as a boon for younger and more highly qualified graduate teachers recruited in the 1990s is perceived as a sticking point for older and non-graduate teachers and administrators whose promotion has been much slower in coming.

To summarise: in the vastly changing scene of career prospects in the Singapore Education Service, it is today possible for high performing teachers to aspire to principalship by their mid- to late-30s as the MOE has created more Senior Education Officers posts in schools. Also, by upgrading the posts of Principals, Vice-Principals and Heads of Department (HOD) for graduate and non-graduate education officers, the MOE has sought to redress the weakness of an earlier system where the remuneration and status of principals was inadequate and inconsistent with the complex nature of their leadership role.

How principals were appraised before 1998

The Staff Confidential Report (SCR)

Up to the end of 1998, the staff appraisal system for education officers was based largely on a standard Staff Confidential Report (SCR) form that was designed by the Public Service Division. There was only one SCR form which had to be completed and submitted annually to the Personnel Division by the reporting officer (RO) of teachers, HOD and principal at the school level. An identical SCR format was used for senior education officers at the MOE HQ. The key word then was an officer's work *performance*. The objective of the annual appraisal exercise was to establish how well each role incumbent was functioning as judged by the RO. Only in the case of an officer who was performing below par and given a 'D' or an 'E' grade would he/she be shown the adverse report. Otherwise, the large majority of officers would not be given more than verbal feedback on their level of performance. In this sense, it was largely a confidential and closed report.

Two broad areas of appraisal are highlighted in the form, namely, Performance of Duties and Personal Qualities. The main difference in the SCR form used for teachers and in versions designed for HOD, vice-principal and that for principal lies in the listing of types of duties that each category of post holders is expected to perform. In the case of teachers, they are appraised for eight areas of duties: Knowledge in Subject Areas Taught*, Delivery of Lessons*, Classroom Management*, Motivational Skills*, Preparation, Assessment, Monitoring, and Extra-curricular Activities. Each area of duties would be graded on a five-point scale, from a high rating of '1' to a low of '5'. Each rating of a dimension is described by a statement, and the RO is required to be as accurate as possible to tick an appropriate rating in the corresponding box for that dimension.

Of the eight duty areas, the first four in the list were identified as critical to a teacher's work and accorded greater weighting for the purpose of working out the overall grading. They are each marked with an asterisk to indicate that they are critical dimensions.

The form designed for use with principals is differentiated in terms of the list of duties performed by principals. Under the heading of Performance of Duties, ten attributes or dimensions are listed. Of these, two items are marked with an asterisk, namely, Leadership* and Professional Knowledge*, these being considered the critical dimensions in the duties of a principal. They would carry a heavier weighting compared with the remaining eight attributes which are Supervision, Interest in Welfare of Staff and Pupils, Planning Ability, Organisational Ability, Decision Making, Written Communication, Oral Communication, and Involvement in Related Organisations. If a principal were given a 'C' grade in any of the two crucial attributes, it would automatically mean that the whole appraisal grade for that officer is a 'C' even if the RO has given a 'B' grade for the majority of the remaining eight attributes.

Under the second heading, Personal Qualities, are seven separate dimensions of which the first two, Conduct* and Professionalism*, are marked with an asterisk to indicate that they are relatively more important than the rest. These are: Work Attitude, Responsibility, Initiative, Adaptability to Change, and Interpersonal Relationships. Once again, as in the first section on Performance of Duties, each dimension is graded from a high of '1' to a low of '5'. There is no difference in the items or wording of this part of the SCR used for teachers, HOD or principals. An additional dimension that applies to the assessment of principals and other professional staff who hold financial responsibilities in the school is Financial Management Competency, which includes financial compliance with MOE guidelines. For principals, it is assessed under two Personal Qualities dimensions, namely, Responsibility and Work Attitude, and under two Performance dimensions; Supervision and Organisational Ability.

An overall grade of an officer's performance and personal qualities is worked out by taking into account all the grades given by the RO for each item. If an officer is judged to have far exceeded the normal requirements of his/her current substantive grade in all areas of work and perceived to be making positive contributions in areas beyond his/her immediate areas of responsibility, he/she is deserving of an 'A' grade. An overall 'C' is considered 'Satisfactory' performance for all levels of education officers. A lower rating of 'D' or 'E' is defined as adverse. The descriptive statement for a 'D' is that 'the officer is just able to meet the requirements of his current substantive grade in his work'. An 'E' grade would only be given if the officer is deemed to be unable to meet the requirement of his/her current grade appointment.

The Reporting Officer's role in appraising the principal

As a supervisor to the principal, each RO is expected to work closely throughout the school year with the direct report. This can be achieved by making regular visits to the school and through telephone and email communication about school matters. The school inspector will have to ensure that new educational policies and changes in work procedures are implemented accurately and speedily.

Principals are required to submit to their inspectors regular reports of their school annual and semestral activities, such as their internal self-appraisal reports and compilation of statistical data concerning staffing and student population, achievement and physical fitness scores collected for the HQ. Annual self-appraisal of the school is undertaken by the principal and his/her school leadership team which focuses on four key areas of work: School Organisation, the Instructional programme, Pupil Management, and the school's Extra-curricular Activities programme. In this sense, it would be extremely important for a principal to have a good working relationship with the inspector as the latter can be a critical friend and source of helpful information on how to improve the school's effectiveness and examination results.

The inspector clearly functions both as a staff developer and an appraiser to the principal. During the external school appraisal exercise conducted once in four to five years, the principal's inspector accompanies the external appraisal team of ten MOE senior officers (other inspectors, subject specialist inspectors from the Curriculum Planning and Development Division and an Assistant Director from the Schools Division) to evaluate the school programme. By including the school's inspector during the week-long appraisal period, the inspector would be able to provide additional information about the principal's leadership and management behaviour and characteristics of the school community to the inspectorate team. The data gathering process on the principal's ongoing performance and leadership style is quite similar to how an inspector operates during his/her regular visits to the school: through observations of a sample of teachers' classroom activities, interviewing teachers, pupils and parents, and examining a variety of documents generated by the teaching and administrative staff members. But during the external appraisal period, the inspector is more that of a senior school team member who is required to take appropriate measures to guide the principal in action planning for school improvement. By working closely with their own schools, the ROs would be in a position to appraise their principals' strengths and weaknesses as measured by the SCR form.

On completion of the SCR forms at all levels of the school hierarchy for professional staff members, the RO has the responsibility of giving feedback about the subordinate's shortcomings, if there are any, and monitoring the officer's progress in regard to performance of duties. The countersigning officer's responsibility is to ensure that the performance report is an objective account of the officer's strengths and weaknesses in his/her areas of work. Principals' SCR forms are then submitted to their respective Assistant Directors or Senior Inspectors of the Schools Division who are their RO or countersigning officers (CO). Adhering to a schedule of deadlines for appraisal work, the forms are subsequently submitted for further processing by the Personnel Division of the MOE.

The Staff Appraisal Report (SAR) in the post-1998 period

The appraisal system of principals had remained unchanged over the last three decades up to 1997/1998 when the Public Service Division (PSD) piloted the implementation of a new set of Staff Appraisal Report forms. By September 1998, it took a further step of revising the Work Review Form and Potential Report for Education Officers which was renamed the Development Form. The PSD announced its decision to use the revised Staff Appraisal Report (SAR) forms for the 1999 year of assessment. The new appraisal system used by the MOE comprises three components, each of which is appraised by three different forms: the Work Review Form, the Development Form, and Performance Form. It is noteworthy that there is now only one version for the set of three forms to be used for all levels of education officers, including those in the MOE HQ.

Taken together as an instrument for appraising all levels of education officers, the introduction of the three-part SAR system signals a significant departure from the way teachers and administrators were evaluated in the earlier period. The new appraisal procedure can be seen as a more effective administrative measure of translating into operational terms additional planning and monitoring mechanisms to evaluate the work performance and career development of education officers. At the same time, it has been designed to deal with the management of talent in the education service. In recent years, 'potential' has emerged in the Civil Service as a central concept and it has given rise to innovative ways of retaining and recruiting promising officers to the public sector. But, as will be discussed further on, the attempt to gauge an officer's potential has resulted in some implementation difficulties, particularly at the early stage of employing such an instrument. Each part of the SAR will now be described in some detail.

The Work Review Form

This new component of the appraisal system in the Civil Service serves as a very comprehensive tool to review officers' professional work ranging from their contribution to work improvement teams (WITs) and education staff suggestion scheme (ESSS) at their workplace, to target-setting for their annual work and training plans for their professional and personal development. For the first time in the Education Service, the creation of such a form provides a means of integrating various elements of a principal's or teacher's duties and responsibilities. Applied across the board, it can be a powerful device to monitor how actively senior education officers (who serve as RO and CO) are able to implement work processes aimed at instilling quality assurance through regular staff supervision and participation in decision making at all levels of the education bureaucracy. It was not surprising that detailed written guidelines and a training guide were issued by the PSD to all MOE supervisors to explain the philosophy and rationale of the new appraisal system.

The Work Review Form as used for principals is designed to serve as a joint working document between the RO and the officer to discuss work targets and review achievements and new initiatives on a regular basis. After setting targets for the new work year and assessment period, they would be required to agree on the next date to review achievements, priorities and the principal's training plans. There is a separate section on the principal's personal Training Plans which is jointly discussed with the RO to establish the type and level of training, such as inductive, basic, advanced, extended or continuing training. There is a column for indicating the number of hours anticipated for different forms of training. The five-page form provides adequate space for the RO to write a summary of additional points that have been discussed with the principal. The latter can write comments on what was discussed and then sign the form.

A new feature of the 1999 revised form are the extra columns and boxes to record the principal's level of involvement in giving staff suggestions each year as well as how actively teachers and heads of departments of that officer's school organisation participate in school-based work improvement teams and staff suggestion schemes. There is a formula for calculating statistical data on the ratio of suggestions, participation and implementation of the school's WITs and ESSS given as an annex to the form. For the first time, the appraisal exercise has made it mandatory for principals to make a count of statistics pertaining to each school regarding the Civil Service's initiatives to instill work productivity concepts and encourage all teachers to become regularly involved in staff training activities. Such additional appraisal data could now be factored into the consideration of officers' promotion as well as the use of performance indicators.

The Development Form

For the third year running since 1998, the new Development Form was implemented but this time round it was modified for use in the Education Service. The revised version incorporates two new elements about readiness for promotion and additional information that could be provided about the officer by the CO who is in direct contact with the principal. Compared with the Work Review Form, the Development Form is focused largely on appraising the strengths and weaknesses of the principal in terms of nine Appraisal Qualities, the Helicopter Quality, and Other Qualities.

Comprising ten sections, the seven-page form seeks to draw out from the RO information about the principal's leadership skills and disposition, and personal qualities as demonstrated in the work context. The Appraisal Qualities are: Power of Analysis, Imagination, Sense of Reality, Achievement Motivation, Political Sensitivity, Decisiveness, Capacity to Motivate, Delegation and Communication. A singular item, called the Helicopter Quality, is included in the first section of the form to appraise the principal's 'ability and drive to look at a problem from a higher vantage point with simultaneous attention to relevant details', the capacity for systems thinking and sensitivity to business, social, political and technical environments. Each of the ten qualities is rated on a four-point scale from 'High' (defined as 'sufficient for more than two grades higher than his/her substantial grade'), 'Exceeding' (defined as 'sufficient for one or two grades higher than his/her substantive grade'), 'Meeting' (defined as 'enough for his/her substantive grade, not enough for a higher one') to 'Below' (defined as 'present job performance is suffering because of weakness in this quality').

Three other qualities are appraised: Commitment to Job, Integrity and Teamwork, and the RO has to indicate in an appropriate response box the magnitude ('Highly Committed to the Job' to 'Lacks Commitment') and frequency for four accompanying statements to define how Integrity is operationalised. There is an item to determine whether the principal has the aptitude to be a specialist staff in the MOE HQ, followed by an item that elicits comments from the RO on the officer's character, strengths/weaknesses, special aptitudes and skills.

The Development Form also carries a large section on Potential which requires the RO to consult with the CO on the principal's Currently Estimated Potential (CEP) and the Key Appointment Likelihood (KAL). What each construct seeks to do is to provide some prediction of how well a principal (or any other education officer) could advance in his/her career path from the present job level and substantive grade in the Civil Service, taking into account the incumbent's current work performance and appraisal qualities. The term 'potential' is not treated as a static construct, which has the effect of foreclosing the chances for a principal's further career mobility in the Education Service. Thus a principal with a high CEP could theoretically be promoted to a Superscale E grade. Unlike the CEP, the Key Appointment Likelihood construct seeks to establish what is the next higher level of appointment of a principal in the next three years, which could be up to the position of a divisional director in the MOE HQ if the officer has the makings of one.

The next section of the Development Form is on 'Development' which takes the concept of 'potential' further by asking how an RO could recommend the principal's direction for development within three years and over a longer time. The need for further training for the principal's development is also elicited from the RO in the form. The principal's overall performance assessment is based on how the RO evaluates his/her current work performance and five letter grades (from A to E) are provided, each with a defining statement. A 'D' grade indicates satisfactory performance while an 'E' grade indicates that the officer is unable to meet the requirements of his/her current grade of work, where shortcomings are more than additional contributions. The RO would have to communicate to the principal in writing that an 'E' grade is given, following a prototype of a written notification of unsatisfactory performance. If the Personnel Division endorses the adverse grade, the officer would be put under a performance review process for a year and be closely monitored by the RO.

The Performance Form

The Performance Form, which used to be called the Staff Confidential Report before 1998, has remained unchanged and is used in the Education Service. Its contents have been described in an earlier section under the heading, Staff Confidential Report (SCR). The only difference is the instruction that the RO will only be required to submit the SCRs of officers who receive 'D' or 'E' grades and for all new officers who are on probation in the Education Service. In the SCR form, the fine details of attributes and qualities required for the job are spelled out and would serve as a helpful tool for the RO to point out the officer's shortcomings under Performance of Duties and Personal Qualities. Otherwise, each officer's Performance Form is completed annually and filed for personal reference.

The next step of processing the SAR forms of principals submitted by various school inspectors or superintendents is more involved and complex. They would get together for the purpose of cross-ranking principals and re-assign individual grades if necessary. At this stage of the exercise, deputy directors of the Schools Division and the director of schools will join in and seek to ensure that there is uniformity of standards used for the appraisal process. The final rank of all principals is then submitted to the Personnel Division for its follow-up work. The Schools Division has the primary responsibility of making recommendations for principals' promotions and implementing guidelines for the use of the SAR forms.

How principals have responded to the new appraisal system

With the help of relevant background information on principal's performance appraisal and the fast-changing landscape of education in Singapore, it is now possible to comment on how principals perceive the new appraisal system and to suggest some consequences for the operation of the school system. While there is no large-scale survey available at this early stage of the implementation of the SAR system, there is some data based on interviews with ten principals (Chew *et al.* 2000) on how policy changes in work appraisal and career development have affected their work and sense of well-being.

Inevitably, not all principals have been equally elated with the improved remuneration and status of senior education officers given the differential salary structure of graduate and non-graduate principals. Another important variable is the age differential between the older and experienced principals appointed more than five years ago compared to younger officers who have begun to enjoy the effects of the upgrading of principalship announced by the MOE in 1995.

Ambivalence and perceived subjectivity of the concept of potential

Perhaps the most contentious issue is in the interpretation of an officer's 'currently estimated potential' (CEP) and how the new concept is viewed against the previous use of a single yardstick of job performance with which most established principals are familiar. With the introduction of the revised Development Form in 1999, all principals and other supervisors are expected to be able to operationalise the term 'CEP' in their appraisal of teachers and other subordinates. Some principals have expressed a reservation that undue weightage has been placed on an officer's potential for higher office than their actual performance. As two secondary school principals put it in reply to an interview question on how the SAR has affected the motivation of school heads in Singapore:

> CEP is very subjective. You are predicting the potential of the person without giving the officer time to show from his/her performance. In the past, promotions were based on how well the officer performed in his/her capacity but now it is based to an unbalanced extent on the CEP.
>
> (Principal, aged 43, in his sixth year of appointment)

> Promotion has caused a lot of unhappiness through its link with ranking. It is not promotion per se that has caused the problem. It's the lack of transparency or fairness of it. . . . It's not transparent because on the one hand those in charge say that it's based on potential while others see it as performance.
>
> (Principal, aged 53, who is into his tenth year of headship)

Such sentiments appear to be fairly widespread amongst principals who would compare their slower and seemingly hard-earned promotion with that of younger graduate officers some who have been given higher postings, a few as superintendents, or who are placed on a Superscale grade. Until the Personnel Division and Schools Division clarify further the basis for recommendations for certain officers' promotions, many older principals are inclined to believe that the ground rules have changed to their disadvantage. Younger graduate officers who are motivated to work towards faster promotion will be perceived as a threat to the career advancement of non-graduate and even older graduate colleagues.

For this reason, the Education Service has encouraged more non-graduate teachers in their late twenties to forties to pursue a part-time bachelor's degree course at the Singapore Institute of Management–Open University Development Programme. The MOE has also liberalised the Study Leave Scheme in 1998 for non-graduate teachers to pursue full-time undergraduate studies (Chiang 1999). This has been accompanied by a growing emphasis on teachers' continual education and professional development since 1997, the landmark year when major policy initiatives were announced to reposition the MOE as a driving force for bringing about education reform for the twenty-first century (MOE 1998a).

Regular monitoring of work for estimates of potential and performance

Beginning in 1997 the concept of Cluster Schools was introduced by the MOE where up to ten schools are identified on the basis of their physical proximity to be supervised by cluster superintendents (MOE 1998b: *Contact* July issue). Quite like the senior inspectors and assistant directors who used to appraise principals' performance and recommend promotion in the pre-1998 period, superintendents are required to work very closely with their ten school principals to facilitate school improvement and to initiate collaborative projects for curriculum and management areas. In fact, cluster superintendents spend much of their time getting to know their schools and mingling with teachers and middle-management staff in order to facilitate new leadership tasks for cluster principals. They are responsible for reporting on the principals' work each year and do so by completing SAR forms.

As described earlier, there are now clear-cut procedures in which superintendents are expected to schedule review meetings with their principals about their work targets and aspirations for furthering their professional development. Such close monitoring of work will enable the supervisor to appraise their principals and also to rank them by performance and by their CEP. This step is followed by another to cross-rank principals by cluster superintendents and the deputy directors of the Schools Division.

Under the present appraisal system, it becomes crucial for principals to be able to get along with their supervisors and to demonstrate that they are innovative and able to collaborate with other cluster principals. Through informal conversations with principals who have worked longer in cluster schools, there is growing evidence of much 'contrived collegiality' (Fullan and Hargreaves 1992), with principals having to put on their best on-stage performance for their attitude towards innovations and willingness to try new things. Thus, impression management on the part of the principal can become a matter of great concern. The dichotomy between 'potential' and performance will continue to vex many principals since Singapore schools are now encouraged to work on complex innovations in curriculum processes and organisational learning as a means of realising long-term strategic plans.

In practice, so far, some principals have felt that an officer's work performance has been de-emphasised and that any serious attempt to measure potential should not be done by discounting an officer's actual performance. At the initial period at least, there is a need for principals to be convinced that the recent seeming preoccupation with 'currently estimated potential' will not result in a lowering of motivation on the part of longer serving officers who have been graded lower for their CEP compared to younger colleagues.

In conclusion, the new appraisal system of principals has introduced many new challenges and increased tensions in the way school personnel are managed and developed for career advancement, since the Education Service has been overhauled to enable the school system to compete for higher quality teachers and aspiring school leaders from the very small and finite pool of university graduates and non-graduates. While many policies have been implemented to make education an attractive career option for graduate officers, including measures to upgrade the qualification of younger non-graduate teachers, there is a need to ensure that older teachers and principals are not overshadowed despite their commitment and length of service in schools. But it is quite clear that the future looks very rosy for highly qualified and younger officers who joined the service more recently. How the MOE will succeed in encouraging them to remain highly committed and productive will be interesting to watch since schools are now expected to participate actively in curriculum improvement and the delivery of a new education system.

Notes

1 The Minister for Education revealed the magnitude of the retirement phenomenon in July 2000 when he gave the projected number of 3,500 teachers who would retire by the year 2005. They constituted 30 per cent of the teaching force in 2000.
2 Principals in Singapore do not apply for principalship but are appointed on the basis of their job performance as classroom teachers and proven track record as effective leaders in middle-management posts such as heads of department and vice-principalship. The Schools and Personnel Divisions handle the appointment of new principals.
3 The Masterplan for Information Technology in education was launched on 28 April 1997. It sets out national standards for the use of IT in schools by the year 2002 and schools are given some flexibility in determining how quickly they can meet national standards before 2002, depending on their readiness to use IT meaningfully to meet learning objectives. The IT Masterplan is integral to ongoing innovations in Singapore education to produce a high-tech workforce for the twenty-first century.
4 National Education was launched as a compulsory programme in the school and tertiary education system on 17 May. At a Teachers' Day rally on 8 September 1996, the Prime Minister Mr Goh Chok Tong described it as 'an exercise to develop instincts that become part of the psyche of every child'. Like IT, it is an integral part of the government's strategies in education to prepare Singaporeans for the twenty-first century.
5 'Thinking Schools, Learning Nation' has become the central concept in guiding the process of education reform since its launch on 1 June 1997. The aim is to create a thinking environment in schools where all administrators, teachers and students can be encouraged to seek continuous improvement, be ready to experiment with new ideas and creativity, and engage in organisational learning. Work improvement teams and staff suggestion schemes are examples of how educators can seek to contribute ideas and suggestions on ways of increasing the effectiveness of the school as a productive problem-solving educational unit.

References

Chew, J., Stott, K. and Boon, Z. (2000) 'On Singapore: the making of secondary school principals'. Conference paper presented at the CCEAM Symposium on Small Island States: the Making of Secondary School Principals, held in Tasmania, Australia, 10–14 September 2000.

Chiang, C.F. (1999) Speech by Permanent Secretary, Ministry of Education, at the Continuing Education Graduation Ceremony held on 11 September 1999 at the National Institute of Education, Singapore.

Fullan, M. and Hargreaves, A. (1992) *What's worth fighting for in your school*, Buckingham: Open University Press.

Goh, C.T. (1997) 'Shaping our future: "thinking schools" and a "learning nation"'. (Full text of the Prime Minister's welcome speech at the 7th International Conference on Thinking held in Singapore from 1–6 June, 1997.)

Lee, Y.S. (1996) 'Shaping up the Education Service for the 21st Century'. (Statement by the Minister for Education delivered to Parliament on 20 March 1996.)

Ministry of Education, Singapore (1997a) Launch of Masterplan for IT in Education. Press Release dated 28 April 1997.

—— (1997) Launch of National Education. Press Release dated 16 May 1997.

—— (1998a) 'Expanding our horizons through continuous learning', *Contact*, January issue, 1998: 4–9.

—— (1998b) 'Cluster schools and its challenges', *Contact*, July issue, 1998: 1–2.

—— (1999) Education Statistics Digest.

—— (2000) Directory of Schools, Singapore.

Tan, T. (1998) 'What must Singapore do to prosper in the 21st century?' Speech by the Deputy Prime Minister and Minister for Defence at the National Day Dinner of the Singapore Chinese Chamber of Commerce and Industry held on 18 August 1998.

Tay, J. (1999) 'Public service reforms in Singapore'. Article contributed by the Singapore Government in the website of the UNDP Bureau for Development Policy Management and Governance Network. (http://magnet.undp.org/Docs/psreform/civic_service_reform_in_Singapore.htm)

Teo, C.H. (2000) Speech by Minister for Education on 'Building the 21st Century Teaching Force – Challenge and Response' delivered at the 2nd Teaching Scholarship Presentation Ceremony held on 15 July 2000.

Wong, S. (1999) Senior Minister of Education's speech on Teacher Training at the Committee of Supply, Ministry of Education, 17 March 1999.

Chapter 4

Criteria for appraising school leaders in an accountable policy context

Kenneth Leithwood

Introduction

Personnel evaluation policies must concern themselves with many questions: What are the objectives for the evaluation? What criteria and standards will be used as the lenses through which actual practice is judged? What data will be collected about such practice and how will be it be amassed, analysed and reported? How and when will feedback be given to those being evaluated? and How will the actions to be taken as follow-up to the evaluation be decided? Such policies usually address, as well, questions about the training of evaluators, and other matters related to policy implementation.

But among the questions addressed by any comprehensive evaluation policy (at least any one aimed at the improvement of practice), none is more critical or more difficult to answer than the criteria question. No question is more critical because feedback to evaluatees concerning their performance will contribute little to the development of their organisations if it does not focus on what make them effective in their roles; indeed, the absence of both clear and clearly communicated criteria contributes to the politicisation of the evaluation process (Davis and Hensley 1999). No question is more difficult because of the considerable debate about effective practices in many educational roles, including the role of school leader. So the purpose of this chapter is to help those charged with the development of school leader evaluation policies to identify the most defensible criteria to incorporate into their policies.

Job descriptions, LEA or district missions, the charge given the school leader on appointment, annual targets for student achievement, goals to be accomplished over the course of a year as set by governors or school councils, results of research on effective leadership, standards for administrator performance, the collective opinion of a committee of administrators – each of these is the main source of the criteria being used to evaluate some school leaders somewhere at the present time. But none of these sources, considered individually, stands much chance of yielding defensible criteria for evaluating school leaders. Each source misses some critical aspect of school leaders' work that ought to be reflected in the criteria used for their evaluation.

Those school leader evaluation policies which aim to be formative and growth-oriented, must draw their criteria from a combination of at least three sources. One of these sources is evidence about leadership practices that are productive in almost all organisational contexts. Such practices are relatively stable, changing over time only as the knowledge base about such practices changes. Increasing school leaders' abilities to engage in these practices represents a long-term investment in the leadership capacity of the school district as a whole. Such practices are the 'basic skills' of leadership on which additional, more contingent, expertise is built, even though such skills cannot be assumed on the part of many existing school leaders. Like the basic skills of a professional athlete, neglecting them inevitably results in their erosion.

A second source of evaluation criteria is evidence about leadership practices demonstrably productive in the external policy context which always frames a portion of what leaders are able to do in their schools. This policy context may be relatively unstable, changing in concert with the political platforms of newly elected governments. Modifications of the United Kingdom's Thatcher-era, conservative educational policies, introduced by Tony Blair's Labour government, requiring schools and their leaders to become much more skilled in interpreting and working with quantitative evidence about their students' achievement is a case in point (Gray et al. 1999).

A third source of criteria is the unique characteristics, challenges and aspirations of leaders' individual schools and local communities. School improvement planning often provides a framework for addressing such challenges, and those leadership practices which are effective in accomplishing specific school improvement goals are important criteria to include in school leader evaluation policies. Leadership practices of this sort depend on either the initial possession, or eventual acquisition, of targeted (or 'domain specific') knowledge about the school's problems or challenges and promising responses to such challenges. The knowledge needed by a leader to assist her or his school in improving students' early literacy skills, for example, is quite different from the knowledge needed to help the school develop more effective partnerships with local businesses. A substantial portion of the variation in school leaders' problem solving expertise is explained by the possession of such domain-specific knowledge (Leithwood and Steinbach 1995).

However, identification of these three sources of criteria for school leader evaluation policies is only a modest beginning toward the specification of practical evaluation criteria. The most complex part of the task is to draw defensible conclusions about what each of the sources has to say about leadership evaluation criteria. This task calls for considerable judgement on the part of evaluation policy developers, and different people will often arrive at different conclusions about what evaluation criteria are suggested by the same source. This chapter aims to significantly reduce, but by no means eliminate, this ambiguity by outlining one set of defensible conclusions to be drawn from two of the three sources of leadership evaluation criteria. It is, of course, not possible in a chapter such as this to identify criteria which take into account the unique features of individual schools and communities.

Evidence about leadership practices that are productive in most contexts

> The ideal leader in most cultures and organisations is transformational not transactional. Transformational leadership and charismatic leadership are generally more effective and more satisfying than transactional leadership. This is true above and beyond situational effects.
>
> (Bass 1997: 541)

Evidence from many schools varying in size, location, level and cultural context provides support for this claim in the context of educational organisations (e.g. Leithwood, Jantzi and Steinbach 1999a; Day *et al.*, 2000; Southworth, 1998). For this reason, practices associated with transformational school leadership offer one set of defensible criteria for school leader evaluation.

What does such leadership look like? Part of a cluster of related approaches termed 'new leadership' by Bryman (1992), transformational leadership has become the subject of systematic empirical inquiry in school contexts. This approach to leadership fundamentally aims to foster capacity development and higher levels of personal commitment to organisational goals on the part of leaders' colleagues. Increased capacities and commitment are assumed to result in extra effort and greater productivity (Burns 1978; Bass 1985). Authority and influence associated with this form of leadership are not necessarily allocated to those occupying formal administrative positions, although much of the literature adopts their perspectives. Rather, power is attributed by organisation members to whomever is able to inspire their commitments to collective aspirations, and the desire for personal and collective mastery over the capacities needed to accomplish such aspirations.

Contemporary leadership literature offers no unitary concept of transformational school leadership. Kowalski and Oates (1993), for instance, accept Burns' (1978) original claim that transformational leadership represents the transcendence of self-interest by both leader and led. Dillard (1995: 260) prefers Bennis' (1959) modified notion of 'transformative leadership – the ability of a person to reach the souls of others in a fashion which raises human consciousness, builds meanings and inspires human intent that is the source of power'. My own work has been influenced by another modification of Burns, this one based on Bass' (1985) two-factor theory in which transactional and transformational leadership do not represent opposite ends of the leadership continuum, as Burns suggested (Leithwood 1994). Bass maintained that the two actually can be complementary, building on one another. Leithwood identified six factors that make up such leadership. Hipp and Bredeson (1995), however, reduced the factors to five in their analysis of the relationship between leadership behaviours and teacher efficacy. Gronn (1996) notes the close relationship in much current writing between views of transformational and charismatic leadership, as well as the explicit omission of charisma from some current conceptions of transformational leadership, my own included.

The most detailed specification of transformational school leadership practices describes six categories of such practices: building school vision and goals; providing intellectual stimulation; offering individualised support; modelling professional practices and values; demonstrating high performance expectations; developing structures to foster participation in school decisions; and developing productive working relationships with parents and the wider community (Leithwood *et al.*, 1999a). Each category includes many specific practices and the thinking that gives rise to such practices has been described by Leithwood and Steinbach (1995).

Most models of transformational leadership are flawed by their under-representation of transactional practices which my colleagues and I interpret to be 'managerial' in nature. Such practices are fundamental to organisational stability. For this reason, four categories of management practices have been added to my own model based on a review of relevant literature (Leithwood and Duke 1999). These include: staffing, instructional support, monitoring school activities, and community focus.

There is a modest quantity of compelling empirical evidence concerning the effects of this form of leadership exercised by principals on a wide array of school conditions, teacher motivations and practices, as well as on student outcomes. Leithwood *et al.*'s (1996) review of twenty studies of such effects reports over-whelmingly positive results. More recent research by Leithwood *et al.* (1999), has demonstrated significant effects of transformational leadership on a handful of carefully selected school conditions and student engagement with school. Together, this evidence is sufficient to justify including those categories of transformational leadership practices discussed in this section, along with the management practices also mentioned, among the criteria to be included in policies for school leader appraisal. These are the 'basic skills' of school leadership.

Leadership practices in an accountable policy context

Transformational leadership practices are a necessary but not sufficient part of the full set of criteria for school leader evaluation. In addition, such criteria need to reflect those leadership practices uniquely suited to the external policy context in which leaders find themselves. In this chapter we focus on a policy context common to school leaders in many countries around the world at the present time, one dominated by the demand for schools, and the people who work in them, to be publicly more accountable. Educational reform initiatives guided by the 'New Right' (Marchak 1991) and closely related political ideologies are largely responsible for this context.

The framework used for identifying school leader evaluation criteria which acknowledge this context is a fourfold classification of approaches to accountability developed as part of a recent study of educational accountability policies in seven countries (Leithwood *et al.* 1999). Labelled market, decentralisation, professional, and managerial, each category of approaches to accountability is described in this section along with the school leadership practices needed to implement them.

Market approaches to accountability

Sometimes referred to as the exit option, this approach to accountability increases the competition for students faced by schools. It is an especially prominent approach currently, with versions of it evident in several European countries, and in Canada, the United States, New Zealand, Australia and parts of Asia. Specific tools for increasing competition among schools for student-clients include allowing school choice by opening boundaries within and across school systems, school privatisation plans, the creation of charter schools, magnet schools, academies and other specialised educational facilities. Competition also is increased by altering the basis for school funding so that money follows students (e.g. vouchers, tuition tax credits), and by publicly ranking schools based on aggregated student achievement scores. These tools are often used in combination.

The common thread binding together these different tools for increasing competition is a belief that schools are unresponsive, bureaucratic, and monopolistic (Lee 1993). Such organisations are assumed, by advocates of this approach, to have little need to be responsive to pressure from their clients because they are not likely to lose them. In relation to schools, this means that they will come to view their major task as offering programmes that *they* believe are good for their clients. Such organisations, it is argued, seek efficiency on their own terms and are prone to view clients as objects to be treated rather than customers to be served.

Advocates of this approach to educational accountability (e.g. Chubb and Moe 1990) hold a series of assumptions about how such competition is likely to result in greater student achievement. First, increased competition allows parents and students to select schools with which they are more satisfied and which better meet their educational needs. Second, parents who are more satisfied with their child's school provide greater support to that school and to their child's learning. Third, students are likely to be more engaged when their own learning styles are matched to a particular school. Fourth, when teachers have chosen their work settings and have been active in designing their own schools' programmes, they will be more committed to implementing those programmes effectively. Finally, all of these outcomes will combine to increase student achievement, attendance, and educational attainment (Elmore 1990; Raywid 1992).

Market approaches to accountability assume an ideal set of responses from school leaders (Kerchner 1988). Of course, having a good 'product' to sell is the first order of business. These leaders are able to market their schools effectively, develop good customer/client relations, and monitor 'customer' (student and parent) satisfaction. To prosper in such contexts, school leaders continuously redesign their organisations in response to fast-changing market conditions. They collect data about competitors' services and prices and find niches for their schools. They have exceptional levels of clarity about their missions because these missions are viewed as a central criterion in parent and student choices.

Evidence about how school leaders actually respond to increased market competition, while still relatively limited, suggests a more complicated reality, however. First, choice arrangements vary considerably in the autonomy awarded principals. As an explanation for the few differences found in the practices of US principals of magnet and non-magnet schools, Hausman (2000) pointed to the wide array of district policies regulating all principals in the district. Second, evidence demonstrates that some school choice settings actually put very little pressure on leaders and schools to compete. This is the case when a school is oversubscribed (Hausman 2000), or when it serves parents and students who, for economic and other reasons, feel unable to travel to a school outside their own neighbourhood (Lauder and Hughes 1999). Finally, school leaders facing the same competitive conditions may respond quite differently for reasons associated with their individual abilities, values, beliefs, and motivations.

Grace (1995) interpreted his evidence as capturing three quite different responses by individual school leaders to increased competition for students. One group of leaders welcomed the more managerial role they believed was implied in policy changes. A second group were preoccupied with the loss of a professional orientation to schools, and concerned about managerialist values encroaching on their work. The third group of school leaders actively opposed those features of market approaches to school reform which they believed were unlikely to lead to school improvement. Other evidence suggests that competition has unpredictable effects on the propensity of school leaders to engage in instructional leadership, some finding little time for it while others increase their attention to it (Hausman 2000).

This brief review of theory and evidence suggests, most obviously, that school leaders implementing market solutions in truly competitive environments need marketing and entrepreneurial skills, and that evaluation of their work should seek evidence of these capacitates. By themselves, however, such skills do not acknowledge the growing evidence that market approaches to accountability can be, and usually are, highly inequitable (Lauder and Hughes 1999; Lee 1993). Communities in which equity is a strongly valued goal will want to add criteria to their school leader evaluation policies which reflect the effort of leaders to market their schools in ways that make access possible even for those children and families from diverse and economically disadvantaged backgrounds.

Decentralisation approaches to accountability

When decentralisation or devolution of decision making is used for purposes of increasing accountability, one of its central aims often is to increase the voice of those who are not heard, or at least not much listened to, in the context of typical school governance structures. When this is the goal, a *community control* form of site-based management (e.g. Wohlstetter and Mohrman 1993) typically is the instrument used for its achievement. The basic assumption giving rise to this form of site-based management is that the curriculum of the school ought to directly reflect the values and preferences of parents and the local community (Ornstein 1983). School professionals, it is claimed, typically are not as responsive to such local values and preferences as they ought to be. Their responsiveness is greatly increased, however, when the power to make decisions about curriculum, budget, and personnel is in the hands of the parent/community constituents of the school. School councils in which parent/community constituents have a majority of the membership are the primary vehicle through which to exercise such power.

Devolution of decision making, however, is sometimes rooted in a broader reform strategy for public institutions, which Peters has referred to as 'new managerialism'. According to Peters (1992: 269), new managerialism '. . . emphasises decentralization, deregulation and delegation'. While there are variants on this approach to accountability among countries, they share in common a shift in emphasis:

(a) from policy formulation to management and institutional design;
(b) from process to output controls;
(c) from organisational integration to differentiation; and
(d) from statism to subsidiarity.

(Peters 1992)

In countries such as New Zealand and Australia where school reform has been substantially influenced by the philosophy of new managerialism, creating more efficient and cost effective school administrative structures is a second central goal for devolution. Typically, this goal is pursued through the implementation of an *administrative control* form of site-based management which increases school-site administrators' accountability to the central district or board office for the efficient expenditure of resources. These efficiencies are to be realised by giving local school administrators authority over such key decision areas as budget, physical plant, personnel, and curriculum. Advocates of this form of site-based management reason that such authority, in combination with the incentive to make the best use of resources, ought to get more of the resources of the school into the direct service of students. To assist in accomplishing that objective, the principal may consult informally with teachers, parents, students or community representatives. Site councils are typically established to advise the principal but with membership at the discretion of the principal.

Decentralisation approaches to accountability assume a role for school leaders as teachers of those with newly found voices, usually parents and/or teachers. This approach to accountability assumes that the school leader's role is to 'empower' these people and to actively encourage the sharing of power formerly exercised by the principal. School leaders, it is assumed, will act as members of teams rather than sole decision makers. This role entails teaching others how to make defensible decisions and how to clarify their decision responsibilities. As well, school leaders will embrace the belief that, through participation in decision making, teachers and parents will not only be more committed to the results of such decision making, but that the decisions themselves will be better. The school leader becomes the keeper of the process, not the outcome of the process.

Evidence of the effects on school leaders of decentralisation or school based management in its various forms is quite extensive (e.g. Bullock and Thomas 1997; Wildy and Louden 2000; Tanner and Stone 1998; Leithwood and Menzies 1998). These data indicate that, while assumptions about the role of school leaders in decentralised settings sometimes describe what actually happens in practice, it is often not the whole story. Decentralisation is associated, as well, with a radically increased emphasis on budgetary considerations and less attention to providing leadership in curriculum and instruction. Decentralisation greatly increases the time demands on school leaders and the need for more attention to time management, intensifies their role and, in quasi-market conditions, may isolate them from other administrative colleagues outside their own organisation.

When parent-dominated school councils are part of decentralisation, principals often provide leadership in respect to both internal and external processes associated with councils. Internally, principals often find themselves setting the agenda, providing information to other council members, assisting council decision making, and developing a close working relationship with the council chair. Externally, principals often act as strong, active supporters of their school councils, communicating with all stakeholders about council activities, and promoting the value of councils for the work of school staffs.

As an approach to accountability, site-based management is widespread, and experience with it relatively long-standing. Considerable empirical evidence suggests, however, that by itself it has made a disappointing contribution to the improvement of teaching and learning (Leithwood and Menzies 1999). In those exceptional cases where teaching and learning have benefited from this approach to accountability, school leaders have, for example, adopted a supportive leadership role themselves, nurtured leadership on the part of others, and strongly encouraged councils to adopt a capacity-building agenda (Beck and Murphy 1998; Leithwood *et al.* 1999b). Leadership practices such as these which transform an otherwise impotent strategy into at least a modest force for improving teaching and learning are important to be included among the criteria for evaluating school leaders.

Professional approaches to accountability

There are two radically different accountability strategies that have a professional orientation. One of these approaches manifests itself most obviously in the implementation of *professional control* models of site-based management. The other approach encompasses the professional standards movement as it applies to the practices of teachers, administrators. What both strategies share in common is a belief in the central contribution to their outcomes of professional practice in schools. They differ most obviously on which practices they choose for their direct focus. In the case of professional control site-based management, the focus is on school-level decision making, whereas classroom instructional practices and school leadership practices are the primary focus of the professional standards movement.

Professional control site-based management (Murphy and Beck 1995) increases the power of teachers in school decision making while also holding teachers more directly accountable for the school's effects on students. The goal of this form of site-based management is to make better use of teachers' knowledge in such key decision areas as budget, curriculum, and occasionally personnel. Basic to this form of site-based management is the assumption that professionals closest to the student have the most relevant knowledge for making such decisions (Hess 1991), and that full participation in the decision-making process will increase their commitment to implementing whatever decisions are made. Participatory democracy, allowing employees greater decision-making power, is also presumed to lead to greater efficiency, effectiveness and better outcomes (Clune and Witte 1988). Site councils associated with this form of SBM typically have decision-making power and, while many groups are often represented, teachers have the largest proportion of members.

A standards approach to accountability in the traditional professions emphasises heavy control of entry to the profession by government, with responsibility for subsequent monitoring of accountability turned over to members of the profession itself (e.g. colleges of physicians, lawyers' bar associations). Such an approach requires clear standards of professional knowledge, skill, and performance, something the professional standards movement in education set out to define beginning in the US, for example, in the early 1980s. Different products of the standards movement are available by now as the basis for the licensure of entry-level teachers (e.g. INTASC's Model Standards for Beginning Teacher Licensing, Assessment and Development) and school administrators (e.g. State of Connecticut Department of Education) as well as for recognising advanced levels of teaching (e.g. The National Policy Board for Teaching Standards), and school administrator performance (e.g. Education Queensland's 'Standards Framework for Leaders').

Professional approaches to accountability imply an increased need for school leaders to stay abreast of best professional practices and to assist staff in the identification of professional standards for their work. School leaders in the context of professional approaches to accountability need to set expectations and create conditions for professional growth. It seems likely, as well, that these leaders will find it productive to monitor progress of staff toward the achievement of professional standards, buffer staff from external distractions, and assist parents to understand and appreciate such standards. It has been suggested, as well, that school leaders will need to mobilise resources to meet not just higher but more sophisticated standards. They will need to be vigilant about such unintended side effects of standards as the narrowing of curricula. Maintaining teacher morale in schools identified as low-achieving, and helping ensure equitable treatments for needs of students, also seems a likely challenge for school leaders to be responding to this form of accountability (ERIC Clearinghouse 1999).

There is a dearth of systematic evidence about the extent to which these implications for school leaders are actually effective in implementing professional approaches to accountability. So, criteria included in a school leader evaluation policy reflecting this approach need to be used in an especially tentative manner. Furthermore, the professional standards approach to accountability and school improvement is severely limited by its focus on the capacitates of individual professionals. While improving the capacities of teachers and leaders one at a time is undoubtedly worthwhile, the collective effort of these professionals has a significant impact on what students learn. Among the criteria included in school leadership appraisals, therefore, should be practices which foster collective capacity identified in recent research about 'professional learning communities' (Louis and Kruse 1995), 'organisational learning' in schools (Leithwood and Louis 1999), and 'collective teacher efficacy' (Goddard *et al.* mimeo) Many of these are transformational practices, as described earlier in this chapter.

Management approaches to accountability

Not to be confused with 'new managerialism', this approach includes systematic efforts to create more goal-oriented, efficient and effective schools by introducing more rational procedures. The main assumption underlying this approach is that there is nothing fundamentally wrong with current school structures. The effectiveness and efficiency of schools will be improved, however, as they become more strategic in their choices of goals, and more planful and data-driven about the means used to accomplish those goals. This approach encompasses a variety of procedures for 'strategic planning', especially at the LEA level, as well as multiple procedures for school improvement planning (see the states of Illinois, Florida and Missouri, for example), school development planning (Giles 1997), and monitoring progress (e.g. the accountability reviews managed by New Zealand's Education Review Office).

Management approaches to accountability assume that effective school leadership conforms to what is sometimes labelled 'strategic management'. Heads or principals exercising this form of leadership are skilled in collecting and interpreting systematically collected data. They develop with their staffs clear, manageable goals and priorities for school improvement. Progress in accomplishing such goals is carefully monitored and plans refined accordingly. Because district resources and cooperation often are needed to accomplish school priorities, school leaders find it productive to develop especially good working relations with their LEA colleagues.

Evidence reviewed by Southworth (1998) suggests that these assumptions about effective leadership for school improvement have considerable real-world validity but that they are only part of the picture. In the context of two projects carried out by the University of Cambridge Institute of Education, successful school improvement appeared to depend on establishing and sustaining a culture of enquiry and reflection, a commitment to collaborative planning and staff development, high levels of stakeholder involvement, and effective coordination strategies. Establishing these conditions depended on school leaders emphasising the use of systematic evidence, focusing on student learning, and encouraging careful monitoring of both teaching and pupil progress. 'Strategic management' in these projects also entailed developing school improvement plans from the results of enquiry and reflection, and carefully monitoring and evaluating the implementation of those plans.

While often used as part of other approaches to accountability, the establishment of student standards, widespread student testing of their achievement, and judgements about both schools and leaders based on the results, is a strategy most often associated with management approaches to accountability. There is, however, considerable evidence that this strategy can have disastrous unintended consequences. Such consequences include, for example, minimising individual differences among students, narrowing the implemented curriculum, consuming enormous amounts of valuable instructional time, negatively influencing schools' willingness to accept students with weak academic records, and providing incentives for cheating (e.g. McNeil 2000; Ohanian 1999; O'Neil and Tell 1999). In the face of such risks, the evaluation of school leaders should include attention to practices designed to minimise or eliminate them.

Conclusion

In this chapter I argued that, for school leadership evaluation policies to serve growth-oriented purposes, they should include not just those criteria which acknowledge school-specific challenges faced by leaders. Such criteria also should reflect leadership practices:

- known to be productive in almost contexts, as well as
- those demanded by the external policy contexts in which leaders find themselves working.

Transformational leadership practices, it was argued, seem likely to be productive in many contexts and so serve as one promising source of school leadership evaluation criteria. Since increased demands for greater school accountability is a dominant part of the context in which present school leaders are working, practices effective in implementing such demands is a second source of evaluation criteria; these include practices capable of ameliorating the sometimes disastrous, unintended consequences of those demands for greater accountability.

As the chapter pointed out, most approaches to increasing accountability in schools make one of four quite different sets of assumptions about the status of schools and what is required to improve them. Because of these assumptions, each approach places unique demands on school leaders, for example: market approaches assume significant marketing skills; decentralisation approaches count on considerable expertise in group facilitation and empowerment; professional approaches demand high levels of knowledge about instructional effectiveness and skills in diagnosing and building such skills among teachers; and management approaches depend on leaders engaging in regular forward planning, as well as possessing quite sophisticated data interpretation and organisational monitoring skills.

As this summary of expectations and requirements illustrates, different types of accountability policies require at least partly distinctive responses on the part of school leaders to be 'effective'. Putting aside, for the moment, possible disagreements with the assumptions on which each set of accountability policies are built, leading school reform premised on any one of the four approaches to accountability is likely to be a manageable task. But almost no one uses the term manageable in reference to the job of principals or heads these days. 'Manageable headship' (like 'airplane food') has become an oxymoron. And one of the most plausible reasons is that most reform initiatives are eclectic. They bundle together into a single reform platform elements of all, or most, of the four approaches to accountability touched on in the chapter (also see Adams and Kirst 1999), and in the process create significant leadership dilemmas (Wildy and Louden 2000). So school leaders attempting to respond to their governments' demands for change can be excused for feeling that they are being pulled in many different directions simultaneously, because that is precisely what is happening – they *are* being pulled in many different directions simultaneously.

By now, however, considerable evidence (e.g. Fullan 1991) suggests that much of the variation in the extent to which externally initiated reforms actually result in school improvement can be explained by the ability of potential implementors to make sense of the reforms – to find them meaningful. So, in the face of policy eclecticism and the resulting sense of confusion and uncertainty, school leaders, with their staffs, parents, and other stakeholders need to locate and adopt elements of external initiatives that cohere with their schools' directions, that make sense in light of the school's goals and priorities. No matter the particular nature of the eclectic mix of policies and assumptions faced by a school, effective leadership will always include, for example, buffering staffs from their conscientious tendency to feel they must respond comprehensively to demands for policy implementation from governments. It will include, as well, providing individualised support to staff, challenging them to think critically and creatively about their practices, building a collaborative culture, developing structures that allow for collaboration to occur, and fostering parents' involvement in the education of their children. Policies for evaluating school leaders need to reflect these broader strategies if they are to foster school improvement.

References

Adams, J.E. and Kirst, M. (1999) 'New demands and concepts for educational account-ability: striving for results in an era of excellence', in J. Murphy and K. Louis (eds), *Handbook of Research on Educational Administration*, second edition, San Francisco: Jossey-Bass.

Bass, B. (1997) 'Does the transactional/transformational leadership transcend organiza-tional and national boundaries?', *American Psychologist* 52: 130–39.

Bass, B. (1985) *Leadership and Performance Beyond Expectations*, New York: Macmillan.

Beck, L. and Murphy, J. (1998) 'Site-based management and school success: Untangling the variables', *School Effectiveness and School Improvement* 9(4): 349–57.

Bennis, W. (1959) 'Leadership theory and management behaviour: The problem of authority', *Administrative Science Quarterly* 4(1): 259–60.

Bryman, A. (1992) *Charisma and Leadership in Organizations*, Newbury Park: Sage.

Bullock, A. and Thomas, H. (1997) *Schools at the Centre? A Study of Decentralization*, London: Routledge.

Burns, J. (1978) *Leadership*, New York: Harper & Row.

Chubb, J. and Moe, T. (1990) *Politics, Markets, and America's Schools*, Washington, DC: The Brookings Institute.

Clune, W.H. and Witte, P. (1988) *School-based Management: Institutional Variation, Implementation, and Issues for Further Research*, New Brunswick, NJ: Eagleton Institute of Politics, Center for Policy Research in Education.

Davis, S. and Hensley, P. (1999) 'The politics of principal evaluation', *Journal of Personnel Evaluation in Education* 13(4): 383–404.

Day, C., Harris, A., Hadfield, M., Tolley, H. and Beresford, J. (2000) *Leading Schools in Times of Change*, Buckingham: Open University Press.

Dillard, C. (1995) 'Leading with her life', *Educational Administration Quarterly* 4(1): 260.

Elmore, R. (1990) 'Choice as an instrument of public policy: Evidence from education and health care', in W.H. Clune and J. Witte (eds), *Choice and Control in American Education, Volume 1: The Theory of Choice and Control in Education*, New York: Falmer Press.

ERIC Clearinghouse on Educational Management (1999) 'Accountability', *Research Roundup* 16(1).

Fullan, M. (1991) *The New Meaning of Educational Change*, Toronto: OISE Press.

Giles, C. (1997) *School Development Planning: A Practical Guide to the Strategic Management Process*, Plymouth: Northcote House Publishers.

Goddard, R., Hoy, W. and Woolfolk, A. (mimeo) 'Collective teacher efficacy: its meaning, measure and impact on student achievement', Ohio State University.

Grace, G. (1995) *School Leadership: Beyond Education Management*, London: Falmer Press.

Gray, J., Hopkins, D., Reynolds, D., Wilcox, B., Farrell, S. and Jesson, D. (1999) *Improving Schools: Performance and Potential*, Buckingham: Open University Press.

Gronn, P. (1996) 'From transactions to transformations: a new world order in the study of leadership', *Educational Management and Adminstration* 24(1): 7–30.

Hausman, C.S. (2000) Principal role in magnet schools: Transformed or entrenched?', *Journal of Educational Administration* 38(1): 25–46.

Hess, G.A. Jr (1991) *School Restructuring Chicago Style*, Newbury Park, CA: Corwin Press.

Hipp, K. and Bredeson, P. (1995) 'Exploring connections between teacher efficacy and principals' leadership behaviour', *Journal of School Leadership* 5(2): 136–50.

Kerchner, C.T. (1988) 'Bureaucratic entrepreneurship: The implications of choice for school administration', *Educational Administration Quarterly* 24(4): 381–92.

Kowalski, J. and Oakes, A. (1993) 'The evolving role of superintendents in school-based management', *Journal of School Leadership* 3(4): 380–90.

Lauder, H. and Hughes, D. (1999) *Trading in Futures: Why Markets in Education Don't Work*, Buckingham: Open University Press.

Lee, V. (1993) 'Educational choice: The stratifying effects of selecting schools and courses', *Educational Policy* 7(2): 125–48.

Leithwood, K. (1994) 'Leadership for school restructuring', *Educational Adminstration Quarterly* 30(4): 498–518.

Leithwood, K. and Duke, D. (1999) 'A century's quest to understand school leadership', in J. Murphy and K. Louis (eds) *Handbook of Research on Educational Administration*, San Francisco: Jossey-Bass.

Leithwood, K. and Louis, K. (eds) (1999) *Organizational Learning in Schools*, The Netherlands: Swets & Zeitlinger.

Leithwood, K. and Menzies, T. (1998) 'A review of research concerning the implementation of site-based management', *School Effectiveness and School Improvement* 9(3): 233–86.

Leithwood, K. and Menzies, T. (1999) 'Forms and effects of site-based management', *Educational Policy*, 11(3): 233–85.

Leithwood, K. and Steinbach, R. (1995) *Expert Problem Solving*, Albany, NY: Suny Press.

Leithwood, K., Edge, K. and Jantzi, D. (1999) *Educational Accountability: The State of the Art*, Gutersloh: Bertelsmann Foundation Publishers.

Leithwood, K., Jantzi, D. and Steinbach, R. (1999a) *Changing Leadership for Changing Times*, Buckingham: Open University Press.

Leithwood, K., Jantzi, D. and Steinbach, R. (1999b) Do school councils matter? *Educational Policy* 11(4): 467–93.

Leithwood, K., Tomlinson, D. and Genge, M. (1996) 'Transformational school leadership', in K. Leithwood (ed.) *International Handbook of Educational Leadership and Administration*, The Netherlands: Kluwer Academic Press.

Louis, K. and Kruse, S. (1995) *Professionalism and Community*, Thousand Oaks, CA: Corwin Press.

Marchak, M. (1991) *The Integrated Circus: The New Right and the Restructuring of Global Markets*, Montreal: McGill-Queen's University Press.

McNeil, L. (2000) *Contradictions of School Reform: Educational Costs of Standardized Testing*, New York: Routledge.

Murphy, J. and Beck, L. (1995) *School-based Management as School Reform*, Thousand Oaks, CA: Corwin Press.

Ohanian, S. (1999) *One Size Fits Few: The Folly of Educational Standards*, Portsmouth, NH: Heinemann.

O'Neil, J. and Tell, C. (1999) 'Why students lose when tougher standards win: A conversation with Alphie Kohn', *Educational Leadership* 57(1): 18–23.

Ornstein, A.C. (1983) 'Administrative decentralization and community policy: Review and outlook', *Urban Review* 15(1): 3–10.

Peters, M. (1992) 'Performance indicators in New Zealand higher education: Accountability or control?', *Journal of Education Policy* 7(3): 267–83.

Raywid, M. (1992) 'Choice orientations, discussions, and prospects', *Educational Policy* 6(2): 105–22.

Southworth, G. (1998) *Leading Improving Primary Schools*, London: Falmer Press.

Tanner, K.C. and Stone, C.D. (1998) 'School improvement policy: Have administrative functions of principals changed in schools where site-based management is practiced?' *Education Policy Analysis Archives* 6(6): 1–14.

Wildy, H. and Louden, W. (2000) 'School restructuring and the dilemma of principals' work', *Educational Management and Administration* 28(2): 173–84.

Wohlstetter, P. and Mohrman, S.A. (1993) *School-based Management: Strategies for Success*, New Brunswick, NJ: Rutgers University.

Chapter 5

The issue of ethics in principal appraisal

New Zealand

Wayne L. Edwards

Introduction

In today's era of reform in education, appraisal of performance has become a fact of life for teachers, principals and administrators. Almost daily, one seems to meet someone in education who is ready to chat about his or her recent appraisal experience. The stories vary from, 'It was great!' to 'We simply went through the formalities', to 'I felt totally inadequate, put down or demeaned!' – depending on who is telling the story and his or her perspective on the appraisal experience. Similarly, there is also no shortage of 'how to do it' resource material on the task of appraisal. The process is now embedded in many education systems and this is certainly true in New Zealand.

To institutionalise the task among teachers required time and effort while, quite predictably, the time was soon to arrive for principal appraisal to come to the fore. As with teachers, principals typically report a range of satisfactions (or dissatisfactions) with their experiences. As with teachers, the written advice is strongly focused on the process by which appraisal might occur. The steps are made clear, the potential benefits are delineated and the possible documentation is presented in sample form. All that remains is to 'get on' with the process.

From a personal perspective, as I listened to appraisees' stories, I found my own interest becoming less concerned with process and product. The growing concern was with the reports of people's feelings about their appraisals, the way in which the process was undertaken and the way in which they perceived they had been treated during that process. In addition, teachers were heard to make such comments as: 'We certainly never hear anything about the principal's appraisal. The staff get no feedback and aren't asked for any views', or, 'I don't even know whether or not our principal is ever appraised!' To begin reflecting on such issues, inevitably, takes one well beyond the confines of process or product and into the deeper field of examining issues which are ethical in nature.

Once one enters this field of thinking, the conclusion soon follows that, in fact, addressing ethical issues in appraisal might well be at least as (and probably more) important than becoming slavishly addicted to designing and implementing some form of appraisal process. In short, *the ethics* which underlie the process might be even more important than *the technicalities* of that process. The literature rarely takes readers into this dimension. One soon begins, therefore, to address the issues which underlie the overt process.

The field of ethics – what is it?

Stated simply and in popular terms, ethics is concerned with 'doing right things' as distinct from 'doing things right'. Ethics might be seen as a moral code or set of moral principles. After having been closely involved in the protracted negotiation of a senior level employee's grievance and future in an organisation, the writer learned, at first hand, about the importance of the concept of natural justice.

Certain elements of the case were disturbing. Decisions had been made about the person's duties and standing in the organisation without consideration of this person's views or wishes. In the subsequent negotiation and reconciliation process, however, the importance of natural justice was brought to the fore. Clearly, the affected person should be treated with respect and in an open manner in which any allegations could be answered, in which all evidence would be tabled for examination and in which the person's views could be expressed and given every consideration. Laura Weintraub (1998: 113) explains, although focusing on the legalities and the rights of students:

> Natural justice means that those involved can participate in and respond to the proceedings. . . . One of the occupational obligations of educators and educational administrators is to consider, integrate, and protect the principle of natural justice.

Although performance appraisal processes might not normally involve a high degree of attention to legalities, this fundamental principle should, in my view, be clear in the minds of all parties involved in activities concerned with any evaluation of one's work performance. Clark (1997: 160) notes this principle simply as, 'being fair to all concerned'. He goes further (pp. 159–60) by listing a group of ethical principles which ought to underpin all spheres of human contact and which can readily be applied to the appraisal process:

- Promoting good and minimising harm (i.e. beneficence).
- Treating people with dignity (i.e. respect).
- Endeavouring to tell the truth and being committed to the pursuit of truth.
- Advancing the freedom of the individual to a degree which is consistent with the maximum liberty for all.

Each of these ethical principles, on reflection, was important in the case mentioned above. In principal appraisal, too, they are easily applied: for instance, the process should help to enhance the principal's performance in leading the school as an educational place (beneficence); the people should interact in a dignified manner throughout the entire process (respect) while the process should draw on useful and reliable information in order to be worthwhile in itself (truth). But, first, what provisions or demands exist for the appraisal of school principals in New Zealand?

The appraisal of principals in New Zealand

Since 1 January 1997, the provision of performance management systems has been a mandatory feature of New Zealand schools. Each school's board of trustees (which is largely comparable to governors in the British system) is required to have established and implemented policies and procedures for managing the performance of all teachers as well as the school's principal. Teachers and principals are required to take part in the appraisal of their performance at least once per year. Typically, teacher performance management and appraisal are delegated to the principal while the responsibility for undertaking the principal's appraisal lies with the board of trustees.

The board's role is enshrined in legislation in New Zealand, as described in the Ministry of Education's *Principal Performance Management* (1999: 4). The State Sector Act 1988 requires boards to have personnel policies that provide for the 'Fair and proper treatment of employees in all aspects of their employment'. The Education Act 1989 explains the roles and responsibilities of boards and principals: 'A school's principal is the board's chief executive in relation to the school's control and management.' The Act further requires boards to ensure that:

(a) the school is managed, organised, conducted and administered for the purposes set out or deemed to be contained in the charter, and

(b) the school, and its students and community, achieve the aims and objectives set out or deemed to be contained in the charter.

The Act provides legal authority for the National Administration Guidelines (commonly termed 'the NAGs'). Guideline 2 of the NAGs (explained in *Governing and Managing New Zealand Schools*, 1997: 20–3) refers to personnel policies and the performance management of staff, including principals. This guideline contains two requirements for boards of trustees which must:

(i) develop and implement personnel and industrial policies, within policy and procedural frameworks set by the Government from time to time, that promote high levels of staff performance, use educational resources effectively, and recognise the needs of students.

(ii) be a good employer as defined in the State Sector Act 1988 and comply with the conditions contained in employment contracts applying to teaching and non-teaching staff.

Principal appraisal – the Ministry of Education

The Ministry of Education's publication, *Principal Performance Management* ('PPM', in brief: 1999) provides boards and principals, in a dozen pages, with advice for developing and implementing performance agreements and appraisal. The remainder of the publication consists of two dozen pages of samples of board policy statements on these topics and job descriptions for principals, performance objectives for principals and, in quite detailed form, sample indicators of the professional standards which principals are required to meet in the course of their work.

The PPM document contains two major sections (pp. 3–13) first, principal performance management and, second, performance appraisal. 'Principal performance,' the document notes, 'formalises the relationship and accountabilities between principals and their boards, and links these to the annual planning and review cycle.' The joint process between principals and boards should, 'help keep them on track' as they work through clarifying board expectations and developing the principal's performance agreement, ensuring that the agreement's objectives link with the school's strategic plan, identifying professional development objectives, monitoring the principal's performance and providing feedback, to principal and board, which is based on the performance appraisal.

The annual performance agreement highlights priorities for the principal's performance and professional development. The agreement therefore seeks to draw together four elements: the principal's job description, the published Professional Standards for Principals, the results which the principal is expected to achieve and the objectives for increasing the principal's knowledge and skills where appropriate. In the latter area, PPM suggests that at least one such objective should be identified each year.

The PPM document continues (p. 9):

> A principal's performance appraisal is based on the performance agreement signed at the beginning of the performance management cycle between the principal and board of trustees. The process of monitoring and giving feedback needs to be ongoing throughout the year. The arrangement works best when principals and board chairs have regular contact, and an open style of communication based on high levels of trust and understanding.

The document notes (p. 9) that the process usually involves principals and board chairs although a small sub-committee might be appointed by the board in order to undertake the task. Maintaining confidentiality is specifically noted as being important while, at the beginning of the appraisal cycle, principals and board chairs should decide on the proposed timeline, the kinds of information which will be used and the people who will be involved in the process. The appraisal should be based on the same four sources of information noted in developing the performance agreement.

A number of options are suggested (pp. 9–10) as appropriate sources of information for the process, including peer appraisal, self-appraisal, board members, staff, students, parents, the community, neighbouring schools and various kinds of written information. The latter items might include, for example, board reports, newsletters, evaluation reports on the school, various school records and plans and information which might be available in reports of professional development activities emanating from government agencies (such as the Education Review Office or the New Zealand Qualifications Authority). The possible involvement of outside consultants is also discussed.

Other PPM guidance includes (p. 10):

- Information is usually collected throughout the year.
- Regular contact between board chairs and principals is normal practice in order to keep up with current issues and events, goals and deadlines.
- Sufficient uninterrupted time for the appraisal interview is important.
- The principal and chair should establish the focus and priorities for the appraisal.
- There should be a balance between quantitative and qualitative aspects of the principal's performance.

The PPM document advised (p. 11) both principal and board should receive feedback based on the performances agreement. Board chairs should normally provide principals with an overview of the information which was collected for appraisal purposes while a subsequent written report should be able to be subject to the principal's response. Any amendments to the report should be signed by both parties. Board chairs, in reporting to their boards, should describe the process which was undertaken and a summary of the 'points agreed to by both parties'. The PPM further indicates (pp. 11–12): 'Any discussion should be in committee, and should focus on the processes used and the extent to which the principal met the requirements in the performance agreement.' The final step, after each formal appraisal, is that of board and principal reviewing the performance agreement prior to signing a new agreement which either confirms or changes the job description, sets new performance and development objectives and either confirms or changes the performance indicators.

Principal appraisal – The School Trustees' Association

The New Zealand School Trustees' Association publication, *Guidelines for Boards of Trustees: The Management of the Principals by the School Board of Trustees* (NZSTA 1999: 2–19) provides guidance for boards as the employers of their principals. The remaining twenty-one pages of the publication consists of reiteration of the professional standards for principals in addition to samples of the appraisal process, job descriptions, principal appraisal policies and a sample performance agreement.

The School Trustees' Association ('STA', as it is popularly termed) is clear in recognising the legal place of boards in the system of education administration in New Zealand. The first paragraph of Section One notes (p. 2) 'Legislation establishes boards of trustees as the employer in state schools in New Zealand. The board has all the rights, duties, and powers of an ordinary employer.' At the foot of the page, the document reiterates the point that the State Sector Act 1988 and the Education Act 1989, '. . . gives the board the duties, responsibilities, and privileges as an employer.'

On the roles and relationships of board and principal, STA interprets (p. 3) the Education Act 1989 as, 'the board managers the manager, and the manager manages the school.' This responsibility, STA explains, is subject to board policies determining the board direction for running the school through the principal's day-to-day management, with board resolutions providing the basis for the principal's actions and the performance objectives established by the board and the performance standards which the principal is required to achieve. Further, STA notes: (p. 3)

> The principal is charged under section 76 of the (Education) Act with the complete discretion to manage the school. . . . This allows the principal the judgement to manage the school according to the curriculum requirements and other National Education Guidelines within board policy. The principal also has specific responsibilities with respect to management of staff, health, education, suspensions, etc.

STA notes, too, (p. 4) that the National Education Guidelines and the National Administration Guidelines make it clear that boards must aim at providing an environment in which high levels of performance are promoted while, at the same time, acting as a good employer and complying with the terms and conditions contained in employment contracts. The greater part of the STA document is concerned with performance appraisal which is described (p. 7) as:

> Performance appraisal or performance review of a principal is a tool by which the board can measure whether the objectives set for the school are being met. Through performance appraisal, the board and the principal can ascertain whether the elements of a job description, the performance objectives, and the outcomes are achievable and productive and take both the individual and organisation forward.

Trustees are reminded (p. 8) that the Government introduced the requirement for a board's performance management system to include a performance appraisal process for principals and teachers: 'It is therefore, a mandatory requirement that boards of trustees will review the performance of their principal through the performance appraisal process.' In a substantial section of its document (pp. 11–14) STA provides guidance on establishing the performance agreement: determining overall and specific objectives and indicators, determining the appraisal process, determining good performance and formally approving the performance agreement. Some advice is then provided (p. 15) for deciding whether or not to use the services of a consultant in the appraisal process. STA's guidance concludes (pp. 17–18) with 'The Review/Appraisal' process itself. First, interim assessments might help a board to anticipate unforeseen circumstances and make adjustments during the course of the year. Second, the nature of an appraisal is discussed. The uninterrupted appraisal meeting (p. 18) is about:

- *Acknowledging* success and achievements.
- *Providing* performance feedback.
- *Recognising* where professional development is required.
- *Improving* the quality of the day-to-day management of the school.
- *Fulfilling* the board's contractual obligations as the employer.
- *Supporting* the principal by an established process.
- *Evaluating* effectiveness.
- *Resourcing* ongoing development needs.

Results should be summarised in writing (including agreed plans, dates and indicators) and provided to the principal for comment before being presented in committee to the full board. Three copies of the final document should be provided – one for the principal, one for the board (secured in a safe place) and one for the principal's personal file.

STA's guidance concludes with a note on making any decisions which concern any proposed bonus, after the consideration of the appraisal report – without the presence of the principal. Finally, STA indicates (p. 19): 'However, there are occasions (though relatively few) when there is a disagreement either as to the process itself and / or the outcome of the performance review.' Where disagreement continues to exist, secondary principals have the right to attach written comments to the final performance agreement. However, the views of principals in other types of schools (primary, intermediate, area or middle schools) must be considered by their boards although any subsequent decisions of the board shall be final. The importance of good communication skills is highlighted during the development of process and content.

The emphasis in both documents

In the two New Zealand documents that were described above, the major concerns centre almost entirely on establishing a workable *process* for principal appraisal. Rights and responsibilities of boards and principals are clarified as is the mandatory requirement for the appraisal of principals. Advice is provided for establishing the process, for collecting information, for identifying appraisers, for undertaking the appraisal interview and for reporting to the board and establishing the future performance agreement. Procedures for handling disagreements also receive some attention. Both publications provide examples of various types of documentation which might be associated with the process – job descriptions, principal appraisal policy statements, performance agreements and development objectives. In the wider literature, it is not difficult to locate other items with similar focus (e.g. Poster and Poster 1993; Gane and Morgan 1992, ch. 5). However, this major concern with process overshadows a number of other important issues which underlie a principal's appraisal.

Issues in the appraisal of principals

The appraisal of principals (and perhaps other senior staff members with major responsibility for an institution or significant sections of it) is quite different, and probably more complex and far reaching, than is the case with the majority of staff members. There are, for example, some questions which are crucial to the success of the appraisal process for such key staff members:

- How open should the process be?
- What kinds of staff, and other, consultations should occur as part of the process?
- Who should undertake the appraisal task itself?
- Should 'outsiders' be involved – and on what basis should they be selected and by whom?
- What level of involvement should be available for all members of the governing body which collectively carries responsibility for the task and for the principal's performance?
- To what extent should the process be linked to future performance (i.e. being formative in nature) or to performance rewards (i.e. being summative in nature)?
- What sort of information should be reported more widely after the appraisal event?
- Whose meanings and whose values should drive the principals' appraisal process?

These questions raise a number of significant ethical issues or dilemmas in the appraisal of principals. Discussion of several such issues should serve as illustrative 'think pieces' at this point.

Issue One: Key values such as fairness, honesty, transparency, trust and respect

This group of values relates closely to the notion of nature justice which was noted earlier. Several aspects are important.

First, today's teachers are well-used to participating in performance appraisal. They should rightly expect that the demands of similar appraisal processes will be applied throughout their schools – from the principals to the most newly appointed staff members. In this sense, it is only fair that *all* staff are required to participate in processes which will enable their professional performance to be effectively evaluated. Boards face a dilemma if some staff seem apparently free of this demand. The first response from teachers is likely to be the cry, 'It's just not fair!' Janet Thomson (1992: 85) principal of a school in England, explained the point effectively: 'I would consider that observation of their headteacher taking part in appraisal must also engender trust and understanding of appraisal among the staff.'

Second, the actual processes for appraising any specific principal should not remain the privileged knowledge of the few people directly involved in the event. Open and public disclosure of the process might not only indicate that the task was carefully planned and rigorously implemented but also that the board takes seriously its responsibilities as a 'good' employer in monitoring the professional performance of its chief executive and in seeking to enhance his or her opportunities for development in order to function as an effective principal. The dilemma, of appearing to be either lax or off-handed towards its responsibilities or becoming secretive in its dealings, faces boards which do not openly publicise the principal appraisal process.

Third, of course, the process should be undertaken in a dignified fashion in which there is mutual trust and respect between appraisers and principal and, in particular, where the concept of natural justice is fundamental to the process. Without the presence of such key values, boards will ultimately face dilemmas in maintaining harmonious and workable appraisal relationships and in being able to effectively defend the integrity of their appraisal processes and purposes. Respect, therefore, for both the persons and process is important. Janet Thomson reported on one particularly sensitive moment in her experience of being appraised as headteacher of an English school:

> If this appraisal had been a mechanistic exercise to grade my performance and assassinate my character I would have packed my bag and left at this moment. Because of a number of factors to do with quality of relationships – trust, respect, security, confidence and the underlying philosophy of our appraisal process – I complied.

Issue Two: The purpose of a principal's appraisal, and Issue Three: The nature, limits and responsibilities of participants in disclosing outcomes with people beyond the appraisal group (e.g. staff members, fellow board members, parents, students)

These two issues are intertwined. Chester (1992: 73) in discussing headteacher appraisal in England, noted: 'It should be acknowledged that the case of head-teachers is distinctly different from that of teachers in general.' He also noted the complexity of the headteacher holding full membership of the school's governing body and being responsible for implementing that body's policies. Chester continued:

> Since the headteacher is held accountable . . . it is tempting to turn to the appraisal of headteachers to provide input into that accountability process. To do so is to make a fundamental error about the nature and purpose of headteacher appraisal. It is not there primarily to provide accountability. Its principal function is to contribute to professional development to which headteachers are entitled as much as other teachers.

While the professional development purpose of principal appraisal is important, as Chester suggests, such an appraisal must necessarily go beyond appraising only against a narrow job description. Consideration should be given to the principal's part in leading towards school goals and in implementing the school's strategic plan, in promoting better teaching performance, in working towards school improvement and in managing a cohesive school environment.

There are, too, a number of people and groups upon whom a principal's performance has a significant impact and who might be expected to take more than a passing interest in the performance appraisal of that principal. Such stakeholders are also likely to be keen to be told more than that 'our principal has been appraised'. This concern raises the issue of reporting on a principal's appraisal. With their overview and ultimate responsibility for the school's performance and for the meeting of strategic goals and for the implementation of overarching policies, the principal is not only a key player in the total life of the school but also he or she has significant responsibilities which affect the working levels and performance (with impact, too, on personal lives) of the board itself and of teaching colleagues, parents, students and the school's community.

The dilemma is for a board to report meaningfully to such stakeholders without breaching the privacy of the principal. In conjunction with the principal, the board needs to identify and agree on the precise information that can be communicated, from or about the principal's appraisal, to a wider audience. Perhaps, in fact, the first task might be to identify the personal, private or confidential information which will be held entirely within the keeping of the board and the principal. A simple statement which informs people that the appraisal occurred and that the process covered a number of (listed) areas of interest to others might be the very least kind of communication. However, an agreed statement, between board and principal, might indicate, once again, that the appraisal occurred and some flavour might be provided about the discussion on major areas of achievement and the objectives which have been established for the future. Such an example might state that: The principal's appraisal occurred recently. In general, both board and principal agreed that the school has successfully moved forward in a number of important areas in the current year – especially in the following curriculum and pastoral areas. . . . In addition, the board and the principal agreed that the further development of the school's professional development programme would be given priority during the coming year. Etc, etc.

However, the privacy of the individual in relation to the rights of the school (and other members of the school community) is important. There is little shortage of advice on privacy matters in relation to appraisal. In general, the same points apply to principal appraisal. Appleby (1995: 1) lists a dozen principles for 'information privacy' in relation to New Zealand's Privacy Act 1993, including:

- *purpose* (collection of information must be lawful)
- *advice* (individuals must be aware that personal information is being collected)
- *collection* (personal information should not be collected unlawfully or intrude on an individual's private life)
- *access* (individuals should be able to access their personal information)
- *correction* (individuals have the right to correct their personal information)
- *use* (personal information must be used only for the purpose for which it was sought)
- *disclosure* (personal information must not be disclosed to any other person, body or agency, unless the disclosure is related to the purpose for which the information was obtained).

Boards need to be aware of these principles and, as Cascio (1991: 440) suggests, as employers, 'after reviewing their policies, they should articulate, communicate and implement fair information practice policies'.

The problem in addressing these and other such complex issues lies in the degree of 'firmness' with which we establish our principles in order to solve the ethical dilemmas which can play a part in any principal appraisal process.

Ethical theory – two bases

In considering such ethical dilemmas in a way which will suitably underpin the implementation of its planned principal appraisal process, a board must decide the degree to which these policies will be firmly or immovably 'set in concrete' or the degree to which it will be subject to, at least, some amount of flexibility and interpretation in order to enable circumstances or competing forces to be considered in any particular situation. Clark (1997: 153) explains this dichotomy:

> First in establishing principles, we can aim to construct rules which must be followed regardless of the consequences. In this sense, a principle becomes a promise which should be kept in all circumstances.

Clark terms this a *deontological* approach.

> In the context of appraisal, an act is morally good if the promise is kept but wrong if the promise is broken. It is irrelevant to take into consideration either

any special circumstances which might operate or any potential consequences which might arise.

Second, we can aim to be more utilitarian in constructing rules (or guidelines) which place considerable emphasis on the possible consequences of an action. In this sense, the greatest satisfaction for the greatest number of people is important.

Clark terms this a *teleological* approach and goes on:

> In the context of appraisal, an act is morally right when it promotes more good than harm but morally wrong when there is a greater balance of harm over possible good.

Clark's explanation is useful in helping us to appreciate the difficulty of 'legislating' in areas which involve the consideration of ethics, while Cascio (1991: 437–8) reminds us that ethical behaviour is not governed by hard and fast rules but it adapts to changing social norms and in response to the needs and interests of those served by a profession; for example, the deep interviews, the prescribed standards of dress and the lack of access of employees to their own files would be considered improper today.

Perhaps the best course of action for boards is that they become fully aware of the ethical issues and of their potential for impacting on the appraisal process. Discussion of ethical issues in principal appraisal, therefore, is vital at board level when such processes are being planned. The fruits of these discussions, very likely, will be not only greater understanding of what is really happening in a principal's appraisal but also the construction of guidelines to firmly underpin any implementation of the planned system. Board members, therefore, need to consider the 'inflexibility–flexibility' dilemma and, similarly, they should seek to identify the features of their principal appraisal which will be 'non-negotiable' and those for which some degree of flexibility may be possible. Although writing about the broader field of human resource management, Cascio (1991: 451) provides a useful summative perspective:

> Ethical choices are never easy, the challenge of being ethical in managing human resources does not lie in the mechanical application of moral prescriptions, but rather in the process of creating and maintaining genuine relationships from which to address ethical dilemmas that cannot be covered by prescription.

Principles for principal appraisal: Ten suggestions

What might be a set of suitable ethical guidelines for a principal performance appraisal process? This is the major question! A possible answer might include:

1 Key human values stemming from a concern for natural justice will form the basis of the principal appraisal process.
2 The purpose of the appraisal will be clear to board and principal.
3 Board members and their principal will discuss the purpose and design of the proposed principal appraisal process.
4 The appraisal process will have integrity and it will be open to disclosure.
5 The rights, interests and privacy of the principal as an individual will be protected as will the same features of the school as an organisation.
6 Confidentiality of sources of information will be ensured.
7 Information used in the appraisal will be reliable – not based on hearsay or bias.
8 There will be commitment to act on results.
9 Principals will have the opportunity to respond to and discuss the foreshadowed judgement arising from the appraisal process.
10 A useful and appropriate statement on the process and the outcomes will be provided to stakeholders.

What else might be suggested? It might be tempting for appraisers to simply 'lift' such a battery of points for use in their own situation. However, any real value is much more likely to come from a board carefully considering the ethical issues of principal appraisal themselves and then constructing their own list of points prior to building any process which might be followed in undertaking the task of principal appraisal.

In conclusion

This chapter began with a couple of disturbing quotes which indicated that some principal appraisal experiences might seem irrelevant or inadequate, poorly conceptualised, unfair or demeaning, surrounded in mystique or just a way of 'going through the motions'. Reflection, by boards and principals, on the deeper issues which underlie the appraisal of principals, is likely to produce processes which take account of significant ethical issues and, hence, which engender shared awareness of the essential foundations of principal appraisal. Gane and Morgan (1992: 35–6) argue persuasively:

> . . . appraisal is much more than a mere checking device; it is also a powerful instrument for bringing about improvement in performance, as a result of colleagues being enabled, through a properly structured process, to share ideas and working methods, and to collaborate purposefully in enhancing the quality of their work. It is developmental, not only for appraisees, but also for appraisers who benefit several times over from their contact with each appraisee, and from the privilege and advantage of being able to share their accumulated wisdom and increased expertise with their colleagues.

A well founded, ethically driven approach to principal appraisal holds enormous potential not only for enhancing the abilities and performance of the principal as an individual educator but also, and more importantly, for helping that principal to function with greater effect and influence as the key professional leader in his or her school's journey towards greater school improvement. We should look forward to many more principals commenting on their appraisal experiences with, 'It was great!'

References

Appleby, R. (1995) 'Does your organisation comply with the privacy act?', *Leading Issues*, New Zealand Institute of Management, Wellington, Issue 11.

Cascio, W.F. (1991) *Applied Psychology in Personnel Management*, Englewood Cliffs, NJ: Prentice Hall.

Chester, H. (1992) 'School governance and the appraisal of headteachers', in M. Hattersley (ed.) *The Appraisal of Headteachers*, London: Cassell.

Clark, J. (1997) *Educational Research: Philosophy, Politics, Ethics*, Massey University, Palmerston North: ERDC Press.

Gane, V. and Morgan, A. (1992) *Managing Headteacher Appraisal*, London: Paul Chapman.

Ministry of Education (1999) *Principal Performance Management*, Wellington: MoE.

Ministry of Education and Learning Media (1997) *Governing and Managing New Zealand Schools: A Guide for Boards of Trustees*, Wellington: MELM.

New Zealand School Trustees Association (1999) *Guidelines for Boards of Trustees: The Management of the Principal by the School Board of Trustees*, Wellington: NZSTA.

Poster, C. and Poster D. (1993) 'Headteacher appraisal', in M. Preedy (ed.) *Managing the Effective School*, Buckingham: Open University Press.

Thomson, J. (1992) 'She would say that, wouldn't she?', in M. Hattersley (ed.) *The Appraisal of Headteachers*, London: Cassell.

Weintraub, L. (1998) 'Subversive record keeping', in *SET Research Information for Teachers*, New Zealand Council for Educational Research, Wellington, No. 2 Item 10.

Part II

Performance appraisal and teacher development

The chapters in this part offer different perspectives on the ways in which managing teacher performance and its appraisal may or should influence teacher development. In Chapter 6, Stephen Jacobson and Catherine Battaglia describe the starting point in the USA as one where teachers are on 'the lowest rung on the educational hierarchy' and their development is little more than remediation. They describe a project in which teachers' attitudes, as well as their practice, was transformed by a much greater emphasis on the teachers as people and as learners. They draw out the lessons for educational leaders as being to move towards sharing the assessors' role with others, recognising and therefore influencing the environment of teachers' work, and towards a greater emphasis on collaborative thinking. Perhaps this is what is often described as performance appraisal as being something you do *with* people not *to* them.

In the new landscape of the post-apartheid New Republic of South Africa, Michael Thurlow describes in Chapter 7, with Shamella Ramnarain, how the legacy of past practice in teacher appraisal has led to intense suspicion of new practice. The current proposals inevitably pay much attention to processes that must be seen as democratic but may run the risk, as the authors point out, of being bureaucratic and, by offering a 'one model fits all' approach, of undermining some of the principles described in the chapters in Part I.

The issue of separating professional development within the performance appraisal process leads to what Tanya Fitzgerald in Chapter 8 sees as a paradox and a considerable potential tension. She shows that teachers are anxious that statutory requirements for professional development to meet stated standards for accountability reasons may have negative effects. Some schools in her New Zealand study had integrated processes in place in 1998 but she argues that there may well be compliance at a minimal level in the future. Since the principles in the New Zealand scheme, including those concerning pay and promotion, are close to the UK ones, there may well be lessons for managers elsewhere.

In Chapter 9, David Middlewood describes the pendulum swings in the UK of the way teacher performance and its appraisal has been managed. A 'soft' form of appraisal, focused almost exclusively upon professional development, was pronounced as 'discredited' by the government and its supporters, but the new forms of performance management were introduced with minimum consultation. Middlewood argues that there were valuable lessons to be learned from the earlier model which school managers need to absorb to ensure that the new management works to best effect. Research showing teachers' concerns about divisiveness supports the view that there are fundamental principles that managers need to establish in developing any scheme. Above all, they need to take a long-term view and ensure that any imposed scheme fits with the strategic aims that the school has for its performance and that of the teachers who work there.

Chapter 6

Authentic forms of teacher assessment and staff development in the US

Stephen L. Jacobson and Catherine F. Battaglia

Introduction and overview

More often than not, teacher assessment and staff development in the US are not closely aligned and, even when they are, the connection between the two tends to communicate a 'relatively impoverished view of teachers, teaching, and teacher development' (Little 1993: 130). Staff development is often perceived as little more than instructional remediation that necessarily follows assessment. In part, this is because assessment and staff development mirror the overarching approach to leadership that governs education at any point in time, and often school governance views teachers as the lowest rung on the educational hierarchy.

In this chapter, we will present a case for viewing appraisal as a natural, systemic part of the life-long learning of a teacher, especially when considered within the framework of a transformational approach to leadership that seeks to elevate the status of teachers. We will look at self-directed, job-embedded forms of professional development, such as self-assessment, collegial circles, peer coaching, and action research. Although underutilised, these forms of evaluation can provide a conceptual link between staff development and teacher appraisal. But, to be implemented successfully, they demand a redefinition of central and site-based leadership, especially with regard to the relationship between teachers and administrators and the development of organisational structures that support the context for such initiatives. Specifically, the development and implementation of such appraisal tools reflect an evolution first from managerial to instructional approaches to leadership, both of which are characterised by traditional 'top-down' organisational hierarchies, and then to a 'flatter' type of learning organisation that many transformational leaders believe schools can become.

We begin this chapter by painting our canvas in broad strokes to capture the landscape of educational governance and leadership that existed in the US over the past century. First, we consider the emergence of schools as organisations fashioned on an industrial model during the first half of the twentieth century, which was followed by a recommitment to instruction as the central purpose of schooling during the 1970s and 1980s. We conclude this section by examining the 'systemic' reform movement that has characterised the close of the century.

The hallmarks of this movement are centrally determined learning standards and greater site autonomy and accountability in the achievement of those standards. These reforms have increased the need to build the professional capacity of all educators, teachers and administrators alike and, in so doing, these efforts have forced educators to reconsider school leadership and the forms and functions of appraisal and staff development that best support it.

To better understand these changes in teacher assessment and staff development and their relationship to school governance and leadership, we next use a finer brush to represent these same issues on a smaller scale, through examples of school initiatives currently underway in one US school district. We conclude the chapter by offering a few lessons learned from the experiences of this district. We hope that by reducing our examination of authentic forms of teacher assessment and staff development to a single case, we can best present both the complexity and potential of the approaches we endorse.

The growth of the school organisation

The latter part of the nineteenth century was a time of rapid population growth and immigration in the US. While just over four million youngsters aged 5–17 years-old attended schools in 1850, there were seventeen million in 1900, a fourfold increase in fifty years (Bureau of the Census 1976). This period was also a time of rapid economic development and industrialisation in the US. In response, American industry needed public schools to create a large, cheap labour force that had a common language and work ethic, factors necessary to make workplace supervision easier and less costly.

Principles of scientific management, with its inherent concern for efficiency, were thus introduced to education early in the twentieth century (Callahan 1962). Over the next seventy years, one manifestation of scientific management was that schools were centralised and consolidated in order to create economies of scale. Between 1930 and 1970, the number of public school districts in the US declined markedly from 130,000 to 18,000, while enrolments continued to grow rapidly – from 29 to 51 million (Bureau of the Census 1976). As a result, the average US school district's enrolment mushroomed from roughly 200 to over 3,000, a fifteenfold increase in just forty years (Jacobson 1998).

This rapid growth in district size brought with it a managerial approach to leadership that often requires individuals to suppress personal needs for the sake of achieving organisational goals. Commitments are, therefore, specified through formal contracts and policies. As Leithwood *et al.* (1999: 14) point out:

> Managerial leadership assumes that the focus of leaders ought to be on *functions, tasks, or behaviours* and that if these functions are carried out competently the work of others will be facilitated.

From this perspective, one can imagine the school functioning as an assembly line, with each worker (teacher) having a highly specific, carefully time-managed task, turning out products (students) in an efficient, 'scientifically' determined fashion. Accordingly, as is the case in a factory, a hierarchical structure emerged in these larger scientifically managed educational organisations that assumed that one's position in the governance hierarchy reflected one's professional expertise. As Sergiovanni (1994: 216) writes:

> Those higher in the hierarchy are presumed to know more about teaching, learning and other matters of schooling than those lower, and thus each person in a school is evaluated by the person at the next higher level.

Assessment and development under such a governance structure is quite simplistic, often reduced to checklists of observable behaviours and then the remediation needed to enable teachers to 'get it right'. There is no place for professional judgement and/or self-assessment under such a scheme.

Schools rediscover instruction

In the aftermath of James Coleman's influential 1966 report, *Equality of Educational Opportunity*, policymakers in the US began to question the value-added contribution of formal public schooling over and above that of the social capital contributed by students' parents. The fact that parental socio-economic status (SES) was the best predictor of student performance was not a surprise, but the fact that school factors contributed so little to achievement was both a surprise and a disappointment to educators. As a result of this concern, educational researchers began to examine the unique organisational characteristics of high performing inner-city elementary schools serving low-SES, minority students (Rosenholtz 1985). This line of research, which came to be known as the Effective School Movement, found that organisational factors account for 32 per cent of between-school variance in student achievement, even when controlling for random error (Rowan *et al.* 1983). To many educational policymakers, this was good news because it signalled the fact that schools could make a difference if the following characteristics were in evidence:

1 strong principal leadership;
2 clear mission and purpose;
3 safe and orderly climate;
4 high expectations for all teachers and students; and
5 consistent, standardised measures of performance.

(Brookover and Lezotte 1979; Edmonds 1979)

At the state level, this work ushered in the so-called 'first wave' of school reform which focused on instructional standard-setting that included initiatives to:

•   raise high school graduation requirements;

- tighten curriculum controls around the content, sequence, and pacing of instruction; and
- mandate state-wide testing.

(Fuhrman *et al.* 1993)

At the school level, managerial leadership began to give way to instructional leadership. Instructional leadership is similar to managerial leadership in that authority is allocated to administrators based upon their relative position within the governance hierarchy. Thus, there remains the presumption that administrators have expert knowledge (Leithwood *et al.* 1999). But where instructional leadership differs from managerial leadership is in the fact that the focus is primarily on the principal and 'the behaviours of teachers as they engage in activities directly related to the growth of students' (Leithwood *et al.* 1999: 8).

Concurrent with this renewed focus on instruction, important changes began to emerge in the way schools were configured and governed. Peters and Waterman (1982) found that excellence in the private sector could often be attributed to 'chunking', i.e. companies decentralising into smaller, more manageable units. Picking up on this lead, educational policymakers began to argue that bigger was not necessarily better when determining the optimal size for units of educational governance. In fact, there was a growing realisation that smaller, site-based units of governance might offer students and community members significant educational and social benefits that outweighed efficiencies gained through economies of scale. This 'second wave' of restructuring reforms was subsequently implemented by a number of large urban school districts in the US, most notably in Chicago, where in 1989 considerable control was shifted from the central school bureaucracy to local councils in each of the city's 592 schools (Hess 1993).

Not surprisingly, the focus of staff appraisal on professional development during this period was teacher behaviours presumed to directly influence student performance. The exemplar of that period was Madeline Hunter's 1982 work on the Essential Elements of Instruction. Although never intended, Hunter's work offered administrators a seemingly straightforward set of guidelines for evaluation, improving on past evaluation checklists only in its emphasis on empirically tested instructional behaviours. However, this approach still perpetuated the top-down model of appraisal that had formerly characterised managerial leadership.

Systemic reforms to transform schools

In the early 1990s, a new approach to school reform emerged, one that attempted to combine the first and second waves into a third 'systemic' wave of reform. This strategy sought to work by simultaneously:

> . . . increasing coherence in the system through centralised coordination and increasing professional discretion at the school site. Thus while schools have the ultimate responsibility to educate thoughtful, competent, and responsible citizens, the state – representing the public – has the responsibility to define

what 'thoughtful, competent, and responsible citizens' will mean in the coming decade and century.

(Smith and O'Day 1991: 254)

In essence, systemic reform seeks to coordinate top-down state mandates with bottom-up local initiatives. The state mandates create standards for accountability, which are best realised by allowing local flexibility and creativity. To accomplish these goals, school leaders need to transform the culture in schools from one in which collegiality is fostered through structural arrangements and appeals to personal self-interest, to one in which relationships rely on interdependence, emerging from 'the binding of people to common goals, shared values, and shared conceptions of being and doing' (Sergiovanni 1994: 219).

Since transformational leaders focus on 'the commitments and capacities of organisational members', authority in transformational leadership, unlike either managerial or instructional leadership, is more personal than positional, and power is attributed to 'whomever is able to inspire their commitments to collective aspirations' (Leithwood *et al.* 1999: 9).

This change in orientation is so different from past practice as to require a change in leadership and governance that is:

... more in tune with meaning and significance, and the shared values and ideas that connect people differently. And these new connections would require that we invent new sources of authority for what we do, a new basis for leadership.

(Sergiovanni 1994: 218)

Part and parcel of this new orientation is the need to develop alternative ways to view teacher assessment and professional development. To examine how this new orientation is beginning to emerge in practice, we move our study closer to the ground and examine changes in evaluation and staff development that have taken place in one school district over the past decade and a half.

Assessment and staff development: One district's experience

The focus of our study is an inner-city school system located in Western New York, which includes approximately 9,300 students and a staff of 1,195 instructional and classified personnel. At the time of writing, there are nine elementary schools, three middle schools, one senior high school, a Centre for Young Parents, a day school for adult basic education, and a school for students in need of an alternative educational environment.

As an outgrowth of the Effective Schools Movement, the school district formed an interim staff development committee in the spring of 1985. The group had two purposes: first, it functioned as a central advisory committee to plan and coordinate training activities on an efficient, cost-effective basis. It reviewed all proposed activities from the schools, prioritising them according to system-wide needs and available funds, and made recommendations accordingly to the Deputy Superintendent (the second in command in the district). Second, it served as a resource to principals by providing information and supportive services to help meet building-level staff development needs.

At this juncture, the district was organised in a traditional bureaucratic fashion, and management determined decisions about teachers' professional development. Building level administrators and central office personnel planned professional development for the staff members they supervised and provided the means for such experiences to occur. Routinely, this was accomplished in one-day, 'one-shot' in-service training sessions or 'Superintendent's Conference Days', that informed, inspired, and entertained staff members in mostly benign, unobtrusive ways. Such events were typically characterised by 'the workshop' and built upon the expectation that teachers would take ideas from training sessions and integrate them into practice. Support for such services was usually contracted from outside the organisation and delivered by consultants with specialised expertise in designated areas.

Teacher appraisal was also bureaucratically managed, with professional staff supervised and evaluated by building administrators. The district utilised a Behaviourally Anchored Rating System (BARS) to assess teaching proficiency and rate performance. The scale was intended to monitor and enhance teaching competency and was designed to answer two key questions:

1 Is the teacher doing the job according to the established standards of the school district?
2 In what areas might the teacher develop and extend his/her knowledge and professional repertoire of technique and skill?

Despite the fact that BARS offered an objective, standardised method for conducting teacher appraisal, it was predicated on the belief that teachers lacked the ability to set goals or assess their own performance. Thus, it suggested that teacher knowledge is best derived from people and places outside the context of the classroom.

As noted earlier, about this same time, educational reform reports were painting a less than optimistic picture for how schools would fare if restructuring did not occur. These reports altered traditional conceptions of student learning and advocated the inclusion of social discourse, personal reflection, and collaborative inquiry in an effort to shift learning from a consumer orientation to one that encouraged active participation. The reforms were strongly supported by research in cognitive science and constructivist approaches to learning:

> To know something is not just to have 'received' information, but also to have
> . . . elaborated on it and questioned it, examined it in relation to other

information . . . and to 'build knowledge structures' . . . in this way, knowledge becomes truly generative . . . and can be used to interpret new situations, to solve problems, to think and to reason, and to learn.

(Resnick and Klopfer 1989: 4)

When the rhetoric of restructuring was applied to teachers' practice within the school organisation and teachers, rather than students, became the focus of reform, an incongruity emerged. This prompted the district to reconceptualise the role of 'the teacher' in light of what it meant to be 'a student'. If teachers were to become participant learners in a learning community, it was clear that a redesign of the appraisal system was needed.

The staff development committee recommended the initiation of a district-wide staff development programme focusing on the then popular tenets of instructional theory and practice (Hunter 1982; Gentile 1988). To meet this objective, three full-time staff developers were hired to design and deliver the programme (Battaglia 1997 was one of these three). A course entitled ITIP – Instructional Theory Into Practice – was offered to all full-time, tenured staff members, with a minimum of five years' experience in the district (three years by the tenure requirement). The intent of the seminar was to update teachers' instructional skills and knowledge and encourage professional dialogue about teaching and learning. The course offered teachers the opportunity to study and work with colleagues from different buildings, grade levels, and disciplines.

Although coursework was based on research regarding effective teaching, content was structured to downplay the technical, positivistic interpretations of teacher practice. The district's version of ITIP endeavoured to present teaching as a creative, complex, decision-making activity, rather than a mechanical act relying on field-tested recipes. The course offered a more constructivist approach and teachers were encouraged to reflect on and make sense of information presented as it applied to the conditions of their work.

Among the many benefits of the ITIP programme was that it provided teachers with a common body of knowledge in all disciplines and at all grade levels. Since it focused on instructional theory, teachers were less apt to talk about methods and more inclined to engage one another in conversation related to learning theory. Those comfortable with the language were inclined to use it in discourse about practice with supervisors who came to evaluate them. The expectation at the time was that teachers needed to know pedagogy and be able to explain their instructional actions within broader theoretical terms. Because there was also the expectation that in order to supervise and assess instructional practice principals needed to know and understand instructional theory, the ITIP programme provoked a shift from managerial to instructional leadership.

However, ITIP was a training programme and, as such, it did not operate without its share of problems. A disturbing consequence when training teachers in this fashion is 'de-skilling', wherein teacher learning is treated as a commodity and appraisal erroneously labels those with the most tools and techniques more competent (McNeil 1988). Such a view postulates that there are general solutions to practical problems which can be developed outside the classroom, tested independently, and disseminated to practitioners with the expectation that they will accept and utilise the information (Schon 1983). This technical rational approach implies a top-down hierarchy, which assumes that practitioners passively apply theoretical knowledge that has come to them from outside the context of practice (Sparks and Loucks-Horsley 1990). It further purports that those closest to the problems of practice are least qualified to deal with them and must, instead, rely on the influence of more reliable experts. This view of teachers-as-implementers contradicts the image of teachers-as-reflective-educators and further solidifies their status as impotent technicians. If teacher expertise was to become a legitimate voice in school improvement, the ITIP would have to evolve.

The ITIP programme ran from 1988 until 1993, when the district underwent a major restructuring effort to decentralise decision-making and develop a site-based model. This was a natural outgrowth of the shift taking place at the time towards instructional leadership, but also a precursor of systemic reform, as state-level mandates proliferated. Consequently, staff development initiatives became part of school-site plans, prompting both teachers and principals to request more in-class assistance and support. Informally, many began coaching one another and small study groups, called 'collegial circles', formed where teachers fleshed out deeper understandings of instructional practice.

When ITIP was first conceived, plans included the concept of support but did not specifically address what it would look like or how it would be implemented. Subsequently, a formal coaching component was integrated into the ITIP programme to provide for sustained, in-classroom support. This action temporarily satisfied the need for more contextual, job-embedded staff development. What was becoming clear, however, was the need to develop a model of professional learning and development that focused on relationships between educators and the environment surrounding professional activity (Goodlad 1987).

This new model needed to attend to the diverse needs and interests of individuals and espoused a 'working-with' rather than a 'working-on' stance towards teacher appraisal (Lieberman 1986). A 'working-with' perspective treats teachers as both partners in their own assessment and active agents of change. This emphasis on shared leadership, horizontal relationships, contextual learning, and reflective decision-making and assessment reinforced the tenets of school restructuring at that time. Such a model, when combined with meaningful collaborative involvement and self-directed inquiry, while not perfect, was promising because it recognised that although teachers need guidance and support, they bring considerable expertise to their own development. This deviates from more traditional bureaucratic approaches to teacher remediation by promoting instead teacher learning to help build organisational capacity (Smylie 1996).

Action research as a strategy to restructure appraisal and professional development for teachers

Provoked by the challenge to redesign professional development for teachers, the district investigated using action research methodology as one way to encourage teachers to improve by systematically studying practice 'on the job' and in the company of colleagues. In the spring of 1993, the district's Board of Education approved a pilot project entitled the *Professional Growth Plan* (PGP), to study the efficacy of using action research (AR) as a professional development / alternative assessment option for teachers (Battaglia 1997).

Based on Lewin's (1946) assertion that the best way to improve and study practice is to change it, AR was considered because it is:

> ... the study of a social situation with a view to improving the quality of the action within it. . . . (The) total process – review, diagnosis, planning, implementation, monitoring effects – provides the necessary link between self-evaluation and professional development.
>
> (Elliott 1982: ii, 1)

Moreover, AR is:

> ... concerned with the everyday practical problems experienced by teachers, rather than the theoretical problems defined by pure researchers within a discipline of knowledge.
>
> (Elliott, 1982: 1)

Winter (1989: 4) elaborates:

> Professional workers are not to be thought of as the 'objects' of research into professional practice but always (at least) as collaborating research workers and (ideally) as well placed to initiate and carry out the investigation and development of the practice and understandings in which they are involved. . . . Hence the complete phrase which describes the activity is 'practitioner action-research'.

While each author conceives professional inquiry and research in slightly different ways, the thematic link is the concept of teachers' thinking. If, as the reform reports conclude, students are expected to graduate from schools with the capacity to inquire into their world, it was apparent that teachers also needed to be encouraged and supported in their critical inquiry. Thus, through the use of AR, teachers could utilise the social setting of the school as a starting place for systematic, intentional investigation where personal knowledge construction and theory building are nurtured.

However, this model demands a new form of leadership, one that is less focused on managing teacher behaviour and more intent on creating an environment for teacher learning to occur. Conceptually, AR provides such a process and establishes conditions where teachers and students have opportunities to:

- identify problems and issues important to them;
- select materials and study information pertinent to their issues;
- choose ways to implement new ideas and solutions to problems;
- target specific areas of their practice where improvement and growth are desired;
- develop as inquirers and learn new methods for carrying out research in their classrooms in an effort to add to their professional knowledge; and
- initiate and lead restructuring efforts within the school community.

Essential qualities of AR, according to some writers, are cooperation and collaboration, thus bringing together attributes of community and collegiality consistent with transformational leadership approaches. 'Two of the ideas which were crucial in Lewis's work were the ideas of group decision and commitment to improvement' (Kemmis and McTaggart, 1988: 6). Collaboration may take the form of working with team members who affiliate with a thematic concern or as an individual participating with others to share perceptions, interpret data, and act as 'critical friends' (Costa and Kallick 1993). This is important to note, because it represents a significant shift in teacher culture. For example, Little (1993) suggests that teachers are more inclined towards superficial congeniality than critical collegiality. The development of a 'critical community of equal voices' where teachers are engaged in studying and appraising practice is recognised as a possible first-step to commence change (Noffke and Stevenson 1995).

AR methodology provides teachers with the opportunity for choice, reflection, empowerment and collaboration, and supports principles of adult learning theory. In addition, the establishment of collaborative communities where individuals 'own' and profit directly from their research endeavours upholds democratic traditions (Kincheloe 1991), and is consistent with the aims of transformational leadership.

The project

The general plan involved working with volunteer teachers in a three-year AR pilot project to study and engage in critical discourse about practice. The project rested on the premise that teacher appraisal and staff development needed to be more closely aligned; therefore, it aimed to study and develop ways for teacher learning to become job-embedded, and eventually part of the culture of the district. Little (1993: 130) emphasises this point, stating:

> In the midst of current reform, traditional, bureaucratic management of teachers' professional development appears incompatible with profession-

alism. Choice, reflection, inquiry, and collegial support need to become standard and not unique when looking at teachers' learning environments.

Such literature offered advice about where improvement could start, emphasising the fact that teachers needed both the time and opportunity to work together. Collaboration, inquiry, and continuous learning stood out when thinking about restructuring teachers' professional development. With this as a backdrop, the PGP project endeavoured to modify professional development and teacher appraisal by providing teachers with the means to:

- create new knowledge about practice;
- engage in reflective discourse with members of their profession;
- achieve a higher degree of autonomy about professional growth and development; and
- enjoy lifelong learning within the school community.

Prior to the commencement of the PGP project, and common to teacher practice in general, teachers were reluctant to subscribe to ideas tested in experimental settings outside the classroom. Workshops and graduate courses were criticised by teachers for being 'too theoretical', which was a way of claiming, 'It won't work here'. This lack of transfer from workshop to workplace is a key reason why staff development training has often had negligible effects on teacher practice and short-term impact on meaningful school improvement (Joyce and Showers 1988).

After a three-year pilot study, substantive evaluations were conducted to assess the use of AR as an alternative assessment option. The cadre of teachers who engaged in the project was enthusiastically supportive of the potential for including AR as a professional development appraisal option. The goal now was to bring the PGP project to scale and to have it negotiated into the teachers' contact as a bona fide alternative to augment the BARS assessment. Several key issues emerged that inform both the future of the process within this district and provide insights that might be generalised to other educational contexts.

Lessons learned

First, attempting to move quickly from a principal-directed, administratively managed model such as BARS was simply too big a change for many teachers and principals, many of whom had little or no understanding of AR tools, reflective processes, or job-embedded assessments in general. This prompted the need to include additional appraisals that might help the staff shift toward the rigour of the AR model in a more incremental fashion. Therefore, along with AR and BARS, self-assessment and peer coaching were negotiated into the district contract to provide teachers a continuum of assessment options from which to select. Quite simply, the lesson learned was that when change of this magnitude is instituted, it is necessary to proceed slowly and provide sufficient teacher appraisal options in order to bring staff and school leaders along.

Second, prior to its site-based initiative, the district had attempted 'multiple interventions' at school improvement, but like many other districts in the US, the connections between these interventions could best be described as 'low coherence' (Fuhrman et al. 1993). When the district finally began to institutionalise a more systemic planning process to guide school improvement, it became necessary for everyone at the school-site to be moving toward common targets. However, unlike prior district practices under managerial and instructional leadership, it was no longer necessary for central office and building level administrators to mandate 'how' to hit these targets. Under those earlier forms of leadership, teacher appraisal and professional development were SUPERvised, i.e. determined by those with superior status in the educational hierarchy. This approach predominated until the district moved to site-based governance, where SUPERvision had to be replaced by superVISION. To accomplish this, leaders at both the school-site and district levels needed to embrace a new vision of collegiality and a sense of how to achieve district goals though teacher self-assessment. These new relationships would grant teachers more authority over their own professional development, thus lessening the authoritative role of the administrator in this domain. It was found that teachers could play significant roles in providing this type of leadership because, through their personal authority, they could inspire their colleagues to work and learn together.

However, even the most respected teachers were not in the position to make key decisions required to facilitate a more collaborative work environment. Therefore, it was still necessary for administrators to exert their hierarchical authority in order to allocate the time, space, and fiscal resources that would permit such work among teachers to occur.

That said, an unexpected consequence of this change was that administrators at the school-site were confused about what role they were to play in these new forms of appraisal and began to ask questions such as: 'Where do I fit in this new relationship?' 'How do I enter this conversation?' and 'Who is ultimately responsible for teacher evaluation?'

Some principals even expressed concern that less than competent teachers might use these new forms of appraisal to avoid detection and, thus, the intervention of their supervisor. To address these concerns, only tenured teachers were granted permission to participate in the alternative assessment options, and building administrators were required to sign-off on the involvement of any teacher in such a plan. The reader should be aware that these were expedient responses, not preferred approaches. Ultimately, we would hope to see the creation of a professional culture that would preclude the need for such restrictions.

In addition, the district learned some important lessons in regard to the preparation necessary to support job-embedded appraisal structures. It became apparent that it was crucial for staff to learn to utilise the language of critical friendship, or what Little (1993) calls 'informed dissent', in order to familiarise staff with the processes and strategies of alternative appraisal options such as peer coaching and action research. Because the professional culture of educators rarely encourages this kind of collegial discourse, administrators and teachers are not always prepared to either engage in, or facilitate, conversations in which colleagues can 'agree to disagree'. It was recognised, therefore, that various forms of training and coaching should be provided so educators can integrate the language of critical reflection into practice. Leaders, in turn, must have this on their agenda as a priority, be able to model it, and be ready to support such conversation if transformation of a school culture is to occur. More importantly, reflective inquiry cannot commence when a person first enters a school or assumes a leadership position; tools of inquiry and critical reflection must be taught and become part of an educator's professional preparation (Jacobson *et al.* 1998). Quite simply, another lesson learned is that teachers and administrators alike need to understand these new forms of appraisal and their respective roles within them and develop the prerequisite tools necessary to best utilise them.

Moving from the specifics of leadership transformation at the building level, another point gleaned from this experience was the importance of altering governance at the district level as well. Specifically, it was recognised that many district-wide policies and practices precluded opportunities for collegial engagement to occur at the site level. For example, principals complained about the difficulty of providing time to accommodate teacher collaboration and suggested the modification of school calendars and reallocation of staff development days to provide time so that teachers could collaborate to reflect about practice. These adjustments routinely reside with leaders in central office who have the ability to influence school board policies and practices. Given this dynamic, it is imperative that central office administrators delegate greater authority to administrators at the building level so that the critical allocations of time, space, and fiscal resources noted earlier can occur unimpeded and be context specific.

Perhaps the most ambitious challenge for leaders at both the school-site and district level is for them to become authentic members of the learning communities they endeavour to create and don new behaviours for facilitating inquiry-based collaborative work. If they simply mimic, or choose merely to manage the processes of inquiry without applying the same processes to their own professional learning and growth, attempts to change school or district culture will, at the very least, lead to staff scepticism and non-compliance (Emihovich and Battaglia 2000; Jacobson, 1998; Leithwood *et al.* 1999)

As noted in the introduction, our goal in this chapter was to provide the reader with a better understanding of the relationship between educational leadership and authentic forms of teacher assessment and staff development by focusing on change efforts in one US school district. It should be clear from this case that reforming a school system's approach to appraisal may require changes in its approach to leadership and vice versa. Ultimately, the goal for districts pursuing this work would be to develop simultaneously forms of leadership, teacher appraisal, and professional development that are interconnected, complementary, and consistent in ways that will eventually align school structures with sustained learning and improvement for the whole of the educational community. The analysis undertaken with this district holds promise for expanding this work beyond its modest beginning and has sparked a number of broad issues relevant to the field that may serve as points of departure for further inquiry. However, there is still much to be done.

References

Battaglia, C. (1997) 'Creating a reflective teaching community: Action research squared', unpublished doctoral dissertation. New York: University at Buffolo.

Brookover, W. and Lezotte, L. (1979) *Changes in School Characteristics Coincident with Change in Student Achievement*, East Lansing, MI: State University, College of Urban Development.

Bureau of the Census (1976) *Historical Statistics of the United States, Colonial Times to 1970*, Part I Education (Series H 412–789) Washington, DC, US Department of Commerce.

Callahan, R. (1962) *Education and the Cult of Efficiency*, Chicago: University of Chicago Press.

Coleman, J. (1966) *Equality of Educational Opportunity*, Washington, DC: US Government Printing Office.

Costa, A. and Kallick, B. (1993) 'Through the lens of a critical friend', *Educational Leadership* 51(2): 49–51.

Edmonds, R. (1979) 'Effective schools for the urban poor', *Educational Leadership*, 37, 15–24.

Elliott, J. (1982) *Action Research: A Framework for Self-evaluation in Schools*. Working Paper No. 1, Teacher-Pupil Interaction and the Quality of Learning, London: Schools Council.

Emihovich, E. and Battaglia, C. (2000) 'Creating a culture of collaborative inquiry: The role of instructional leaders', *International Journal of Leadership in Education, Theory and Practice* 3(3).

Fuhrman, S., Elmore, R. and Massell, D. (1993) 'School reform in the United States: Putting it into context', in S. Jacobson and R. Berne (eds), *Reforming Education: The Emerging Systemic Approach* (pp. 3–27), Fourteenth Yearbook of the American Education Finance Association, Thousand Oaks, CA: Corwin Press.

Gentile, R. (1988) *Instructional Improvement: Summary and Analysis of Madeline Hunter's Essential Elements of Instruction and Supervision*, Cleveland, OH: National Staff Development Council.

Goodlad, J. (1987) 'Structures, process, and an agenda', in J. Goodlad (ed.), *The Ecology of School Renewal* (pp. 1–19), Chicago: University of Chicago Press.

Hess, A. (1993) 'Decentralisation and community control', in S. Jacobson and R. Berne (eds), *Reforming Education: The Emerging Systemic Approach* (pp. 66–86), Fourteenth Yearbook of the American Education Finance Association, Thousand Oaks, CA: Corwin Press.

Hunter, M. (1982) *Mastery Teaching*, El Segundo, CA: PIP Publications.

Jacobson, S. (1998) 'Preparing educational leaders: A basis for partnership', in S. Jacobson, C. Emihovich, J. Helfrich, H. Petrie, and R. Stevenson (eds), *Transforming*

Schools and Schools of Education: A New Vision for Preparing Educators (pp. 71–98), Thousand Oaks, CA: Corwin Press.

Jacobson, S., Emihovich, C., Helfrich, J., Petrie, H. and Stevenson, R. (1998) *Transforming Schools and Schools of Education: A New Vision for Preparing Educators*, Thousand Oaks, CA: Corwin Press.

Joyce, B. and Showers, B. (1988) *Student Achievement Through Staff Development*, New York: Longman Press.

Kemmis, S. and McTaggart, R. (1988) *The Action Research Planner* (third edn). Geelong: Deaking University Press.

Kincheloe, J. (1991) *Teachers as Researchers: Qualitative Paths to Empowerment*, London: Falmer Press.

Leithwood, K., Jantzi, D. and Steinback, R. (1999) *Changing Leadership for Changing Times*, Buckingham: Open University Press.

Lewin, K. (1946) 'Action research and minority problems', *Journal of Social Issues* 2: 34–46.

Lieberman, A. (1986) 'Collaborative work', *Educational Leadership*, 43: 4–8.

Little, J. (1993) 'Teachers' professional development in a climate of educational reform', *Educational Evaluation and Policy Analysis* 15(2): 129–51.

McNeil, L. (1988) *Contradictions of Control: School Culture and School Knowledge*, New York: Routledge.

Noffke, S. and Stevenson, R. (eds), (1995) *Educational Action Research: Becoming Practically Critical*, New York: Teachers College Press.

Peters, T. and Waterman, R. (1982) *In Search of Excellence*, New York: Harper & Row.

Resnick, L. and Klopfer, L. (1989) *Towards the Thinking Curriculum: Current Cognitive Research*, Alexandria, VA: Association for Supervision and Curriculum Development.

Rosenholtz, S. (1985) 'Effective schools: Interpreting the evidence', *American Journal of Education* 93(3): 352–88.

Rowan, B., Bossert, S. and Dwyer, D. (1983) 'Research on effective schools: A cautionary note', *Educational Research* 12(4): 24–31.

Schon, D. (1983) *The Reflective Practitioner*, San Francisco, CA: Jossey-Bass.

Sergiovanni, T. (1994) 'Organisation or communities? Changing the metaphor changes the theory', *Educational Administration Quarterly* 30(2): 214–26.

Smith, M. and O'Day, J. (1991) 'Systemic school reform', in S. Fuhrman and B. Melen (eds), *The Politics of Curriculum and Testing* (pp. 233–67), Bristol, PA: Falmer Press.

Smylie, M. (1996) 'From bureaucratic control to building human capital', *Education Researcher* 25(9): 9–11.

Sparks, D. and Loucks-Horsley, S. (1990) 'Models of staff development', in W.R. Houston (ed.), *Handbook of Research on Teacher Education* (pp. 234–50), New York: Macmillan.

Winter, R. (1989) *Learning from Experience: Principles and Practice in Action Research*, Philadelphia, PA: Falmer Press.

Chapter 7

Transforming educator appraisal in South Africa[1]

Michael Thurlow with Shamella Ramnarain

Introduction

South Africa has committed itself to a fundamental transformation of its social institutions and the values which underpin and shape them, and this commitment finds its clearest expression in the country's new Constitution (Republic of South Africa 1996a), as well as in a variety of policies and emerging legislation.

Since 1994, within the broad context of transformation, the national Department of Education has refocused the vision and direction of the South African education system through a series of policy initiatives, several of which have been formalised in legislation (Department of Education 1996: 11). The range of these initiatives, undertaken during the first five year term of the democratic government, as evidenced in successive annual reports of the Department of Education, has been extensive and impressive. In terms of restructuring, a single education system has been developed out of the previously existing nineteen, racially based departments and the administration of the system has been devolved substantially from national to provincial levels. The establishment of school governing bodies, through the enactment of the South African Schools Act (Republic of South Africa 1996b), has resulted in considerable decision-making authority being allocated to schools, giving rise to the assertion that South Africa is now firmly pointed towards a school-based system of education management (Department of Education 1996: 12). Among the other initiatives, of which there are too many to enumerate here, significant developments have included the mapping out of a national qualifications framework for education and training, the development and staged implementation of an outcomes-based approach to curriculum, and a variety of measures aimed at increasing access to schooling and greater equity and redress in resourcing.

While the achievements of the first five years have been substantial, the Director-General of the national Department of Education has observed:

> Despite the many changes however, the challenge to make a significant impact on the quality and extent of learning attainment for the majority of our people remains elusive.

> (Department of Education 2000a: 3)

The promotion and achievement of quality in schooling, and the education system more generally, would appear to lie at the heart of the Department of Education's corporate plan for the five years 2000–2004, with a particular emphasis being placed on implementation and improved service delivery. The Department's plan is based upon its political mandate from the Minister of Education, which was set out in a ministerial statement entitled 'Call to Action: Mobilising Citizens to Build a South African Education and Training System for the 21st Century' (1999), with its accompanying slogan of 'Tirisano' or 'working together', indicating the partnership that exists between the national and the nine provincial departments of education. This plan addresses nine priorities, identified by the Minister, through five programmes, which clearly are set out in such a way as to emphasise a commitment to action, delivery and accountability (Department of Education 2000b).

Of particular relevance for present purposes is Programme 2: School Effectiveness and Educator Professionalism which, among other things, deals with development of the professional quality of the teaching force. One of the strategic objectives identified for Project 4 (Status and Quality of Teaching), which is one of the seven projects subsumed in this programme, is 'to develop a framework for educator development that promotes and enhances the competence and professional skills of educators' (Department of Education 2000a: 16). While considerable work has been completed already on the development of norms and standards for initial teacher education (Republic of South Africa 2000), action identified for this strategic objective includes the development of a policy for educator development, the development of programmes for educator development and the implementation of the educator appraisal system (Department of Education 2000a: 29–30).

It must be presumed that reference to implementing the educator appraisal system refers to an intention to renew efforts to implement the system. The history of the transformation of educator appraisal in South Africa predates the election of the country's first democratic government, in 1994, and an extended process of negotiation and development culminated in an agreement on the introduction of developmental appraisal in the Education Labour Relations Council, during 1998, (ELRC 1998) and the gazetting[2] of the new scheme early in 1999 (Republic of South Africa 1999). Since that time, an attempt has been made to implement the scheme which, as we shall suggest, has been somewhat less successful than was anticipated.

In the remainder of this chapter, we shall summarise the conditions which gave rise to discontent and dissatisfaction with what passed previously for appraisal of educators and will describe the initiatives which gave rise to the development of a transformed appraisal system. Having set out briefly the characteristics of the new system, we shall attempt to offer an early assessment of it, and to raise some issues which remain problematic.

A context for change

> The current system of teacher appraisal is one of the most vehemently contested aspects of the present system, and hence one of the most important factors negatively influencing the quality of education. There is an urgent need to move away from the present summative, authoritarian practices. . . .
>
> (ANC 1994b: 7)

The nature and extent of the inequities and injustices which characterised the provision and practices of education generally during the apartheid era, together with analyses of the resistance engendered by these, are well documented (see, for example, Christie 1985; Kalloway 1984; Nkomo 1990; Unterhalter *et al.* 1991). While it must be obvious that the causes for the rejection of appraisal practices at that time were linked inextricably to the wider context, nevertheless it is possible to identify some of the more specific sources of discontent and disillusionment. However, in doing so it needs to be borne in mind that, because of the fragmented nature of educational administration and substantial differences in levels of resourcing between the various education departments at the time, appraisal practices and the quality of relationships between educators and the inspectorates varied considerably. Whereas the experience of appraisal and relationships with the inspectorate of those employed in the white departments, although not entirely unproblematic, were largely positive, the experiences of the majority of black teachers were substantially different. In the latter case, so strong was the rejection of what was perceived to be an illegitimate system that, after 1989, as a result of a campaign by 'progressive' educators, inspectors and subject advisers were forced to suspend their activities throughout large parts of the country.

However, while in a context exhibiting wide variations in practice and experience one is forced to generalise, it is safe to argue that it was the rejection of existing appraisal procedures and practices, as experienced by the majority of black educators, which provided the effective impetus for transformation initiatives.

In their discussion of teachers' perceptions of prevailing appraisal practices, Chetty *et al.* (1993: 3) identified a range of criticisms, among which the following are especially illuminative:

- the prevalence of political bias in the system;
- the unchecked power which inspectors wield;
- the incompetence of inspectors;
- the irrelevance of some evaluation criteria;
- the arbitrariness of scores given for appraisal;
- the secrecy which surrounds the appraisal;
- the difficulty of challenging inspectors' assessment; and
- the absence of contextual factors in the appraisal.

The significance of these criticisms is that they illustrate how, from the educators' perspective, dissatisfaction apparently was focused both on the methods and processes of appraisal and the inspectorates responsible for the administration and conduct of these. Quite clearly, while the perceptions of educators alone could not be taken to represent a definitive analysis of the inadequacies of the appraisal systems, they were important and were reflected substantially in more considered analyses of factors which impacted negatively on the state of educator appraisal.

In the most comprehensive summary of such analyses available, Chetty *et al.* (1993: 4–12) demonstrated considerable quantitative and qualitative short-comings, in relation to the inspectorates, of the various education departments. In particular, they highlighted the unequal, and frequently inadequate, distribution of inspectors (and subject advisers, who were also involved variously in appraisal) between the different departments; the generally limited capacity and capability of those appointed to these positions; marked gender disparity in appointments; minimal availability of training for the role; relatively low selection criteria and even the influence of 'patronage and political rivalries' in appointments.

However, while many shortcomings were identified in relation both to the quality and availability of the agents of appraisal, more fundamental criticism was levelled at the nature of their appraisal functions and the underlying purposes.

In terms of the former, the commentators observed:

> South Africa's system of appraisal has been largely inspectorial and bureaucratic. It shares with all other aspects of the education bureaucracy a top-down, closed, hierarchical and authoritarian character. In the case of black teachers it has been concerned with efficiency and social control rather than professional development.
>
> (Chetty *et al.* 1993: 2)

And, in relation to the latter:

> At the school level in South Africa (particularly in African departments) supervision is oriented towards improving exam results as a narrow objective rather than improving educational processes generally; it is focussed on assessing teachers with a view to monetary rewards; and it is overwhelmingly about compliance with departmental regulations rather than engaging educators about their work (Fehnel 1993). Loyalty to officials and their departments outweighs the interests and needs of teachers. As a consequence teachers' perceptions of the current appraisal system reflect a strong sense of distrust and anxiety. . . .
>
> (Chetty *et al.* 1993: 2)

In essence, criticisms of the prevailing approaches to appraisal revolved around issues related to concerns over legitimacy and control, the underlying purposes of appraisal and the content and procedures associated with the process. However, as Chetty *et al.* (1993: 1) pointed out:

> ... widespread rejection of the existing appraisal system has not been intended as a rejection of appraisal per se: the majority of teachers want appraisal to be an essential part of their professional development – not a mechanism for enforcing state control.

What the educators were demanding was a uniform, national system of appraisal, developed consultatively, which was open and equitable, school-based and focused firmly on their professional development, and consequently on the improvement of the quality of schooling and the restoration of a culture of teaching and learning, most especially in the most disadvantaged and devastated schools.

What the teachers demanded, they initiated, and it was largely through the initiative of one of the major unions, in partnership with an education policy unit, that the process was begun which would lead to a major transformation of educator appraisal in the country.

A process for transformation

Although there is some limited evidence in the literature of discussion around issues relevant to changing appraisal practices in South Africa (see, for example, Beardall 1995; Jantjes 1996; Thurlow 1993; Waghid 1996), the most comprehensive commentaries on the processes of developing and piloting the new developmental appraisal system are found in two publications of the Education Policy Unit of the University of the Witwatersrand (Chetty *et al.* 1993 and Mokgalane *et al.* 1997). The latter source is especially valuable for understanding the process which led to the development and acceptance of the new system. In this section, we draw largely on this source to highlight some key aspects in the development of this new system.

In the context of the situation outlined in the previous section, as early as 1992 the South African Democratic Teachers Union (SADTU) approached the Education Policy Unit (EPU) at the University of the Witwatersrand to assist it in exploring the development of alternative educator appraisal practices. By 1993, SADTU had been joined by the other teacher organisations and unions and the previously existing departments of education, who engaged in an ongoing process of discussion and negotiation around principles, processes and procedures for a new system of appraisal (ELRC 1999: 51), and by 1994, general agreement had been reached on guiding principles which should underpin a new system and a provisional appraisal 'instrument'.

Later in 1994, following the first democratic elections in the country, a conference was held, involving representatives of the new national and provincial education departments, teachers' organisations and relevant non-governmental organisations, at which agreement on the previously identified guiding principles and the nature of the 'instrument' was confirmed. In addition, it was agreed that a pilot project should be undertaken to test the new system with post level 1 educators (unpromoted teachers) prior to implementation, and the EPU was commissioned to lead this project, in conjunction with the major unions (Mokgalane *et al.* 1997: 3).

The principles which it was agreed should govern the new system of appraisal were:

1. Process is as important as product. This means that the involvement of teachers in negotiations of procedure and criteria is as important as the results of, for example, promotion. The appraisal should be considered as a process and not an event.
2. The process should be negotiated.
3. The process should involve peer review.
4. The process should be oriented towards development rather than judgement.
5. The process should take into account contextual factors. This means that there should be a match between evaluation criteria and, for example, available resources, the state of the school, nature and conduct of students, experience of staff, and qualifications of teachers.
6. The process must be nationally instituted.
7. The process should be democratic. This means that evaluators and the process itself must be evaluated and open to review, and that teachers must be part of the process at all stages of the development of the appraisal system.
8. The process must be conducted openly and not in secrecy. This means that all reports issuing from an individual evaluation should be made accessible to the person being evaluated.
9. All parties involved in the evaluation should be empowered to conduct the evaluation. This means that those conducting the evaluation should receive adequate training in new forms of evaluation.
10. A system of teacher appraisal should be developed which considers structurally separating summative and formative evaluation in terms of processes, procedures and products (Mokgalane *et al.* 1997: 5).

The main features of the 'instrument' (a term used, which presumably equated with procedures) included:

- acknowledgement of the significance of context in shaping teacher performance;
- self-appraisal;
- a school-level appraisal team consisting of the principal/deputy, head of department/ subject head, a peer nominated by the appraisee and a subject adviser;
- the right of the appraisee to nominate the appraisal team;
- a process of open discussion and feedback between appraisee and appraisers;

- the right of appeal by an appraisee through a moderation team consisting of a subject adviser, and independent body and representative from the appraisal team;
- a development plan.

(Mokgalane *et al.* 1997: 3)

It is apparent that these principles and features of the 'instrument', agreed in 1994, either in spirit or in fact addressed directly many of the concerns or causes of discontent that had been articulated in relation to prevailing systems. The actual delineation of principles became slightly modified in the eventual appraisal manual, and some of the more ambitious features of the 'instrument' were modified following the pilot project and final agreements in the Education Labour Relations Council.

The pilot project was carried out during 1995 and 1996 in eight of the country's nine provinces (KwaZulu-Natal did not participate), and involved just 93 schools and 186 unpromoted educators. The processes and procedures of the pilot project are fully reported in Mokgalane *et al.* (1997). While the scale and scope of the project might be regarded as somewhat limited in relation to a national initiative of this importance, and while the claim made, in the eventual appraisal manual (ELRC 1999: 51), that the pilot validated empirically the nature, philosophy, processes and instrument of the new appraisal system, remains untested through independent evaluation of the project, nevertheless the findings were judged to be sufficiently positive for the process of introducing the new system to proceed. In short, the pilot project reported a substantially positive response to most aspects of the proposed 'instrument', but identified shortcomings related to aspects of some of the criteria used, the grading and rating system proposed, the length of time required for the process, the size and composition of appraisal panels – which were problematic for some types of school, the additional administrative work involved and the unsuitablity of the language and terms used in the 'instrument' (see Mokgalane *et al.* 1997: 42–5).

The findings and recommendations of the pilot project were used to inform further ongoing discussions and negotiations between the teacher unions, the provincial departments of education and the national Department of Education in the Education Labour Relations Council and final agreement was reached on the new system, which was signed by all parties in ELRC Resolution 4 of July 1998. Essentially, it was agreed that:

- The overall nature of the appraisal system that was piloted should remain, including the guiding principles, the nature of the appraisal process and the use of appraisal panels.
- The 'instrument' to be implemented should be *developmental in nature only* and would be used with all levels of personnel in education, excluding therapists and psychologists.
- Appraisal would be tied to the nature of job descriptions of the specific level of post to which a person may be attached (ELRC 1999: 52).

In respect of generic job descriptions, sets of core duties and responsibilities of educators (school and office based), including principals, deputy principals, heads of department, educators and various categories of personnel working in education offices, were defined and agreement on these was reached and signed in ELRC Resolution 8 of 1998. Both the core duties and responsibilities of educators and the new appraisal 'instrument' were gazetted by the Minister of Education, early in 1999 (Republic of South Africa 1999).

Following up on the signing of Resolution 4 in the ELRC, a National Appraisal Team, with union representation, was established to oversee and monitor the implementation of the new system. A manual for developmental appraisal was prepared (ELRC 1999), which contained a brief introduction to the new system, examples of the various forms to be used together with tabulations of definitions and expectations associated with core criteria for use in the appraisal of various types of educator, and a facilitators' manual for use in familiarisation and training workshops.

In what was termed an 'advocacy campaign' for the new system, a 'cascade model' of training was employed, starting with the national team and involving other teams at subsidiary levels (provinces, regions, districts and circuits). Responsibility for introducing the new system to the schools rested with officials at the lower levels of this chain. At the school level, the new appraisal system was to be initiated, maintained and monitored through newly established Staff Development Teams (SDTs).

It was intended originally that the advocacy campaign should be completed by the beginning of 1999, and that the process of implementation in schools should run throughout the 1999 school year. Ongoing monitoring of the effectiveness of the new system would take place throughout the implementation process and the whole system would be reviewed in April 2000.

However, for reasons on which we shall speculate later, the process did not run as envisaged. The advocacy campaign, with cascade training, was not completed on time, with the effect that the commencement date for implementation in schools had to be put back to July 1999, and the date for the review of the system to September 2000. In May 2000 no documented evidence was available, but 'informal' evidence suggested that many schools had experienced problems and, although the first cycle was due to be completed by the end of June, some schools had not even begun the process of instituting the new system.

A new system for developmental appraisal

Notwithstanding problems which are being experienced with its introduction and implementation, the new system of appraisal clearly is radically different from those which it replaces.

First, it is fundamentally developmental and formative in its intentions and is unrelated to levels of remuneration and promotion decision-making. (The only stage at which it is intended for use in a summative sense is that of the confirmation of probationer educators.)

Second, it was developed through a process of genuine negotiation involving all the major educator unions and the employing authorities, and thus enjoys a greater legitimacy than was the case with earlier systems.

Third, it is inclusive of all levels of educator and individual educators are active and equal partners in their own appraisals.

Finally, the process is open and accountable. Of course, none of these things will have much relevance if the system is not workable and is not made to work. In this section, we summarise the main characteristics of the system – or how it is intended to work.

Staff Development Team (SDTs)

Every school is required to establish an elected Staff Development Team. Among the responsibilities of the SDT are the initiation of the appraisal process; facilitating appraisal training and ongoing support; the preparation and monitoring of a management plan for appraisal; the establishment of appraisal panels and the identification of appraisees; ensuring a link between appraisal and whole school development; monitoring the effectiveness of the appraisal system and ensuring that records are maintained.

Appraisal training

All members of staff in a school must receive appraisal training. To this end, the official publication for the system includes a facilitators' manual outlining the content of the training programme and suggestions for conducting workshops. This programme includes some contextual background material, some advice on procedures, commentary on the forms to be used in the process and very brief coverage on conducting developmental appraisal. Essentially the manual is instructional and operational in nature.

Appraisal panels

The appraisal process for each individual is carried out through an appraisal panel, which comprises the appraisee and at least three others (except in the case of small schools, where the requirement is at least two others). The other members of the panel are drawn from nominated peers, senior management persons, union representatives, and persons from outside the institution (such as someone from the district education office, a college or a university or an non-governmental organisation). Each panel, the composition of which must be acceptable to the appraisee, elects its own chairman, who is responsible for scheduling panel meetings, the conduct of the meetings and reporting progress to the SDT. It is recommended that two panel members should serve as active appraisers.

The appraisal instrument

While the term 'instrument' appeared to have had different connotations in the report on the pilot project (Mokgalane *et al.* 1997), in the official manual it is used specifically to refer to 'the actual tool that is used in the appraisal of educators' (ELRC 1999: 86). The instrument comprises five forms:

1 A Personal Details Form, which is essentially an abbreviated curriculum vitae, completed by the apraisee.
2 A Needs Identification and Prioritisation Form which contains the criteria that are used in an educator's appraisal (see below) and different criteria are identified for the various levels of educator. These forms are used to identify the specific criteria on which the appraisal will be based and to record priorities for development.
3 The Personal Growth Plan, based on the prioritised criteria, is completed by the appraisee, who is required to identify objectives for development, how it is proposed to meet these objectives and within what time period, what resources might be needed and which indicators are proposed to demonstrate attainment of the objectives. As with most forms, the content is discussed and agreed mutually within a panel meeting.
4 The Discussion Paper, completed by the appraisee with the possibility of subsequent modification after discussion with the panel, records information about the extent to which the appraisee has achieved the objectives set, factors which might have affected negatively the pursuit of these, the nature of support received and what might be needed to further improve performance.
5 The Appraisal Report, contains prioritised needs/criteria, identified needs, strengths of the educator, a suggested development programme, suggested development programme providers and dates for development programme delivery. The report must be signed, as agreed, by all members of the panel (ELRC 1999: 88).

In addition to these forms, there is an optional learner questionnaire, and principals or office based educators may use a similar 'client's questionnaire' to assist with self-appraisal.

Criteria and rating

To ensure that appraisal is related to key job functions, core criteria have been identified and defined for each level of educator. These are compulsory elements in the identification and prioritisation of needs. Provision is made for some core criteria, through agreement in the panel, to be deemed as 'optional' in the light of particular contextual factors at a school. Further criteria, defined as 'additional', may be added to reflect the particular needs of the individual or the institution. A simple A/B rating is used in respect of each criterion, with the former indicating a 'priority need for development in the present cycle', and the latter that 'performance is in keeping with the expectation with room for further development in future cycles' (ELRC 1999: 5).

Evidence

Apart from the appraisee's self-completed forms, the official manual appears to make reference to only two forms of collected evidence of performance. The first of these is the requirement that the educator should submit a portfolio to the panel. According to the official manual an educator portfolio:

> ... includes (a) record of an educator's ongoing professional development, learning experiences and achievements. For example, short and long INSET courses, all certificates/awards obtained, research conducted, materials developed, articles written, management plans, mark-book, teaching programmes etc.
>
> (ELRC 1999: 10)

Although the official manual is silent on this, presumably the purpose of submitting such a portfolio is to furnish substantive evidence of attainment and to provide a basis for discussion of achievement and future needs.

The other source of evidence referred to is that of observation of educators in practice. Presumably, in the case of unpromoted educators, this refers to classroom observation, but no indications are given as to what might be involved in observing, for example, the practice of principals. Whatever the nature of such observations, the manual recommends that 'two visits should occur', and that these should be undertaken by an elected person(s) from the appraisal panel.

The process

The process for introducing appraisal into schools, as well as that for the conduct of individual appraisals, is summarised in the following management plan, extracted from the official manual (see also Table 7.1).

The instruction in the official manual is that all educators must first be trained in developmental appraisal prior to implementation and thereafter half of the staff of a school must be appraised in the first six months, and the other half in the second six months, of the first cycle. (At the time of writing, no firm proposal had been made in respect of the frequency of cycles.) The management plan also provides an indication of what is envisaged for the appraisal process, which involves a variety of activities and several meetings of the panel. It appears from the plan that the actual duration of an individual's appraisal is in the order of nineteen weeks from beginning to end. Although the details of the organisation, instruments and overall process, briefly sketched above, are probably specific to the new South African developmental appraisal system, nevertheless the anticipated benefits of the system and its essential components are very similar to

Table 7.1 Process of appraisal in South African schools

Weeks in cycle	Action	Responsibility
Week 1	Head of an institution calls a staff meeting to elect the SDT	Head of institution
Weeks 2–3	Training of staff	SDT
Weeks 4–6	Identification of appraisees for the 1st and 2nd phases of Cycle 1	SDT
	Constitution of panels and election chairpersons	Staff members
	Appraisees complete Personal Details Form	Identified appraisees
Weeks 6–9	Submission of educator portfolios to the Panel	Appraisee
	Observation of educators in practice	Panel
Weeks 9–12	Decide on optional and additional criteria and motivate for the decision on the Needs Identification and Prioritisation Form	Appraisee, Panel and SDT
	Self-appraisal on the Needs Identification and Prioritisation Form	Appraisees
	Peer/Union Representative/Senior appraisal Needs Identification and Prioritisation Form	Two panel members
	Finalise Needs Identification and Prioritisation Form	Panel
	Complete Professional Growth Plan (PGP) Form	Appraisee
	Panel discusses and finalises the PGP Form	Panel
Weeks 11–22	Appraisee implements the Professional Growth Plan	Appraisee
Weeks 23–24	Appraisee fills in the discussion paper in preparation for the review	Appraisee
	Panel works through the discussion paper	Panel
	Appraisal Report is prepared	Panel

Source: ELRC 1999: 8

those identified by Middlewood (1997: 172) as being likely to characterise most appraisal schemes. However, he makes the point that differences in outcome between schemes are likely to depend heavily upon how the schemes are managed (Middlewood: 173) and that the effectiveness of appraisal will be significantly affected by the management of its process. The observations provide the context for the final section of the chapter, in which we offer a tentative early assessment of the South African scheme.

An early assessment

Any attempt to offer an early assessment of the new South African developmental appraisal system might be regarded as being somewhat premature in view of the fact that the first year of its implementation in schools was still in progress at the time of writing. Moreover, no published evaluation studies are available and the first major review of the system was scheduled to begin towards the end of 2000. Consequently, there are no empirical referents for what follows, and it is not possible to construct a coherent critique, based upon indigenous sources.

As we suggested, at the beginning of the previous section, there can be little doubt that the new system differs radically from the systems which existed previously, both in terms of its underlying purpose and its intended mode of operation. The process by which it was developed and the principles which underpin it combine to invest the new system with an unprecedented degree of legitimacy in the eyes of relevant stakeholders. The rationale underlying the system is such that, not only is it likely to be broadly acceptable to South African educators, but also it relates fairly closely to similar systems in other countries which have developed primarily formative appraisal schemes in education.

However, no matter how inclusive and consultative has been the process of its development or how sound the principles upon which it is built, there is a sense in which the new appraisal system seems to resemble several other local educational initiatives. South Africa has developed many policies in recent years which might be argued to be of high quality and of fundamental relevance to the transformational needs of the country's education system. Nevertheless, as Craig (1990) has pertinently observed, even the best policies do not implement themselves! Notwithstanding the extensive body of new policy, South Africa's implementation record in the education system has been less than impressive, and this has been acknowledged by the Minister of Education whose 'Tirisano' programme has been designed to engage the problem (Department of Education 2000a).

Explanations for implementation failures are likely to be numerous and complex and certainly would be likely to include such factors as severe financial and physical resource constraints, as well as a lack of human resource capacity at critical levels in the system. Whatever the causes may be, it is almost certain also that insufficient attention has been given to the processes of implementation and the complex imperatives for the successful management of change itself. It would seem that a precipitate desire to make things happen fast appears often to have resulted in the neglect of these essential considerations, with the effect that innovations have been compromised.

While reiterating that, as yet, there is no published, empirical evidence on which to base a coherent critique, there does seem to be some tentative evidence which suggests that the new appraisal system might encounter problems related broadly to inadequate attention being given to its implementation. In this regard, the following are offered simply to illustrate this possibility.

1   In spite of the many positive aspects of the process through which the new developmental appraisal system was designed, there must be reservations related to the pilot project, which was an influential element in the process. The pilot project was extremely limited both in scope and duration, relative to the importance of the issue, and its methodology and findings, though published, were never evaluated independently. However, perhaps more significantly, the pilot tested only an appraisal system for unpromoted educators and no such study was conducted on the application of the system with heads of department, deputy principals, principals and office-based educators, who subsequently have been incorporated into the new system. The assumption that 'one system fits all' has not been examined, and not only might this state of affairs be regarded as untenable in countries with longer traditions in performance appraisal, but also it may well prove to be a fundamental weakness in the South African system.

2   In the preamble to the official manual, it is stated that:

> In order to achieve the aims of developmental appraisal, the following *requirements* (original emphasis), inter alia, must be met:
>
> * democratic organisational climate
> * learning culture at institutions
> * commitment of educators to development
> * openness and trust.
>
> (ELRC 1999 p. 2)

These represent fundamental changes in the organisational culture and climate of South African schools (see Department of Education 1996) and imply radical changes to the way in which schools are managed. However, nowhere in the training materials or prescribed programme are these fundamental considerations mentioned, let alone addressed. In so far as the effectiveness of appraisal may be argued to be significantly affected by the management of its process, and in so far as the process is claimed to be dependent upon the above, failure to address the implications of these 'requirements' in training must surely represent a major constraint on the potentiality for successful implementation.

3   In a related vein, the facilitators' manual for the training programme (ELRC 1999: 68) states that the developmental appraisal system is integral to the process of whole school development. The case for linking appraisal to school development has been well argued in other contexts (see, for example, West-Burnham 1993). However, while raising the issue, the training programme fails to address adequately what is implied and, in this way, is more likely to confuse trainees struggling to understand and come to terms with the new appraisal system. While the notion of whole school development (and development planning) is gaining currency in South Africa, and a Framework

for Whole School Development (setting out guiding principles for provinces, regions, districts and service providers) is being drafted in the national Department of Education, and while the development of a whole school evaluation instrument is one of the activities in the Tirisano Implementation Plan for the current year (Department of Education 2000a: 28), the process is far from being familiar to the majority of schools at the present time. If the link between appraisal and whole school development is considered to be of central importance and is relevant to the implementation of the new system, then it deserves attention in the training programme.

4   Considerations such as these provide a clear indication that the nature of the training programme itself may be less than adequate for the promotion of effective implementation of the new system and, indeed, may inhibit this. A review of the structure and content of the programme suggests that, while they address fairly fully issues related to background and context, their pre-dominant focus is on the administration of the system, without any real attention being given to fundamental management issues, neglect of which is likely to severely constrain implementation and institutionalisation at the school level.

5   A further major limitation of the training programme is its failure to address, or implicitly to treat as being unproblematic, the fundamental dimension of the collection of evidence for appraisal purposes. Although 'observation of educators in practice' is identified as an element in the appraisal process, the programme is silent on what this involves and how it might be carried out most effectively. Observation of classroom practice, in the case of classroom-based educators, is a far from routine process and there is plenty in the literature which highlights the many factors which need to be taken into account if this is to be a useful source of evidence in the appraisal process (see, for example, Wragg 1987). Apart from classroom observation, there remains the issue of what might constitute appropriate evidence for non-classroom related work, and how evidence of practice might be collected. Admittedly, the submission of educator portfolios is an identified element in the appraisal process, but clearly there is much more to compiling a portfolio than simply assembling a variety of documents (see, for example, Gibbs, 1992; Thurlow 1992). The training programme is silent also on this.

6   Yet another major omission in the training programme is the apparent lack of awareness of the need for the development of appropriate interpersonal skills for the appraisal process. As West-Burnham (1993: 78) points out:

Although the appraisal process depends on the appropriate structures and procedures these have to be reinforced by effective personal relationships. Appraisal is not an administrative procedure, to be effective it requires individuals to talk about their work in an open and analytic way. Because much of a teacher's work can only be understood through perceptions the appraiser requires significant skills to enhance the understanding and analysis of the teaching and management process. The need for these skills is further enhanced by the need for trust. . . .

Given the assertion in the appraisal manual that one of the requirements for the achivement of the aims of developmental appraisal is that of 'openness and trust' (ELRC 1999: 2), and the well documented probability that one of the challenges accompanying the initial introduction of a formative appraisal system is the need to allay educator fear and suspicion, it would seem likely that a failure to address the development of appropriate interpersonal skills might seriously compromise successful implementation in schools.

7 In summary, although it is not intended simply to equate successful implementation with the quality of appraisal training available, nevertheless the latter must constitute a critical element in the process. Even allowing that the cascade training approach, using the existing training materials, was effective in its own terms, and there is enough informal evidence at this stage to suggest that it may not have been, there appear to be sufficient grounds to argue that the programme neglects to address critical issues related to the management of appraisal to the extent that implementation and institutionalisation of the new system are likely to be considerably compromised. It is difficult not to draw comparisons between the limited quality and coverage of the training programme and materials, designed for the South African context, and examples of high quality training manuals available elsewhere, which were available for consultation locally (see, for example, Jones and Mathias 1995; Pratt and Stenning 1989; West-Burnham 1993).

8 In addition to what we have argued are significant limitations in the design and content of training for the introduction of the new appraisal system, there are many other factors that are likely to have a negative influence on the way in which the system is perceived and implemented. These relate both to the process of introduction and the appraisal process itself and a few examples must serve as illustrations.

First, in relation to what has been discussed already, it is likely that the 'advocacy campaign' has been too hastily and superficially conceived and put into action. Not only have timetables proved to have been unrealistic but also it is probable that insufficient time and opportunity have been allowed for careful preparation to be undertaken before responsibility was passed to the schools. Not only is it essential for school managers to be entirely familiar with the procedures and management implications of the new system but also they need to have access to appropriate, ongoing support from relevant personnel in local education offices. Again, there is ample informal evidence that these superintendents (or equivalent) themselves lack sufficient knowledge of and confidence in the system to be able to offer the levels of support which might reasonably be expected. After all, the limitations of their preparation are similar in nature to those of school level managers and they themselves are also having to try to come to terms with the operation of the system in their own contexts.

Second, as Moses (1985) has written: '. . . there can be no staff development without preceding evaluation . . . , and there should be no evaluation without opportunities for staff development.'

An essential tenet of development appraisal is that the needs of individuals, identified through the appraisal process, must be addressed through appropriate professional development activities and experiences. In this connection, the appraisal manual says: 'The primary responsibility for development lies with the educator and the primary site for development is the workplace' (ELRC 1999: 2).

While this may be accepted, it must also be acknowledged that others in the 'workplace' have a responsibility to be partners in an individual's development. This presupposes that schools have the capacity, capability and resources to assist in meeting individual development needs, or know how to gain access to such support. Prevailing conceptions of staff or professional development in South African schools, derived from past practice, have focused mainly on attendance at externally designed and mounted courses or workshops. Although these remain an important source of professional development, schools will need to develop alternative understandings of what might constitute professional development activities and opportunities. It is unlikely that the experience of appraisal will be positive, and consequently the process will not be implemented and institutionalised effectively, unless this issue is addressed and these understandings are acquired and, again, this is an important area of consideration neglected, or taken for granted, in preparatory training.

Third, there are problematic issues related to the appraisal process itself. The requirement that all educators in a school should complete the appraisal process in one of two six-month periods, coupled with the use of appraisal panels comprising at least four persons for each appraisal, suggests that not only are schools likely to experience considerable administrative strain, but also that the quality of the process for individuals is likely to be compromised. Evidence from other countries which have introduced systematic appraisal suggests that even a cycle of one year, employing just one appraiser per appraisee, is difficult to sustain. Furthermore, it is doubtful if good quality appraisal or effective personal or professional development can be achieved in such concentrated periods. It must also be a matter of concern that the issue of the frequency of the appraisal cycle doesn't appear to have been thought through beyond the initial year of introduction. Negative experiences arising from administrative matters such as these clearly represent a threat to successful implementation. The issue further highlights the probable shortcomings of the pilot project, to which earlier reference has been made. This project involved only two appraisees in each of the sampled schools and consequently there was no opportunity to test the practicality of the appraisal process in a whole school context and thus possible administrative and quality problems were not able to be identified in advance of a general introduction of the system.

Fourth, although we do not intend to dissect the appraisal instruments themselves, there is one significant issue related to these, which has particular relevance in the South African context, and may have a negative impact upon the success of implementation. There are eleven official languages in the country but, at least in its first year of introduction, training materials and the appraisal instruments themselves have only been available in English. Although English is rapidly acquiring a status as the 'common language' in the country, there are many schools for which exclusive availability of the materials and instruments in English has created a major problem. By definition, this state of affairs would have a negative impact on the implementation process.

9   However, notwithstanding those factors which we have suggested might be regarded as limitations in the design and content of training, and others which are likely to have a negative influence on the way in which the system is perceived and implemented, there is perhaps one further significant concern related to the fundamental nature of the new appraisal system. This derives from the apparently exclusively developmental character of the system. While this might be understandable in the light of forces identified earlier, which have shaped the development of the new system, nevertheless it raises questions about its potential efficacy in the longer term.

The value of a developmental approach to appraisal for the professional and personal development of educators, with the anticipated transfer of benefit to the quality of students' learning, is hardly open to question. Questions do need to be asked, however, about whether or not an exclusively developmental approach is both realistic and likely to bring about the desired effects.

For example, in the British context, Middlewood (1997: 175) suggests that there is a growing awareness of a need to ensure a 'harder edge' to appraisal, which 'increases its evaluative and accountability aspects, whilst maintaining a developmental and supportive approach'. He cites Morris (1991: 168), who argues that it is 'precious' to represent appraisal as a 'totally non-threatening and (absurdly) non-judgemental process', and Fidler (1995: 4), who asserts that 'it is difficult to defend an appraisal scheme which leaves poor teachers untouched'.

While provision is found in the Employment Educators Act (Republic of South Africa 1998), in association with provisions within the Labour Relations Act (Republic of South Africa 1995), for dealing with 'incapable educators' and the 'discharge of educators appointed on probation', these are not directly integrated within the published appraisal system itself. An early appreciation of the South Africa appraisal system suggests that, for historical reasons which are understood, evaluative and accountability aspects of appraisal are substantially displaced and that this is likely to compromise the envisaged efficacy of the system in relation to the aim of promoting quality in management, teaching and learning.

It would seem likely to be profitable if, during the anticipated review of the system, attention would be directed to such issues of evaluation and accountability. If the system remains substantially or exclusively based on a 'soft' developmental basis, then the appraisal process for individual educators probably will remain little more, to paraphrase Kedney and Saunders (1993: cited in Middlewood 1997), than a school or departmental office confessional!

Conclusion

The African National Congress policy framework for education and training asserted that:

> The reconstruction of education and training stands or falls with the morale, commitment and capacity of the national body of teachers and trainers. The country needs a dynamic system of teacher preparation and development with a clear mission and sufficient scope to perform it.
>
> (ANC 1994a: 50)

Since assuming power, the ANC government, through its Ministry and the Department of Education, has achieved much in meeting this imperative, including laying the foundations for the reorganisation of the teacher education system, a fundamental revision of the nature and content of initial teacher education and an overhaul of the terms and conditions of educator employment. The introduction of the developmental appraisal for educators system must be regarded, alongside these, as another significant innovation.

We have suggested that the impetus for changing appraisal processes in South Africa derived both from the profound dissatisfaction with, and rejection of, previously existing practices and the manner in which they were conceived and operated, together with a firm belief that the effective identification and meeting of the professional development needs of educators should result in desperately needed improvements in the quality of teaching and learning in South Africa's schools.

South Africa's new system for the developmental appraisal of educators is in place and, notwithstanding certain reservations, would appear to incorporate principles and practices which address the previously articulated concerns and hold some reasonable potential to contribute towards improvements in the performance of educators and, consequently, the quality of learning in schools. Whether or not these ends are achieved remains to be judged through future evaluations.

In this connection, Middlewood (1997: 182) has reminded us that:

> Managing the monitoring and evaluation of the appraisal process is easier than evaluating the outcome. . . . Evaluating the ultimate outcome of appraisal is obviously difficult, since its central aim is to improve the quality of learning in the educational organisation.

As we have pointed out, implementation of the new system in South Africa has only recently been initiated and it is too early for evaluations to have been conducted. However, we have speculated on some factors which we believe could have a significantly negative impact on the success of implementation and the institutionalisaton of the system in schools. In particular, we have drawn attention to the following:

- While considerable attention appears to have been given to administration of the system, although significant issues of detail and process still remain unresolved, there appears to have been only a minimal awareness of the complexities involved in implementing educational change.
- The requirements identified for the successful introduction of developmental appraisal (and its integration with whole school development) represent fundamental changes in the organisational culture and climate of South African schools and imply radical changes in the way in which schools need to be managed. The new system appears to neglect substantially the management implications both for its own introduction and for establishing the conditions required for its successful institutionalisation.
- While the forces which have given rise to an essentially 'soft' developmental approach to appraisal are understandable, greater attention probably will need to be given to evaluative and accountability aspects of appraisal if the products of the process are to have any real impact on the quality of teaching and learning in the country's schools.
- The apparently unexamined assumption that, in performance appraisal, one system fits all could be suggested to be eccentric and misplaced, and it is likely that this state of affairs would merit further investigation.

It is hoped that issues such as these, and others which we have neglected unwittingly, will be highlighted when the first review takes place, and steps will be taken to address them, so that the performance of those who teach and the consequent appraisal of how they do this can be both supported and challenged. The innovation is too important for them to be ignored.

Notes

1 Educator: The term 'educator', which now has common currency in South African education, is defined formally in the Employment of Educators Act (Republic of South Africa 1998), and subsumes a wide range of categories and work locations. South Africa's Developmental Appraisal for Educators system incorporates both educators in public schools and those based in departmental offices. The former comprise un-promoted teachers, heads of department, deputy principals and principals, while the latter subsume those with inspectorial and advisory functions as well as educational psychologists and therapists.
2 Gazette/gazetted: The Government Gazette of the Republic of South Africa is a government publication, registered at the Post Office as a newspaper. It is a vehicle through which White Papers, Bills, Acts of Parliament and other Government Notices

are made public. The new Developmental Appraisal for Educators system was 'gazetted' (or published in a Government Gazette) by the Minister of Education in 1999, through a Government Notice which also incorporated a variety of other terms and conditions of employment of educators, in terms of section 4 of the Employment of Educators Act of 1998.

References

ANC (1994a) A Policy Framework for Education and Training, Johannesburg: Education Department, African National Congress.

—— (1994b) Implementation Plan for Education and Training: Summary Report of the IPET Task Teams, Johannesburg: Education Department, African National Congress (Task Team Report on Teacher Development and Support).

Beardall, J. (1995) 'Teacher appraisal and professional accountability in South African education', Perspectives in Education 16(2): 365–72.

Chetty, D., Chisholm, L., Gardiner, M., Magau, N. and Vinjevold, P. (1993) Rethinking Teacher Appraisal in South Africa: Policy Options and Strategies, Johannesburg: Education Policy Unit, University of the Witwatersrand/NECC.

Christie, P. (1985) The Right to Learn: The Struggle for Education in South Africa, Johannesburg: Sached Trust/Ravan Press.

Craig, J. (1990) Comparative African Experiences in Implementing Education Policies, Washington: The World Bank.

Department of Education (1996) Changing Management to Manage Change in Education. Report of the Task Team on Education Management Development, Pretoria: Department of Education.

—— (2000a) Implementation Plan for Tirisano: January 2000–December 2004, Pretoria: Department of Education.

—— (2000b) Corporate Plan: January 2000–December 2004, Pretoria: Department of Education.

ELRC (1998) Developmental Appraisal: Resolution 4 of 1998, Pretoria: Education Labour Relations Council.

—— (1999) Developmental Appraisal for Educators, Pretoria: Education Labour Relations Council.

Fehnel, R. (1993) Education Planning and System Management: An Appraisal of Needs in South Africa, Johannesburg: World Bank Consultancy Report.

Fidler, B. (1995) 'Taking stock after the first round', Management in Education 9(4): 3–4.

Gibbs, G. (1992) Creating a Teaching Profile, Bristol: Teaching and Educational Services Ltd.

Jantjes, E.M. (1996) 'Performance based teacher appraisal: from judgement to development', South African Journal of Education 16(1): 50–7.

Jones, J. and Mathias, J. (1995) Training for Appraisal and Professional Development, London: Cassell.

Kalloway, P. (ed.) (1984) Apartheid and Education: The Education of Black South Africans, Johannesburg: Ravan Press.

Kedney, B. and Saunders, B. (1993) Coping with Incapability, Mendip Paper 51, Bristol: The Staff College.

Middlewood, D. (1997) 'Managing appraisal', in T. Bush and D. Middlewood (eds) Managing People in Education, London: Paul Chapman.

Mokgalane, E., Carrim, N., Gardiner, M. and Chisholm, L. (1997) *National Teacher Appraisal Pilot Project Report*, Johannesburg: Education Policy Unit, University of the Witwatersrand.

Morris, B. (1991) 'Schoolteacher appraisal: reflections on recent history', *Educational Management and Administration* 19(13): 166–71.

Moses, I. (1985) 'Academic development units and the improvement of teaching', *Higher Education* 14: 75–100.

Nkomo, M. (1990) *Pedagogy of Domination: Toward a Democratic Education in South Africa*, Trenton, NJ: Africa World Press.

Pratt, K. and Stenning, R. (1989) *Managing Staff Appraisal in Schools: Training Manual*, London: Van Nostrand Reinhold (International).

Republic of South Africa (1995) *Labour Relations Act (66 of 1995)*, Pretoria: Government Printer.

—— (1996a) *The Constitution of the Republic of South Africa (Act 108 of 1996)*, Pretoria: Government Printer.

—— (1996b) *South African Schools Act (84 of 1996)*, Pretoria: Government Printer.

—— (1998) *Employment of Educators Act (76 of 1998)*, Pretoria: Government Printer.

—— (1999) *Terms and Conditions of Employment of Educators Determined in Terms of Section 4 of the Employment of Educators Act, 1998*, Government Gazette No. 19767, 18 February, Chapter C, Pretoria: Government Printer.

—— (2000) *Norms and Standards for Educators*, Government Gazette No. 20844, 4 February, Pretoria: Government Printer.

Thurlow, M. (1992) 'The compilation of teaching profiles', *Bulletin for Academic Staff*, University of Durban-Westville 13(3): 3–10.

—— (1993) 'Systematic staff appraisal: evaluation for the professional development of teachers', *Journal of Educational Evaluation* 2(2): 9–26.

Unterhalter, E., Wolpe, H., Botha, T., Badat, S., Dlamini, T. and Khotseng, B. (eds) (1991) *Apartheid Education and Popular Struggles*, Johannesburg: Ravan Press.

Waghid, Y. (1996) 'Can a system of teacher appraisal in a changing South Africa be sustainable?', *South African Journal of Education* 16(2): 81–7.

West-Burnham, J. (1993) *Appraisal Training Resource Manual: Implementing Teacher Appraisal in Schools*, Harlow: Longman.

Wragg, E. (1987) *Teacher Appraisal: A Practical Guide*, London: Macmillan Education.

Chapter 8

Potential paradoxes in performance appraisal

Emerging issues for New Zealand schools

Tanya Fitzgerald

Introduction

Since 1997, appraisal has been a mandated requirement of New Zealand schools. While the management of teacher performance is not new, schools are increasingly being faced with difficult and complex decisions regarding the performance and professional development of staff. Currently, most schools have adopted a system whereby appraisal and professional development are inextricably linked. Performance appraisals conducted in schools focused simultaneously on positive aspects of a teacher's performance and indicated areas for professional development. In 1998 a small-scale survey was conducted that investigated links between appraisal and professional development and ways in which schools had established a climate of professional development and accountability. As well, the research examined teacher perception of factors affecting appraisal at school level. It was revealed that a potential tension within a system of performance management was possible if appraisal was linked with teacher competence and performance pay. This chapter examines the development of appraisal and professional development in the New Zealand context and suggests that recent moves by the government to introduce performance pay have created a potential paradox that needs to be understood in order to reveal possible tensions inherent in the current performance management system.

In any educational organisation, appraisal can be considered an important mechanism which provides critical information on individual and institutional performance that leads to organisational development (Blandford 2000). Simultaneously, appraisal can be an effective developmental and an accountability mechanism intended to identify personal and institutional needs that will lead to growth in the organisation as Cardno and Piggot-Irvine (1997) have shown. In other words, appraisal has the potential to improve performance through systematic management and feedback about an individual's performance. In this respect, I would suggest that New Zealand schools are no different from schools in Britain or Australia and the call for performance appraisal to 'provide a positive framework for improving the quality of teaching and therefore learning' (Ministry of Education 1997a: 1) is not new.

This chapter will provide an overview of the development of performance appraisal and professional development in New Zealand and discuss potential paradoxes that have arisen as a result of meshing systems that deal with competency, performance pay and performance appraisal. As well, findings of a small-scale study on key factors affecting the successful implementation of appraisal and professional development in schools will be reported.

Historical background

Like many other Western countries, educational administration in New Zealand was subject to widespread systemic reform in the late 1980s. Similarly, incorporated into the reform agenda was the need for government to address concerns regarding teachers' work and the need to introduce public levels of accountability in the teaching profession. In particular this has led to the introduction of a number of initiatives. These have included the formal registration of teachers with a national body, the Teacher Registration Board (TRB) (1989), the mandated requirement for schools to implement a performance appraisal system (1997) and the introduction of mandatory professional standards (1999). These requirements are applied to all members of the teaching profession from principals to beginning teachers. As well, injected into this framework have been debates raised by the Education Review Office (ERO) concerning criteria for judging what a capable teacher is (ERO 1998), what constitutes instructional time and the nature of the school day (1998). It would seem therefore that underpinning government policy is the drive to ensure that schools are accountable for the quality of teaching and learning that occurs; the core activities of teachers. A cursory glance at the educational landscape might suggest that government is increasingly moving away from describing what might happen in schools to providing prescriptions regarding what should happen in schools. The journey from inspection prior to 1986 to appraisal from 1997 to the introduction of the professional standards in 1999 can be viewed in the light of increasing centrality of control on teachers' professional activities. The move from mechanisms concerned with quality control to systems focused on quality assurance has resulted, in my view, in the polarisation of appraisal and professional development and the surfacing of a number of underlying tensions.

For a variety of reasons, appraisal has been a contentious issue since its formal inception in 1989 (O'Neill 1997; Neville 1997). Much of the disquiet has rested on concerns regarding the monetarist language (Codd 1993) used to describe appraisal processes. This has included terms such as contracts, targets, objectives, evaluation and accountability (O'Neill 1997). Although it has been clearly stated from the outset that appraisal is concerned with accountability and professional development, there has been a level of anxiety that appraisal could be part of teacher competency and disciplinary proceedings (O'Neill 1997). The introduction of professional standards that stipulate the minimum standards at which teachers must perform has created a challenge for schools. On the one hand, schools can integrate the professional standards within current performance appraisal systems. On the other hand, this presents a challenge insofar as it embeds a system that is focused on minimum teacher competency (Ministry of Education 1999) within a performance appraisal system that purports to identify aspects of a teacher's professional growth and development. Or, schools can have two separate systems in operation, both of which require similar data to be gathered for different purposes. In particular, movements from one level to another within the prescribed professional standards are linked with pay progression. A further difficulty is that from 1 July 2000, professional development is now a mandated requirement (Ministry of Education 1999) and teachers who do not engage in regular professional development opportunities cannot receive pay increments. In other words, professional development is non-negotiable. It is possible therefore as anecdotal evidence suggests, for teachers to attend professional development seminars in order to (simply) comply with requirements. Benefits to the individual and the organisation would be difficult to ascertain within this climate. This particular model is not workable as my research has indicated. Research conducted in 1998 with 109 teachers in a range of schools suggests that performance appraisal integrated with professional development conducted within a supportive climate is widely accepted by New Zealand teachers. Recent moves to provide a framework that is linked with performance pay and minimum competence has created new tensions and challenges.

Quality control – inspection

The need for a mechanism to hold teachers accountable for their work has occupied the educational landscape in New Zealand since the introduction of free, compulsory and secular education in 1877. In his first Inspector's report tabled in Parliament in 1878, the Inspector of the Auckland Province, Richard O'Sullivan, commented that there was a difficulty in 'procuring competent teachers' and that 'inspection and examination are needed . . . to note the defects in organization, discipline, classification, methods of teaching etc and to show the teachers how to set them right' (AJHR 1878, Vol. 2, H-1). To address these concerns, O'Sullivan advocated the need for 'standards for teachers' and that teachers be required to prepare for the 'profession of teaching' and the 'art of teaching and school management' by attending a minimum of two days extra instruction in their own time (AJHR 1878, Vol. 2, H-1). In other words, inspection of teachers was designed to bring about a measure of quality control within a newly established national system. To ensure consistency across the six provinces, Inspectors regularly accompanied each other on visits. For teachers and Inspectors there was a requirement that a minimum of two days per year (outside of classroom time) had to be spent in what is now termed professional development. Inspectors were required to table a report each year in the House of Representatives that provided evidence that this was occurring.

Although the above example highlights particular issues government was grappling with at the advent of the state schooling system, inspection and grading of teachers remained in place until the late twentieth century. In that time successive governments re-visited these issues and developed policies regarding teacher training (Ministry of Education 1997a), teacher registration (Teacher Registration Board 1994) and teacher competency (Parliament of New Zealand 1986). The underlying concern across these two centuries was the need to address public concerns regarding teacher education, teacher performance and teacher accountability.

Prior to 1988 and the widespread reform of education administration, schools in New Zealand were under the auspices of the Department of Education. Within this government body, Inspectors were responsible for making professional judgements about teachers. Individual teachers received reports and grades on their performance and this was used as a mechanism for promotion. In addition to making judgements about teachers, Inspectors (usually retired or ex-principals) were required to offer guidance and support. For secondary schools, this system was abolished in the early 1970s whereas for primary schools this system remained until widespread reform of educational administration took place in October 1989.

Quality assurance – appraisal and professional development

In 1986, the *Report on the Inquiry into the Quality of Teaching*, more commonly referred to as the Scott Report, contended that there was widespread dissatisfaction with the Inspectorate. More significantly, the central concern was that there were no mechanisms in place to ensure that teachers could be made accountable for their work (Capper and Munro 1990). The desire to hold teachers more accountable for their work was both publicly and politically motivated.

In order to locate decisions about, among other things, teachers and teacher performance at the school level, widespread reform of educational administration was instigated in 1988 and, consequently, *Tomorrow's Schools: The Reform of Education Administration in New Zealand* was released. The era of self-managing schools was established. One aspect of the reforms was the requirement that all schools conduct annual performance appraisals of their staff. In other words, accountability for teacher performance was located at the local level. The major expectation of government was that public confidence in the quality of teaching would be restored as a direct result of professional accountability being devolved to schools. ERO were required to ensure that schools complied and this formed a part of their accountability audit of schools. It would seem that in one sweep of a pen, schools now adopted the role that the Inspectorate had previously fulfilled. Dilemmas associated with accountability for staff performance and professional development remained and the scene was inherently more complex as these expectations were located at both the organisational and individual level (Cardno and Piggot-Irvine 1997). Although schools were required to make decisions regarding the quality of teaching and learning, *how* this was to be achieved was not made apparent. Consequently, between 1990 and 1995, there was a lack of action by principals, due in part, to their lack of expertise and training in staff appraisal (Peel and Inkson 1993; Cardno 1995).

In 1995, following extensive discussion, feedback and consultation, the *Draft National Guidelines for Performance Management in Schools* was published. In 1996, these guidelines became statutory requirements for assessing the minimum performance of teachers. The term 'teacher' referred to all teachers, including part-time and long-term relieving teachers, guidance counsellors, specialist teachers such as itinerant music teachers, provisionally registered teachers (beginning teachers), those holding limited authority to teach and principals.

It can well be argued that although the official rhetoric suggests that appraisal is concerned with 'professional growth' and professional development of teachers (Ministry of Education 1997b: 1), the reality is that the central concern is individual teacher competence and accountability (O'Neill 1997: xiii). Although the Ministry of Education has indicated that 'effective performance management' and the 'ongoing professional development of individual teachers' is a critical factor in improving the quality of teaching and learning in schools (Ministry of Education 1999), teachers remain somewhat unconvinced. These concerns are not unrealistic.

I believe that the Ministry of Education has moved from a governance role, whereby they offered advice regarding performance appraisal and performance management systems, to a more pivotal role in ensuring that ERO conducts accountability audits of appraisal policy and procedures in schools. Furthermore, since March 2000, principals have been directed to make decisions regarding teacher performance and attest to salary increments for those teachers who have 'met the professional standards at the appropriate level' (Ministry of Education 1999). For those teachers who do not meet the standards within a particular timeframe 'the principal will determine whether there are significant areas of concern to warrant initiating competence procedures or whether a programme of further support and development should continue' (Ministry of Education, 1999: 7). The interrelationship of performance appraisal, professional development and performance pay has the potential for exacerbating the existing tensions that already undermine teacher confidence in appraisal.

Professional development

Prior to 1989, all teacher professional development was centrally organised and funded. That is, the Ministry of Education determined priorities for professional development both at the individual and organisational level. Most of the professional development that was available was related to curriculum development and curriculum delivery, and teachers' colleges and teacher resource centres were funded to deliver (short-term) in-service training. In other words, professional development was tailored to provide training for teachers that related directly to practice and the improvement of teaching, learning and classroom management. Each year the New Zealand government spent approximately $60 million or 2.7 per cent of its total budget for teacher salaries on providing these forms of training (ERO 2000: 1). Professional development that focused on school development (Cardno 1996) and management development (McMahon and Bolam 1990) was not considered a need or a priority as this form of development was not considered to relate 'specifically to identifiable learning activities in which practising teachers participate' (ERO 2000: 3). Government involvement in the provision of teacher professional development therefore was directed at the implementation of national initiatives and local school-based concerns were not fully considered.

With the advent of *Tomorrow's Schools* (MOE 1988) responsibility and funding for professional development was devolved to schools. Decisions about how much funding was allocated and the setting of school priorities were negotiated between the principal and Board of Trustees. As Cardno (1996) has outlined, the role of the principal was critical in securing investment in professional development both at the individual and school level. From 1997 onwards, schools were required to have in place performance management systems that included clearly defined professional development policies. While research conducted in 1998 and reported later in this chapter suggests that teachers clearly see the need for a link between performance appraisal and professional development, anecdotal evidence suggests that not all teachers regularly engage in professional development activities. The introduction by the New Zealand government of mandatory professional development for all teachers has been accomplished in a number of ways.

In the first instance, teacher unions were presented with the notion of compulsory professional development during collective employment contract negotiations in the 1998–1999 period. An integral feature of the resultant teacher employment contracts is the requirement that all teachers engage in professional development for up to ten days per year 'when the school is officially closed for instruction' (ERO 2000: 7). As well, teacher contracts include a clause (NZPPTA 1999: Section 5.3) that states the school's ability to 'call-back' teachers for up to five days per annum. That is, schools can require teachers to attend professional development during five days of any term break. In linking professional development with teacher employment contracts, the New Zealand government has signalled that there is a *contractual* duty for teachers to undertake professional development. The *professional* duty related to professional development as contained in the 1999 *Professional Standards*. While the interrelationship between performance appraisal and professional development is widely accepted and theoretically sound (Blandford 2000; Cardno and Piggot-Irvine 1997; Middlewood 1997a), the compulsion to undertake professional development is at odds with principles of adult learning (Hargreaves 1994; Middlewood 1997b) and the empowerment of teachers through professional development (Fullan 1995).

Second, a revision of the National Administration Guidelines (NAGs), the national operational framework, stipulates that each school must have a strategic professional development plan that meets nationally mandated requirements. Although it is reasonable to conclude that professional development is an integral aspect of teachers' professional work as Hargreaves (1994) has pointed out, questions must be raised as to whether the provision of incentives, albeit pay increases, for teachers to seek professional development is an effective strategy. In New Zealand, the *Professional Standards* (MOE 1999) contain provisions relating to professional development and pay progression. I would now like to look at the *Professional Standards* more closely.

Professional standards

The *Professional Standards*, introduced as 'part of the Government's strategy for developing and maintaining high quality teaching and leadership in schools and improving learning outcomes for students' are intended to strengthen performance appraisal systems (Ministry of Education 1999: 5). These standards describe the key elements of teacher performance and 'provide a base for assessing teachers' progress in relation to pay progression, competency and professional development' (Ministry of Education 1999: 4). The *Professional Standards* however, detail the minimum competencies that a teacher must display.

The introduction of these standards and associated links with performance appraisal create the potential for tensions and paradoxical situations in schools. On the one hand, performance appraisal is linked with professional development and accountability in a positive and non-threatening way (Ministry of Education 1997a). On the other hand, the *Professional Standards* 'provide a framework for performance appraisal, give a clear focus for identifying development priorities and enable a stronger link between performance and remuneration' (Ministry of Education, 1999: 5). The integration of the *Professional Standards* within a performance appraisal framework suggests that performance, development and pay progression are in some way inextricably linked and provide a measure to indicate teacher performance. What has occurred is the surfacing of tensions that create a tug of war within all three systems. This is represented diagrammatically in Figure 8.1.

Figure 8.1 The tensions in appraisal.

What Figure 8.1 shows is that there are a number of tensions underpinning performance appraisal and professional development in the New Zealand context. This has occurred as a result of challenges to schools to introduce a systemic approach to managing teacher performance and teacher accountability. While performance appraisal and professional development may be considered a positive dichotomy, performance pay, minimum competencies and mandatory professional development have the potential to heighten conflict. In particular, the linking of competency, professional development and pay progression may result in acqui-escence on the part of teachers and schools; i.e. they may conform to expected requirements. That is, quality control is assured within a framework of *compliance*. What may become lost in this equation is the ability of performance appraisal as a quality assurance and quality improvement mechanism. Research conducted in 1998 pinpointed the positive view of teachers toward performance appraisal at a school and national level and revealed factors that teachers considered critical to the success or failure of performance appraisal in New Zealand schools.

Recent research

In the latter part of 1998, research on appraisal was conducted in collaboration with David Middlewood (Leicester University). The primary objective of the research was to find out what teachers believed about performance appraisal. The secondary objective was to determine what factors, if any, did teachers consider critical to the (likely) success and/or failure of appraisal in New Zealand schools.

Through the use of focus groups, semi-structured interviews and a questionnaire, we examined teachers' perceptions of appraisal policies and procedures at a local and national level. During the course of the project, 109 teachers from three selected schools participated. The three schools that participated were selected because:

- all three schools were large (in terms of number of pupils) for their size and were inner city schools;
- all were in reasonable travelling distance from UNITEC;
- all were familiar with having researchers working in their schools;
- the principals in all of the schools were well regarded by their community for their vision and contribution to the school;
- all had appraisal systems in place prior to 1996; and
- there was a high level of involvement by staff in professional development.

While three schools and 109 teachers represent a small-scale study, we were interested in ways in which individual organisations had responded to the imple-mentation of performance appraisal and the extent to which teachers considered appraisal to be part of the fabric of their individual and organisational develop-ment. More importantly, we were concerned with how teachers within the three schools both personally and collectively perceived the purposes of appraisal.

In total, fifty-four teachers from the primary (elementary) sector and fifty-five teachers from the secondary (high school) sector participated. In the first phase of the research, the research team interviewed teachers including the principal and senior managers to ascertain their views on appraisal and associated implementation issues in their particular schools. In total ten teachers participated in one in-depth focus group interview that lasted two hours. Once these interviews were transcribed and coded, a questionnaire was developed to investigate whether there was a correlation between the views of principals and senior managers and the views of classroom teachers in the school. The questionnaire was organised according to broad themes to provide a degree of structure.

Research findings

Data collected in the first phase of the study provided a summation of teachers' attitudes toward a national system of performance appraisal. As well, teachers were asked to rate on a scale from 1 to 3 the factors that they considered most important to the implementation of performance appraisal in New Zealand schools.

In all three schools, teachers recognised the need for a system of performance appraisal that was linked with professional accountability and professional development. This finding echoes Cardno and Piggot-Irvine's (1997) view that for performance appraisal to be effective, there needed to be strong links with accountability and professional development. It would seem from the 1998 study that this integrated approach was viewed by teachers as a critical aspect of performance management at individual school level. From the findings indicated in Table 8.1 it would seem that there are solitary voices that do not perceive the immediate benefits of appraisal.

Table 8.1 Performance appraisal in New Zealand schools

Statement	Agree %	Disagree %
1. Some form of teacher appraisal is essential to raise the standards of teaching and learning	98.0	2.0
2. As a professional, I have a right to have my performance appraised	95.4	4.6
3. Appraisal should be primarily to help me identify my professional development needs	88.0	12.0
4. Appraisal should be for both professional development and accountability	99.0	1.0

These findings support Wragg *et al.*'s (1996) research on teachers' views of appraisal in Britain. Wragg contended that teachers generally endorsed performance appraisal as a process for identifying teacher performance although it was also revealed that only 50 per cent of the teachers had changed their classroom practices as a result of appraisal. While a link between appraisal and improving the teaching–learning process was supported by 98 per cent of New Zealand teachers, follow-up research might well investigate whether appraisal had been instrumental in changing teachers' practices. Evidence from interviews conducted within the three schools suggests that change is a goal for those teachers for whom appraisal activity is seen as a core activity in identifying personal and professional development priorities. I would suggest that for the 12 per cent of teachers who do not consider that there is a primary link between appraisal and professional development, it is doubtful whether appraisal would lead to a change in their teaching practice whatever conditions either the organisation or the government imposed.

As a professional exercise, appraisal was considered by 95.4 per cent of teachers to be a professional right. This factor was also apparent in Down et al.'s (1999) research that determined that one of the key aspects of appraisal was that teachers sought to have their work and achievements recognised and valued through the systematic appraisal of their performance. Conclusions forwarded by Down et al. (1999) suggested that teacher self-confidence and morale was enhanced through this formal recognition. Certainly, the New Zealand study pinpoints the level of positive support for appraisal as both a developmental and accountability process.

The second phase of the research moved from teacher perception of appraisal as a nationally mandated requirement to examining factors that teachers considered most important to the implementation of performance appraisal in their own schools. Teachers were asked to respond to a series of statements and rate them in order of preference with 1 being the highest and 3 the lowest. Results are summarised in Table 8.2.

Discussion

This study serves to pinpoint teachers' perceptions of the critical role of leadership and management in schools in relation to the success of appraisal at the local level:

Table 8.2 Teacher attitudes of factors contributing to success and/or failure of performance appraisal in New Zealand schools

Factor	1	2	3	Total	%
1. The quality of leadership/ management in the school	34	16	19	69	63.3
2. The development of an appropriate culture in the school	13	17	16	46	42.2
3. The availability of resources to meet professional needs	10	31	18	59	54.1
4. The availability of pay rewards for good appraisals	6	3	9	18	16.5
5. The integration of appraisal into general performance management	10	11	8	29	26.6
6. The emphasis on teachers' professional development	22	22	25	69	63.3

that 63 per cent of teachers indicated that the quality of leadership and management was a factor that contributed to the success or failure of appraisal in their school. The need for links between appraisal and professional development was also considered by 63 per cent of teachers surveyed to be a factor that contributed to the success of appraisal in schools. This finding is in line with national and international research (Barber *et al.* 1995; Cardno 1996; Cardno and Piggot-Irvine 1997; Timperley 1998) that establishes the need for a strong connection between appraisal, professional development and accountability. This is further supported by an ERO report which indicated that appraisal had been used as a basis for identifying professional development needs for 82 per cent of teachers in 187 New Zealand schools (ERO, 2000: 36). It would seem, therefore, that appraisal and professional development were strongly linked in New Zealand schools.

The emphasis on teacher professional development was, for 63 per cent of teachers, an important component of appraisal. At the time this research was conducted, professional development was not a mandated requirement. In the three schools in which the research was conducted, professional development was well planned and teachers had high expectations that professional development would take place. This further supports conclusions posited by Capper *et al.* (2000) indicating that professional development has become woven into teachers' daily work and is an integral part of their work. A supportive school culture that places high expectations on teacher professional development has the necessary ingredients for organisational growth and development (Middlewood 1997b). In this way, organisations can be credited with producing teachers who can identify their own needs and who are responsible for themselves as professionals. Recent moves by the New Zealand government to introduce pay incentives that are inextricably linked with performance management systems offer a *regulatory* approach that suggests that responsibility and possibly the impetus for professional development and appraisal must move from the school to agencies of the state.

A significant finding of this study is that teachers in all three schools did not support the availability of pay rewards for good appraisals. That 16 per cent of teachers supported the notion of linking pay and performance, and the fact that 83 per cent did not, suggests that links between performance appraisal and performance pay are fraught with difficulties. In particular, previous research has not been able to provide conclusive evidence on whether teacher appraisal improved teacher effectiveness (Stufflebeam and Nevo, 1994; Wragg *et al.* 1996). National level and school level policies in New Zealand schools presuppose that appraisal is a mechanism for improving the quality of teaching and learning. While teachers value the recognition of their achievements through the appraisal process, associated improvements in their teaching have been difficult to prove. Research conducted by Ingvarson and Chadbourne (1997) in Australia indicated that teachers were sceptical about the potential of performance appraisal to make a difference to teaching and learning. Similarly, research conducted by Her Majesty's

Chief Inspector of Schools in Britain in 1996 concluded that the impact of appraisal on teaching and learning had not been substantial. Performance pay is not the way to ensure a positive correlation between teacher performance and student performance. Further work needs to be done in this area in New Zealand schools.

Conclusion

Performance appraisal is a way in which teachers in New Zealand schools can reflect on and improve the quality of teaching and learning in schools. While there is a need to integrate professional accountability and professional development within a cohesive and comprehensive performance management system, the introduction of the *Professional Standards* and compulsory professional development has the potential to create paradoxes for school leaders and managers. The challenge has evolved whereby on the one hand, schools have integrated appraisal and its developmental and accountability mechanisms as the 1998 study has indicated; and on the other hand, schools are now required to comply with regulatory mechanisms that compel teachers to engage in professional development in order to prove they are meeting minimum standards. It could be argued that in order to ensure compliance, teachers will engage in performance appraisal processes and professional development at a minimal level. If this were to surface, potential improvement in teacher performance and student learning will be difficult.

References

Appendices to the Journals of the House of Representatives (1878) Vol. 2, H-1.

Barber, M., Evans, A. and Johnson, M. (1995) *An Evaluation of the National Scheme of School Teacher Appraisal*, DfEE: London.

Blandford, S. (2000) *Managing Professional Development in Schools*, Routledge: London.

Capper, P. and Munro, R. (1990) 'Professionals or workers? Changing teachers' conditions of service', in S. Middleton, J. Codd and A. Jones (eds) *New Zealand Education Policy Today*, pp. 150–160, Wellington: Allen & Unwin.

Capper, P., Fitzgerald, L.M., Weldon, W. and Wilson, K. (2000) 'Technology and the coming transformation of schools, teachers and teacher education', in A. Scott and J. Freeman-Moir (eds) *Tomorrow's Teachers: International and Critical Perspectives on Teacher Education*, pp. 176–99, Christchurch: Canterbury University Press.

Cardno, C. (1995) 'Diversity, dilemmas and defensiveness: Leadership challenges in staff appraisal contexts', *School Organisation* 15(2): 117–31.

Cardno, C. (1996) 'Professional development: An holistic approach', *New Zealand Journal of Educational Administration*, 11, December: 25–8.

Cardno, C. and Piggot-Irvine, E. (1997) *Effective Performance Appraisal: Integrating Accountability and Development in Staff Appraisal*, Auckland: Longman.

Codd, J. (1993) 'Managerialism, market liberalism and the move to self-managing schools in New Zealand', in J. Smyth (ed.) *A Socially Critical View of the Self-Managing School*, pp. 153–70, London: Falmer Press.

Down, B., Hogan, C. and Chadbourne, R. (1999) 'Making sense of performance management: Official rhetoric and teachers' reality', *Asia-Pacific Journal of Teacher Education* 21(1): 11–24.

Education Review Office (1998) *The Capable Teacher*, Wellington: Education Review Office.

Education Review Office (2000) *In-Service Training for Teachers in New Zealand Schools*, Wellington: Education Review Office.

Fullan, M. (1995) *Broadening the Concept of Teacher Leadership, New Directions*, Toronto: National Staff Development Council.

Hargreaves, A. (1994) *Changing Teachers, Changing Times*, London: Cassell.

Her Majesty's Inspectors of Schools (1996) *The Appraisal of Teachers 1991–1996. A Report from the Office of Her Majesty's Chief Inspectors of Schools*, London, OFSTED.

Ingvarson, L. and Chadbourne, R. (1997) 'Will appraisal cycles and performance management lead to improvements in teaching?', *Unicorn* 23(1): 44–64.

McMahon, A. and Bolam, R. (1990) *A Handbook for Secondary Schools: Management Development and Educational Reform*, London: Paul Chapman.

Middlewood, D. (1997a) 'Managing appraisal', in T. Bush and D. Middlewood (eds) *Managing People in Education*, pp. 169–85, London: Paul Chapman.

Middlewood, D. (1997b) 'Managing staff development', in T. Bush and D. Middlewood (eds) *Managing People in Education*, London: Paul Chapman.

Ministry of Education (1988) *Tomorrow's Schools: The Reform of Education Administration in New Zealand*, Wellington: Government Printer.

Ministry of Education (1995) *Draft National Guidelines for Performance Management in Schools*, Wellington: Learning Media.

Ministry of Education (1997a) *Quality Teachers for Quality Learning: A Review of Teacher Education*, Wellington: Government Printer.

Ministry of Education (1997b) *Performance Management Systems*, Wellington: Learning Media.

Ministry of Education (1999) *Professional Standards: Criteria for Quality Teaching*, Wellington: Government Printer.

Neville, M. (1997) 'Equity in performance appraisal – a contradiction in terms', in J. O'Neill (ed.) *Teacher Appraisal in New Zealand: Beyond the Impossible Triangle*, pp. 81–95, Palmerston North: ERDC Press.

New Zealand Post Primary Teachers Association (1999) *Secondary Teachers' Employment Contract*, NZPPTA: Wellington.

O'Neill, J. (ed.) (1997) *Teacher Appraisal in New Zealand: Beyond the Impossible Triangle*, Palmerston North: ERDC Press.

Parliament of New Zealand (1986) *Report on the Inquiry into the Quality of Teaching (The Scott Report)*, Wellington: Government Printer.

Peel, S. and Inkson, K. (1993) 'High school principals' attitudes to performance evaluation: Professional development or accountability', *New Zealand Journal of Educational Studies* 28(2): 125–41.

Stufflebeam, D. and Nevo, D. (1994) 'Evaluation of educational personnel', in T. Husen and T. Postlewaite (eds) *International Encyclopedia of Education*, second edn, Vol. 4, pp. 2123–32, Oxford: Pergamon Press.

Teacher Registration Board (1994) *Advice and Guidance Programmes for Teachers*, Wellington: TRB.

Timperley, H. (1998) 'Performance appraisal: Principals' perspectives and some implications', *Journal of Educational Administration* 36(1): 44–58.

Wragg, E., Wikeley, F., Wragg, C. and Haynes, G. (1996) *Teacher Appraisal Observed*, London: Routledge.

Chapter 9

Managing teacher appraisal and performance in the United Kingdom

Pendulum swings

David Middlewood

Introduction

This chapter describes the development of teacher appraisal in the United Kingdom since the early 1990s, from an almost entirely professional development model to an assessment for performance related pay. It examines the reasons for the lapsing of the original model and lessons that could be learned from that experience.

The new emphasis on performance management is then described. Drawing also on new research, factors are identified which seem essential to the effective management of teacher performance, whichever specific scheme is in use, if it is to achieve its intended purposes.

Teacher appraisal in the UK

Regulations for the introduction of teacher appraisal came into being in 1992 following two contrasting experiences – the piloting of appraisal schemes in a number of authorities and a sometimes bitter struggle over teachers' pay and conditions in 1987. Successive Secretaries of State for Education announced that appraisal would be voluntary, then statutory, in a matter of months. The regulations were to be the responsibility of Local Education Authorities (LEAs), who would themselves appraise headteachers. The scheme prescribed classroom observation (two sessions), an appraisal interview, and setting of targets among its components. All existing teachers were to have at least begun their two-year appraisal cycle by July 1995.

There was considerable attention paid in the regulations to the right of appeal (against choice of appraiser and the final report), and to the confidentiality aspect of the process. A key example of the latter was that individual targets could not be attributed in any reports. For example, only 'aggregated targets' could be presented to schools' governing bodies. Most of the pilot schemes had stressed that for appraisal to work it had to be positive and the emphasis in the scheme lay almost entirely on personal professional development.

Because of this focus upon the teacher as an individual, it was hardly surprising that this particular scheme, having been presented as a 'bolt-on' initiative for hard pressed school managers to undertake, was implemented with energy in many schools in the first phase but then fell into a 'limbo' (Nixon 1995). Other priorities quickly took over for school managers and leaders, notably school inspections in the 1990s. These, in the late 1990s, actually included in any case an overt assessment (by grade) of teachers observed, a process to which teachers inevitably paid more attention. It is interesting to note that, among the hopes of the appraisal scheme, was that it would lead to better informed references for teachers concerning job applications, whereas it was in fact high grades from their external inspections which were being mentioned by teachers in their applications!

Even those schools which had implemented the scheme successfully in the first place found little impetus for the second round, partly because of these new priorities but partly also because of the 'so what?' factor. Schools had found that appraisal had not made a significant difference to their core work, or aided staff motivation, although it had helped some individuals.

In some other schools, despite the 'evidence' of statistical returns to the DfEE, appraisal never began to be implemented, or it was stopped part way through the initial process. For example, in a study in one LEA, Stokes (2000) found that of sixteen primary schools investigated, five of them had never started appraisal, nine had stopped appraisal altogether and only one was on schedule. Similar results had been found in 1996 by an HMI study (OFSTED/TTA 1996) of seventeen primary schools.

A review of evidence of the effectiveness of appraisal was conducted in 1995 with statements concerning revision of the scheme in 1996 or 1997. In fact, not until the Green Paper, *Teachers: Meeting the challenge of change* (DfEE 1998) did proposals emerge with the introduction of 'performance management', based upon a now proposed *annual* assessment of performance. The evidence for this assessment was to include classroom observation, with at least one objective linked to pupil performance and to the achievement of school targets.

The review of appraisal having made clear that, in the view of the Chief Inspector of Schools, appraisal was not sufficiently 'improving teachers' level of performance', (OFSTED/TTA 1996: 25) was a clear prelude to appraisal being seen as part of some kind of management of teacher performance. In the 'Conclusions' to that review, a reference is made to performance related pay – (without, it should be noted, basing it upon any data collected as evidence for the review!) – suggesting that it should be tried.

The 'Technical Consultation Document' (DfEE 1999) which followed the Green Paper set out the aims as being to:

- strengthen school leadership;
- provide incentives for excellence;
- engender a strong culture for professional development;
- offer better support to teachers to focus on classroom teacher;
- improve the image, morale and status of the profession.

The scheme is intended officially to

> develop performance management policies covering both appraisal and pay issues. Appraisals of all teachers will be conducted by senior managers on an annual cycle, and will be based on teachers' individual job descriptions and agreed objectives. The process will lead to a statement assessing each teacher's performance against the previous year's objectives, reflecting factors such as challenge of particular groups of pupils. The statement will also outline new objectives for the coming year. The head will then make a recommendation to the governing body about that teacher's pay, based on the outcomes of appraisal.
>
> (DfEE 1999)

Opposition from the teacher unions to performance related pay, often called 'Payment by Results' in their statements, was diluted by an offer of a substantial salary increase in 2000 for those teachers willing to be assessed for crossing a 'threshold', enabling them to progress on an improving scale. This was only available to teachers with the equivalent of nine years' teaching service.

Reflections on the teacher appraisal scheme

Formal evaluations of the appraisal scheme at national level (Barber *et al.* 1995) and at regional level (e.g. Middlewood *et al.* (1995) for Northamptonshire, Hopkins and West (1994) for Kent and Pennington (1996) for Norfolk) were carried out. All presented pictures of its limited effectiveness. Although the national evaluation suggested that appraisal was contributing to eight of the eleven characteristics of effective schools, the general picture can be summarised as appraisal having achieved:

- only a small impact upon pupil learning;
- only a limited impact upon teacher practices;
- very little linkage between individual appraisals and staff development policies or programmes;
- few perceptions from teachers that it had made a difference to their motivation or career enhancement prospects.

It is possible and important to note some 'pluses' also.

- Some teachers found the opportunity to have professional dialogue with senior managers enlightening and rewarding – for both parties.
- The management culture of some schools was influenced positively by the introduction of systematic feedback on performance.
- The introduction of formal classroom observation broke down in some schools barriers of isolation and the related culture of individualism.

- Many appraisers reported that they learned as much from the process as the appraisees.
- Some teachers found the process of self-evaluation, when formally encouraged, very helpful, enabling them to think more self-critically.

Perhaps the most significant legacy of the now 'discredited' appraisal scheme (the word is used in the Green Paper 1998) is the fact that *it introduced the actual concept of assessment of performance* into the teaching profession, and made it acceptable. Notions of target-setting for individuals, for example, and the relationship of performance assessment and targets to school and pupil achievement are now largely taken for granted. In the first decade of the new century, the issue in England and Wales is not whether teacher performance should be assessed – but *how.*

Why was the scheme not successful?

There were of course issues of implementation process management that contributed to the scheme having only very limited success. The historical background of disputes over pay and conditions and the suspicion of many teachers that any form of appraisal was to weed out poor teachers created an unhelpful climate for this particular initiative. Furthermore, it was *imposed* upon a *mature* profession (the average age of the profession was about 45 years at the time) – all these were ingredients for, at the very least, a definite lack of enthusiasm for change! Research into unsuccessful change is well documented. As Fullan (1997: 206) points out:

> ... planners or decision-makers of change are unaware of the situations that potential implements are facing. They introduce change without providing a means to identify and confront the situational constraints and without attempting to understand the values, ideas and experiences of those who are essential for implementing any changes.

Analysis of the actual appraisal scheme however is more useful in identifying elements to guide performance and review managers in the future.

- The scheme lacked real accountability.

By placing its emphasis almost exclusively upon the professional development of teachers, the scheme was at the 'soft' end of the continuum referred to in Chapter 1. Critics had pointed this out at the commencement. Morris (1991: 168) pointed to the danger of a 'preciousness' about the process 'which inheres in representing appraisal as totally non-threatening and (absurdly) non-judgemental'. Kedney and Saunders (1993) suggested that 'basing staff appraisal solely on the soft option of developmental outcomes is akin to regarding the appraisal process as the college equivalent of the confessional!' and Fidler (1995: 4) said that, whatever merits the scheme had, 'it is difficult to defend an appraisal scheme which leaves poor teachers untouched'.

Even though 70 per cent of teachers said that they had gained personal benefit (Wragg *et al.* 1996), under half of those claimed to have changed their practice as a result of appraisal.

• There was an emphasis on the individual at the expense of the organisation.

As mentioned above, little linkage between an individual's development and the school's policies and programmes for improvement occurred. The secrecy arising from a commitment to confidentiality meant this was almost inevitable. As one staff development co-ordinator commented (Middlewood *et al.* 1995: 15): 'It was difficult to plan for training when I am not privy to the individual targets.'

By focusing on the needs of the individual teacher, the relationship of those needs to the needs of the student could only be implicit, not explicit, hence the very limited impact upon student/pupil learning or indeed classroom teaching practice. Although Barber *et al.*'s (1995) evaluation related appraisal to a majority of the factors involved in school effectiveness, it could not do so for school improvement. The concept of a school implicit in an appraisal scheme in which the focus is upon assessing performance of individual teachers is of an organisation which is staffed *by a collection of individuals*. Research evidence consistently indicates that school improvement is related to a culture of collaboration, sharing and strong professional relationships, from which develop shared goals and aspirations to achieving a shared vision (e.g. Hopkins *et al.* 1994).

• The scheme was essentially a 'bolt-on' initiative in schools.

Evaluations showed that most teachers eventually failed to see a connection between the process they had been through, which had been expensive in terms of commitment and time, and any visible progress for them or the school, e.g. in their own career development. As mentioned earlier, other priorities overtook this process and thus enthusiasm for a second round waned (Nixon 1995: 14). One of these priorities was the new schools' inspection focus in the mid-1990s: headteachers and their staffs quickly realised there was no cross-reference between the two! This was clearly noted by the national evaluation (Barber *et al.* 1995). School inspections paid only perfunctory attention to the appraisal scheme in existence and in any case by the late 1990s teachers were being assessed (graded) by visiting inspectors. It was not surprising that appraisal's bolt-on status paid the price of not being integrated: 'Appraisal was the management jigsaw that never got completed' (Thompson 1998). The cautious recommendations of the national evaluation report that the inspection framework 'needs to be refined to give greater emphasis to the importance of effective appraisal' (Barber *et al.* 1995: 66) perhaps recognised the tenuous status of this appraisal process.

Lessons to be learned

For managers in schools, three clear issues arising from the failure of the appraisal scheme to take root were therefore:

1 Any scheme involving appraisal of teachers needed to be based upon accountability as well as development of the appraisee.
2 The scheme needed to link closely the individual's development to the school's improvement.
3 Appraising individuals needed to be part of a whole school approach to the way staff were managed as a whole.

> The integrating of appraisal, whether through a formal scheme or not, into a whole organisation approach to managing its people seems a prerequisite to its effectiveness. . . .
>
> (Middlewood 1997: 183)

However, there were also lessons to be taken from some of the many positive elements found in the appraisal process through its management in a number of schools. Based upon experience and evaluation of the implementation of appraisal in the UK, I identified in 1994 and 1997 (Middlewood 1997: 173–5) several features of appraisal management which I believe remain important in whatever context it occurs in education. We may see these therefore as a continuation of the above list.

4 Making the process application consistent. Whatever the context and precise form of appraisal, appraisees need to be aware that all are being treated in the same way. Resources for the process management should be allocated equitably, including time and venues for example, and that procedures (e.g. note-taking) are applied consistently.
5 Making the process as objective as possible.

One person evaluating another can rarely, if ever, be free from some amount of subjectivity (compare recruitment and selection management, for example, and the increasing recognition of the fallibility of competences or standards measurements). However, in the appropriate climate of professional trust, where attempts to reduce subjectivity are overt, objectivity can be more nearly attained.

6 Recognising that process may be as important as outcome.

Noting that appraisers said they often learned as much from the process as the people they were appraising is a simple reminder that change for improvement is an ongoing process, not to be measured simply in terms of what has been achieved according to a prescribed list of goals or targets. Most people recognise a situation in which set goals are achieved, a measurable improvement on what existed previously, and then a retreat or relaxation will occur as a reaction to the intense effort and perhaps pressure that has been applied to reach these goals.

In schools where appraisal seemed to work well, teachers felt they had gained something from the process itself and it had affected their attitude to self-development.

7   Acknowledging that appraising staff involves skills.

This is an obvious statement and debate occurs as to which are the skills people need. West-Burnham (1993) argued powerfully that they are above all inter-personal skills, such as listening, focusing, negotiating, problem solving, conflict resolution, etc.

8   Evaluating and reviewing the actual process.

Comparatively few schools were known to have evaluated the appraisal scheme process by the mid-1990s, something which school managers would have considered poor practice in most other management initiatives. Those schools that did evaluate were often among the few that moved to a second round having taken account of, for example, resources and staff views.

To summarise, the above eight points are offered as ones which managers of the appraisal of teachers need to bear in mind when implementing any process which involves this, whether one that is a statutory requirement or one which a school has undertaken voluntarily for its own improvement. Obviously, scope is much more limited when initiatives are statutorily imposed upon managers, but the points are ones which relate to whole school management and if ignored, at least as long-term aims, will undoubtedly set back rather than improve management in the school.

Some of these lessons learned are acknowledged in the DfEE's paper on Performance Management (2000: 3–4) since it refers specifically to:

- an atmosphere of trust
- involvement (encouraging teachers to be fully engaged . . .)
- integration of performance management with the overall approach.

Attitudes of teachers

In the context of proposals for a new imposed scheme, research was carried out in six secondary schools in England in the summer of 1999. The investigation focused upon teachers' perceptions of the new proposals and what they believed to be the factors in effective appraisal. The research focused upon the most common team units in secondary schools – the subject departments – because it was attempting to discern the potential impact upon team cultures, especially upon team unity.

The six schools chosen were all comprehensive schools in the Midlands area, covering five different LEAs. A deputy head in each school was asked to identify three departments in his/her school, one of which was seen as a 'high achieving' department, one a low achieving department, and one somewhere inbetween. All the deputy heads, without prompting, made their selection on the basis of examination results, and terms such as 'average' or 'weak' were seen in the context of other departments in that particular school, not by any national or regional comparisons. The eighteen departments had in total 114 teachers, excluding the six heads of departments who were interviewed as appraisers. All six had had experience of appraisal in the1993–1995 teacher appraisal scheme. Clearly, in terms of gathering data from the 114 teachers, they were not aware as having been nominated in any category such as 'very good' or 'weak', as it was important that individuals responded to the survey instrument, a questionnaire, in an unbiased, non-defensive way. The response rate was over 60 per cent; interestingly, the highest response (70 per cent) came from individuals belonging to identified 'weak' departments.

Data from the questionnaire showed that:

- nearly 90 per cent believed it should contain 'both developmental and judgemental aspects';
- appraisal was seen as 'essential for teachers' accountability' by 80 per cent;
- as an 'entitlement for all teachers' by 70 per cent;
- as 'essential for improvement in student learning' by 70 per cent;
- 48 per cent agreed that it should be used to identify the best teachers;
- only 30 per cent agreed that it should enable the weakest teachers to be identified.

The figures overwhelmingly supported the notion suggested earlier that the case for some form of assessment of teachers is accepted by the profession and that this should involve both recognition that teachers are accountable, especially for pupil/student learning, and that their professional development remains central.

Over 85 per cent of teachers disagreed with the view that appraisal should be used to assess performance linked with pay.

How appraisal should be carried out

Almost 90 per cent supported the principle of their immediate line managers (heads of departments) actually doing the appraisal, and 80 per cent believed that individual schools should be left to develop their own appraisal of performance schemes, within national guidelines.

These figures suggest strong support for the *principle* of individual line management and a recognition of the importance of individual contexts to be taken into account in terms of the development of schemes best suited to those contexts.

When analysed, these figures showed no marked difference across the three categories of department, as 'high-achieving', 'average' or 'weak'.

However, with regard to *teachers' belief in fairness of management*, significant differences were shown. In response to the statement: 'My own school would ensure that teacher appraisal would be managed fairly', the overall response showed that just under 70 per cent agreed or strongly agreed with this. However, *all* the teachers who disagreed or strongly disagreed with this came from either School F where every single teacher felt it would *not* be fairly managed, or from departments identified as 'weak' in four of the other five schools. In three of those schools, all the teachers in the 'weak' departments felt the process would not be fairly managed. This left one school (B) where everyone felt it would be fairly managed, regardless of which department they were in, and one school (A) where this was true of all bar one person.

Two things clearly stood out from the data. In one school, there was a pervasive feeling that, although appraisal of performance was supported as something essential and desirable, staff lacked any confidence in the way it would operate. Secondly, in most schools, teachers who worked in departments which were recognised as 'weak' in those schools also lacked confidence in the fairness of the operation, presumably because of an assumption that their 'results' would count against them. It is further worth noting that, in so-called 'weak' departments, there will obviously be some excellent individual teachers. However, in the weak departments, *all* the teachers lacked confidence in the fairness of the scheme, thus suggesting that whatever the quality of the individual teacher, even excellent teachers felt results of the department would count against them.

In the semi-structured interview held with the head of the perceived weak department in the school where there was a widespread lack of confidence, the head of department was vehement in his view as to the potential unfairness of the appraisal.

> We have no chance – middle managers here are expected to do all the dirty work. Our results are average and in this school we are condemned before appraisal. We would like to improve but it's all criticism, no support.

Apart from the one school (D) where there was an all pervading lack of confidence in Senior Management, there was a clear concern from other interviews that heads of weak departments did not want their departmental team unity destroyed by appraisal.

> I know I am the best teacher in this department – perhaps I shouldn't say that, but I am. But if I emerge and am proclaimed as very good and the rest of my department so-so, I'll be worse off and so will the students. We've got to move together.

At the other extreme, in School A, all the heads of department had clear confidence in the appraisal being managed fairly.

It's that sort of school. Our results aren't great but the head knows why and understands. I mean, he's always nudging us to improve but he's fair and we don't have the results of the 'best' departments shoved down our throats all the time.

(Head of 'weak' department, School A)

Thank goodness, this school is about more than results. I mean, my department gets super results, and I think we should, but the SMT and staff generally care about the students – achievement in the widest sense. It means you keep on trying and trying to get better.

(Head of 'very good' department, School A)

There was clear evidence from the data that teachers saw teaching as a shared task and felt it was virtually impossible to decide who had been responsible for what in the students' total achievement. The head of a perceived average department in School B described a situation:

In September, Sheila and Peter had a middle band group each. In the second half of the Autumn Term, Peter was off sick for the rest of the term. His group had supply teachers in, some good, one or two useless. I set work, Sheila set some. Sometimes other members of the department. Occasionally, we swapped classes so Sheila could take his class – anything to help the students. Sheila marked extra work, so did I – and others. I hope both groups get similar – good results. Peter came back in January. It's not his fault he was sick, is it? I can't say Sheila's better than Peter – he would have done the same for her. It's a team effort, isn't it?

Three-quarters of the teachers involved felt that a particular difficulty in appraising performance in education was that some of the effects of teaching and teaching improvements are long-term. Therefore appraisal which focuses on the 'quick fix' or pays too much attention to immediate impact may be flawed. Some heads of departments related this to professional development.

I think it's a tragedy that the government keeps talking about 'training' not 'development'. We need both. For me, 'training' is simple and related for example to information, improving skills and so on. Development is about something more subtle and it can take time.

(Head of 'average' department, School C)

I have one teacher who's had a tough time but is coming through it. She's learned a lot, is getting more confident and I think in three years or so she'll be very good. Appraisal has got to encourage her – she's not afraid to discuss her weaknesses. But – any judgement that simply said she's a poor performer would set her back. I think she'd leave teaching and the profession will have lost a good'un. She'll spread the word outside teaching, too!

(Head of 'average' department, School B)

Implications of the research

One of the reasons for focusing the investigation into attitudes of teachers on departments, and not just individuals, was to see whether evidence emerged of the importance of (a) ethos of trust and (b) team unity and the perceived impact of these upon performance appraisal and indeed the impact of appraisal upon them.

Ethos of trust

The research in these six schools supported the key notion that underpinning all effective management relationships between the manager and the managed is a climate of trust.

> It is a well worn organisational axiom that trust is always the basis of the manager/subordinate relationship. Any activity that tampers with this trust factor must be viewed as a threat to long-term managerial effectiveness and employee performance.
>
> (Longenecker and Ludwig 1990: 76)

The ethos of trust relates of course to the whole management and leadership processes in the schools concerned, so that a potentially threatening process in which assessment is made of individual performance can be viewed by staff as one which will be managed fairly by those in authority – even where doubts exist as to the validity of the actual scheme. Teachers knew that the scheme of appraisal is imposed upon the school and relied upon their managers to apply it fairly. However, most believed that schools should be free to operate a scheme relevant to their individual context, within national guidelines. The work of leaders and managers in establishing this ethos is therefore critical. The scheme to be operated would presumably be the same in terms of procedure in, for example, School A and School D above; but Longenecker and Ludwig (1990: 68) point to research which showed that: 'a procedurally sound system alone will not necessarily produce effective, accurate, ethical performance ratings'.

Factors other than the actual performance of the employee teacher may inevitably influence the appraisal of that performance (see Figure 9.1), and unless the appraisees have trust in the people operating the process, the appraisal will not achieve its purposes. Townsend (1998: 54) goes so far as to call the failure to establish such an ethos as a 'betrayal'. In her list of strategies for preventing that betrayal she includes: 'Examining the moral and ethical issues of appraisal and reaching local consensus on related action.'

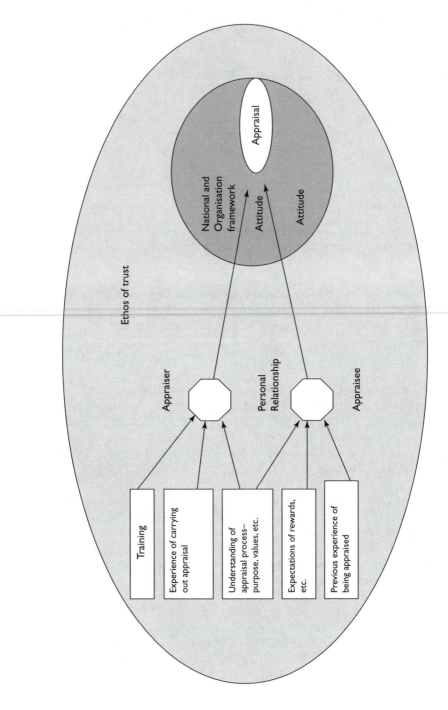

Figure 9.1 Factors influencing the effectiveness.

Team unity

The data from the six schools indicated the importance attached by the teachers to a team ethos, a sense of unity and recognition that teachers work most effectively in a strong, mutually supportive network. This fits of course with the large amount of research into teacher and school improvement, which shows that collaborative cultures are the most effective (e.g. Hopkins *et al.* 1994; Sammons *et al.* 1995). Research into effective departments in schools (Sammons *et al.* (1997); Harris *et al.* (1997)) has also demonstrated the importance of subject departments having cohesive cultures. Despite the fact that classroom teaching at the start of the twenty-first century continues to be largely an isolated activity, the support and challenge of teachers' professional relationship with colleagues remains crucial in achievement.

Proposals for performance related pay being implemented in England and Wales in 2000 were widely viewed by these teachers as being divisive and damaging to the spirit of collegial management. Bassey (1999) and Richardson (1999) both draw on comparisons with other public sector employees to point out that: 'individual performance related pay is perceived as rarely helping teamwork' (Bassey 1999: 22), and both conclude that collegial management is likely to be damaged by the introduction of PRP. Since the first phase of the UK government's performance management implementation is to assess those teachers with nine years' experience or more as to whether they qualify for a pay rise and access to a higher salary scale, there is immediately in all but a few staff rooms a division into three categories of teachers:

- Those who have passed the threshold, at least the first time.
- Those who have failed to pass.
- Those not yet eligible whose assessment is put on hold at present.

However, as most commentators agree, the threshold exercise had very little to do with actual performance management. At worst, it was an exercise which: 'implies that teachers are guilty of incompetence until they can prove otherwise' (Dolton 2000: 23), and at the very least a distraction from the core issue of introducing proper performance management (IiE: 7).

Factors for managing implementation of any form of performance appraisal

From experience in the UK, school managers would do well to learn from the past but also recognise that new arrangements are as certain to change as much as earlier ones did. Performance appraisal in some form is likely to be an important feature of school leadership and management for the foreseeable future. Therefore, identifying factors key to effectiveness in this area is crucial. Evidence suggests that these factors include (with possible actions needed):

- A recognition that teachers do not operate individually. (Link individual, team and whole school plans, targets, etc.; consider team appraisal.)
- An approach that teachers should be regarded as an investment, not a cost. (Indicate that there is a long-term, even lifelong commitment to the individual, whatever the period in the school.)
- An acknowledgement that a teacher's job in a school involves a lot more than classroom teaching. (Avoid focusing on only purely measurable outcomes, otherwise that is all that staff will see as being valued.)
- Understanding what motivates teachers. (Recognise effort and talent; give support and feedback.)
- Development of a climate of trust. (Encourage and exemplify strong professional relationships, critical friendships and self-criticism.)
- A recognition that the aims of education are various. (Set targets, some of which are medium and long term, including those related to professional development.)

Conclusion

Managing and appraising performance in education needs to recognise that the 'product' is people and what happens to them while they are in formal schooling. As I have argued elsewhere (Middlewood 1997), the daily lessons of the teacher and the student form the *transactional* part of the process and it is the part upon which any assessment of the teacher focuses. Education however is a *transformational* process, something powerfully influenced by many factors, some outside of the school's control. For performance appraisal to be effective, it must be part of the whole process of the management of staff in the school, fully integrated into a whole approach to the way in which people are recruited, selected, inducted, mentored, developed and excited. Tinkering with schemes for assessing individuals will neither give incentives to recruits to enter the teaching profession nor allow schools to gain the best from their professionals. The most effective schools recognise this already and can probably manage well even ill-conceived statutory schemes because they have set in place preconditions for success through 'modernised management' (Thompson 1998). Other schools may have to bear the brunt of divisions before they can develop the climate of trust essential to success in the area of performance management.

References

Barber, M., Evans, A. and Johnson, M. (1995) *An Evaluation of the National Scheme of School Teacher Appraisal*, London: DfEE.

Bassey, M. (1999) 'Performance related pay for teachers: Research is needed', *Professional Development Today* 2(3): 15–28.

DfEE (1998) *Teachers: Meeting the challenge of change*, London: DfEE.

DfEE (1999) *Teachers: Meeting the Challenge of Change: Technical Consultation Document on Pay and Performance Management*, London: DfEE.

DfEE (2000) *Performance Management in Schools*, London: DfEE.

Dolton, P. (2000) 'Why it's an obstructed threshold', *Times Educational Supplement*, 29/9/00.

Fidler, B. (1995) 'Taking stock after the first round', *Management in Education* 9(4): 3–4.

Fullan, M. (1997) 'Planning, doing and coping with change', in A. Harris, N. Bennett and M. Preedy (eds) *Organisational Effectiveness and Improvement in Education*, Milton Keynes: Open University Press.

Harris, A., Jamieson, I. and Russ, J. (1997) 'A study of effective departments in schools', in A. Harris, N. Bennett and M. Preedy (eds) *Organisational Effectiveness and Improvement in Education*, Milton Keynes: Open University Press.

Hopkins, D. and West, M. (1994) *Evaluation of Teacher and Headteacher Appraisal*, Maidstone: Kent County Council.

Hopkins, D., Ainscow, M. and West, M. (1994) *School Improvement in an Era of Change*, London: Cassell.

Industry into Education (2000) *Milestone or Millstone? Performance Management in Schools: Reflections on the Experiences of Industry*, Radlett: IiE.

Kedney, B. and Saunders. B. (1993) *Coping with Incapability*, Mendip Paper 51, Bristol: The Staff College.

Longenecker, G. and Ludwig, D. (1990) 'Ethical dilemmas in performance management revisited', in J. Holloway, J. Lewis and G. Mallory (eds) *Performance Measurement and Evaluation*, London: Sage Publications.

Middlewood, D. (1997) 'Managing appraisal', in T. Bush and D. Middlewood (eds) *Managing People in Education*, London: Paul Chapman.

Middlewood, D., Blount, J., Sharman, M. and Fay, C. (1995) *Evaluation of Teacher Appraisal in Northamptonshire*, Northampton: Northants County Council.

Morris, B. (1991) 'School teacher appraisal: Reflections on recent history', *Educational Management and Administration* 19(13): 166–71.

Nixon, J. (1995) 'Appraisal at the crossroads', *Management in Education* 5(3): 41–5.

OFSTED / TTA (1996) *Joint Review of Headteacher and Teacher Appraisal: Summary of Evidence*, London: TTA.

Pennington, M. (1996) *Norfolk Appraisal 1991–1995*, Norwich: Norfolk County Council.

Richardson, R. (1999) *Performance Related Pay in Schools: An Assessment of the Green Papers*, London: National Union of Teachers.

Sammons, P., Hillman, J. and Mortimore, P. (1995) *Key Characteristics of Effective Schools: A Review of School Effectiveness*, London: OFSTED.

Sammons, P., Thomas, S. and Mortimore, P. (1997) *Forging Links: Effective Schools and Effective Departments*, London: Paul Chapman.

Stokes, C. (2000) *Appraisal in West Northshire: Primary Heads' Practice*, Working Papers in Education, No. 1, pp. 51–87, Leicester: University of Leicester Press.

Thompson, M. (1998) 'Modernising appraisal', *Professional Development Today* 2(1): 23–9.

Townsend, F. (1998) 'Appraisal: As a process of betrayal', *International Studies in Administration* 26(1): 45–56.

West-Burnham, J. (1993) *Appraisal Training Resource Manual*, Harlow: Longman.

Wragg, E., Wikeley, F.D., Wragg, C. and Haynes, G. (1996) *Teacher Appraisal Observed*, London: Routledge.

Part III

The way ahead

In this final part, the focus is on possible developments in this whole field. Carol Cardno sees the appraising of performance, especially of teachers, as encapsulating some essential dilemmas that lie at the heart of the way school leaders approach their role and tasks. She argues in Chapter 10 that only by confronting these dilemmas and recognising both 'horns' of the dilemma in an honest way can teacher performance be both effectively and sensitively managed and appraised. She describes a programme for school leaders which appears to have made a major contribution towards this.

Of course, performance appraisal has not only its critics of specific processes but those who believe that its ends may be better achieved through other means altogether. Lawrence Ingvarson suggests in Chapter 11 that a focus on career advancement for teachers through assessment of professional standards is far more significant than such schemes as those involving annual reviews of performance. He compares the schemes in the UK and USA and personally concludes that the US one is more likely to have the right impact because of its thoroughness and the independence of those involved in the assessment.

Finally in Chapter 12, David Middlewood examines many of the issues raised in the book and applies them to possibilities in the way teacher performance and its appraisal will be managed in the future. He suggests that a range of practice will continue to exist internationally because of the wide variety in the factors that influence it, especially cultural, political and historical ones. However, he argues that certain human aspects of the process will remain constant and continue to have a considerable impact upon it, especially the need to recognise professionals' rights to personal development. It is possible that the focus may switch from individual to team performance and the greater involvement of a wider range of stakeholders, especially the students, all of which present continuing challenges to those who manage teacher performance and its appraisal.

Chapter 10

Managing dilemmas in appraising performance

An approach for school leaders

Carol Cardno

Introduction

> A conscious choice must be made to deal simultaneously with both horns of a dilemma if it is to be managed and resolved.

It is in the context of performance appraisal that the most persistent and recurring dilemmas arise for those who are in leadership positions with responsibility for managing the performance of others. Consequently, dilemma management could be viewed as a critical management competency enabling leaders at all levels in the organisation to effectively confront and manage dilemmas rather than avoid them. This implies that they need to attend to both the organisational and individual horns of the dilemma without compromising either one. It also implies that a set of skills associated with this competency has to be developed.

This chapter outlines the nature of appraisal dilemmas and presents research evidence of how a specific *dilemma management* training curriculum has been used to assist senior managers in New Zealand schools to understand and manage the dilemmas that arise in staff appraisal contexts. The approach to dealing with dilemmas presented in this chapter not only assumes that they can be managed but also that this is a critical element of effectiveness in bringing about desired change in performance. It is, therefore, equally important for *all* staff who are involved in appraisal activity to be aware of the nature of dilemmas and how they can be managed.

Understanding dilemmas

We are all too familiar with the universal notion of a dilemma: of finding oneself in a sticky situation or between a rock and a hard place. It is an uncomfortable position to be in because a dilemma is a particular type of complex problem characterised by several features:

- multiple dimensions (or 'horns')
- difficult options
- irreconcilable choices

The term dilemma is generally taken to mean a situation in which a choice has to be made between two equally undesirable or conflicting alternatives – usually creating indecisiveness about which way to turn. Since we think that we have to choose between two equally unattractive choices, it is not surprising to believe that a dilemma cannot be resolved. Because dilemmas are exceedingly complex problems the very idea that they can be managed is viewed by some people as unthinkable. However, an alternative view is that it is both possible and imperative to understand and manage dilemmas in appraisal contexts if we wish to achieve the goals of the organisation and be effective in resolving difficult performance problems, and do this in ways that are moral, humane, collegial and considerate.

Dilemmas in appraisal

Performance appraisal at its best can be one of the most satisfying, supportive and beneficial experiences for those engaged in it. At its worst, it can be a threatening and even destructive tool for control and compliance. Somewhere in between these two extremes it can become merely a formal, technical procedure with little or no commitment to its potential as a vehicle for professional dialogue about improving performance. Alternatively it can remain a highly symbolic goal, espoused by top management but not implemented in any way that actually impacts on improving practice.

There are myriad reasons why appraisal activity can be so difficult for those who participate in the process. Because appraisal has multiple purposes, and is intended to serve both organisational and individual needs, it challenges participants on several levels. This is true for both those being appraised and those responsible for the appraisal of others. It also holds true whatever the context, be it business or education, as a range of research shows (Down *et al.* 1999; Roberts 1998; Timperley and Robinson 1998).

- It challenges us intrapersonally because it engages emotions and beliefs.
- It challenges us interpersonally because it requires us to interact honestly with others at both personal and professional levels.
- It challenges those responsible for meeting organisational goals because it is intended to improve the organisation's performance.
- It challenges those engaged in examining and improving performance because this activity is a complex and often conflicted arena in which dilemmas are present.

Because of the general assumption that any dilemma belongs in the 'too hard basket', leadership dilemmas are usually seen as those tiresome problems about which little or nothing can be done. A further complication is that we often do not recognise that a complex problem is in fact a leadership dilemma with particular characteristics. Failure to recognise a dilemma is one of the main reasons why dilemmas are not confronted or managed in ways that assist their resolution.

As Argyris (1971: 175) in his early work on organisational behaviour reminds us, dilemmas exist and persist for leaders: 'This dilemma between individual needs and organisational demands is a basic, continual problem posing an eternal challenge to the leader'.

In a 'dilemma management' approach, effectiveness is defined as the ability to recognise and solve complex problems so that they remain solved. School leaders in general, and principals in particular, do not have the option of being *either* accountable *or* collegial in dealing with complex personnel management problems. The expectation is that they will achieve both aims.

Characteristics of leadership dilemmas

Dilemmas manifest as significant problems in the context of staff appraisal. School leaders, and others with management responsibility for the performance of colleagues, are placed in an extremely difficult position when they are confronted with such dilemmas, which contain tensions between conflicting value choices and multiple goals. One such dilemma is the conflict between individual needs and organisational demands, and it surfaces in a variety of ways as a *leadership dilemma* (Cardno 1995). For example, it arises at the organisational level when the school is required to implement an appraisal scheme that threatens the autonomy and privacy of classroom practice. Another form of the dilemma is the tension that exists between accountability and development goals because of a historical separation between judging teacher performance, and teacher development initiatives (Cardno and Piggot-Irvine 1997; Middlewood 1997).

Leadership dilemmas are characterised by one or more of the following features:

- diverse goals
- multiple purposes
- conflicting expectations
- values that are at variance
- tension between meeting the needs of the organisation and the needs of the individual
- tension between doing what is best for the school and doing what is best for a colleague
- pressure to be accountable versus pressure to preserve positive collegial relationships.

In essence, these features create conflicting demands and tensions between a leader's concern for accomplishing the tasks of the organisation and a concern for relationships among people in the organisation. The leadership dilemma is particularly highlighted in the context of staff appraisal because appraisal is intended to serve two fundamental purposes: holding people accountable for their performance and supporting the improvement of that performance (Cardno and Piggot-Irvine 1997; Timperley and Robinson 1998). It is concerned with the intermeshed needs of both the organisation and the individual severally and collectively.

Appraisal of performance, however it may be presented or approached, is inherently a threatening activity. This is because it focuses on what we do and involves making judgements about performance. When dilemmas are present threat and anxiety are heightened and create an even greater level of defensiveness in both organisational and interpersonal behaviour. Hence, a critical aspect of capability in dilemma management is an understanding of dilemmas and their attendant defensiveness on the part of both appraisers and appraisees.

Some appraisal dilemmas

A dilemma at the organisational level

A recent external audit of the school identified an aspect of the Performance Appraisal System that needs urgent attention. The board has communicated its concern about this issue to the recently appointed principal and has written into the principal's performance agreement an objective requiring system review and modification to meet nationally mandated requirements. Whilst the school does have a system for appraisal, it is conducted primarily on the basis of informal collegial peer review. Because staff are not appraised by line managers, the person to whom they are directly responsible is not in a position to comment on their performance or to link provision of professional development to specific needs. In short, whilst a formal system appears to exist it is meeting the needs of individual staff to be supported and given feedback by peers but it is not meeting accountability requirements.

The principal finds himself in a double-bind because the staff, who established this regime under his predecessor are strongly committed to and comfortable with the 'warm fuzzy' approach. Yet, he is aware of the need to have a system that serves other 'tougher' purposes as well. What complicates the issue further is the principal's personal belief that collegial peer review is the right way to go and that hierarchical appraisal by managers will reduce the co-operation and trust that has been built up. On the one hand, the principal must achieve school goals and satisfy the demands of the board. On the other hand, the principal is sympathetic to the feelings of the staff and wants to preserve what has been achieved.

A dilemma at the interpersonal level

In this case the principal needs to deal with the unsatisfactory performance of a teacher on the one hand. On the other hand, the principal is concerned about the teacher as a colleague because his/her child is suffering with a terminal illness. How can the principal be both accountable and collegial in this situation? This is a typical dilemma in appraisal because it requires judgements to be made and both parties need to engage in dialogue that enables a satisfactory, long-term resolution of the problem.

This dilemma places the principal in a very unpleasant position. School needs must be served. After all, parents expect their children to be taught well and will not tolerate a situation that detrimentally affects their learning. The principal must ensure that the school's reputation does not suffer. At the same time the principal wishes to be collegial and is genuinely concerned for the welfare of the teacher at this difficult time.

Mapping a dilemma to clarify complexity

One way of clarifying whether or not a problem is indeed a leadership dilemma is to map it under the two basic needs tensions that characterise classic dilemmas. This allows one to articulate the horns of the dilemma in terms of an organisational strand of concerns and a strand of concerns related to interpersonal relationships. An example of such mapping is shown in Figure 10.1.

A CLASSIC LEADERSHIP DILEMMA:
a problem with a staff member
who is not performing as expected by the school

Organisational Concern
On the one hand the leader is concerned because the needs of students are not being met in a manner expected by the school:

An experienced teacher is not meeting the expectations held of him/her in relation to planning and evaluation of teaching.

Other staff, the syndicate leader and team members, have complained that meetings are not attended and that agreed tasks are not being carried out.

The dilemma for the leader is that:
On the one hand
Something must be done to ensure that the expectations of the syndicate are met.

Interpersonal Concern
On the other hand the leader is aware that the teacher has a personal burden which is impacting on performance:

This staff member has been at the school for 12 years and has always performed well in relation to teaching and team expectations.

His/her partner has a terminal illness and sensitivity and great consideration has been shown by colleagues over the year.

On the other hand
The leader wishes to support the teacher as much as possible during this difficult period.

Figure 10.1 A dilemma map.

In short, you will know that you have to deal with a leadership dilemma when:

- a problem you hoped you had solved recurs; and
- the problem challenges you to consider both collegial relationships and school quality goals.

Typical ways of dealing with dilemmas

Remember that all complex problems are dilemmas of one sort or another. Many of these dilemmas lie dormant unless we are prepared to push them to the surface, or they surface themselves because the problem has become acute. When leaders are faced with difficult people-problems, generally related to improving performance, the research consistently reveals that they tend to respond in typical ways (Beer 1987; Bridges 1992; McLaughlin and Pfeifer 1988). One of three approaches is usually adopted in an attempt to deal with a dilemma, especially when we do not recognise all the dimensions of the problem.

Typical approaches are:

- *avoidance* (doing nothing)
- *soft-sell* (being nice)
- *hard-sell* (being nasty)

The first and most common response to dilemmas is *avoidance* – and this is very common, especially when a leader has not recognised that they are dealing with a dilemma. This response takes two forms. Either the issue is suppressed totally and not dealt with – often in the hope that it will go away. Alternatively, the organisational and individual strands of the dilemma are polarised and attention is paid to one horn of the dilemma at the expense of the other. Either way, 'doing nothing' to meet dual dimensions of a dilemma ensures that it persists.

When the response is to polarise the organisational and individual dimensions of a dilemma, further typical avoidance responses have been identified, especially in the way principals and senior managers approach the task of having to give someone negative feedback about their performance.

The second response is the *soft-sell* approach. In this approach the emphasis is on being 'nice' and the driving concern is to be non-threatening. The common activity is pussyfooting in order to protect others and oneself and to be indirect in communicating problems. In these cases, the individual teacher or manager is protected and the organisational goal to improve practice remains unachievable. The third response is the *hard-sell* approach. Sometimes this is used when the soft-sell approach fails to bring about change. In this approach the leader adopts an authoritarian stance, hauls the teacher over the coals, refers to policies and higher authorities, and asserts in no uncertain terms that performance is unsatisfactory. In this approach there is seldom two-way communication of information. In fact, evidence to back up claims may not be available and a bullying stance is a strategy for protecting oneself from having to reveal this. The problem with this 'nasty' approach to dilemmas is that it is unlikely to secure genuine commitment to change. Although the organisation's goals may be met in the short term, collegiality is inevitably eroded and agreement is often of the 'paying lip service' variety.

Defensive responses in appraisal contexts

It is not at all surprising to find that we become defensive when faced with the idea of someone observing and making judgements about what we do as teachers and managers in schools. Argyris (1985), who has written extensively about the routines we use when we become defensive, describes defensiveness as the tendency to protect oneself and others from potential threat or embarrassment. This is a normal human reaction to anything that causes us anxiety or creates unpleasantness and, according to Argyris, defensive responses are culturally taught to all of us early in life and are connected with notions of caring, being thoughtful and being effective in our personal and professional lives.

When we are faced with threat, especially in appraisal situations when we feel vulnerable because we are opening up our practice to the scrutiny of others, or having to communicate information that we feel will be threatening or hurtful to others, we adopt *defensive routines*. Defensive routines are those behaviours that allow us to cover up or bypass threat. We become indirect rather than forthright. We give mixed messages as a way of watering-down or softening the blow. Consider, for example, the common tendency to convey unpleasant news by beginning a conversation with, 'I don't want to upset you, but . . .' as a prelude to saying something that you know will upset the other person. The most common way of covering up or avoiding an embarrassing or threatening situation is to withhold information. Defensiveness leads us to making decisions about what we will or will not say so that we are protected from the response of others, or so that we protect others whether they wish us to or not.

Defensiveness prevents people from learning about and getting rid of the causes of threat and embarrassment because we make sure that these are 'never discussed'. When people in schools are faced with the challenge of having to design and implement appraisal systems that will have multiple goals: to evaluate and improve the quality of our performance, this is a highly threatening matter. It requires us to examine openly and discuss both our strengths and weaknesses and might even require changes to be made to our current practice. There is no doubt that this sort of activity creates risks for those who must appraise the work of others and have their own work appraised. In such situations defensive routines become even more marked because of the human tendency to place blame elsewhere when under threat.

Understanding ourselves and our defensive behaviour against a set of theories about defensive reasoning and practice, and a better alternative that is known as productive reasoning and practice, opens up a new set of options for how we can deal with appraisal dilemmas. The learning involved is presented in the next section as a training curriculum for making a transition from dilemma avoidance to dilemma management. Ideally all staff should be offered the opportunity to learn dilemma management skills. This option would take considerable resourcing and in the interim, learners to date have chosen to engage in this learning rather than be directed to undertake it as part of a national training project. The research reported further on in this chapter draws on data collected by surveying principals and senior managers involved in management development training and education who have taken the first steps in learning that could lead to implementing the dilemma management curriculum in their schools.

Training for managing dilemmas

At the heart of dilemma management training is the skill of engaging in a dialogue that is simultaneoulsy critical and collaborative. It is a skill that, once internalised, enables those who are prepared to use it to articulate a dilemma and work towards its collaborative resolution. It is offered as a powerful tool for creating a culture of openness and honesty, in which productive feedback is offered within appraisal activity to meet the needs of both the organisation and the individual. The training curriculum is intended for use by trained consultants in school-based or workshop settings working with groups of staff.

Implicit in this approach is the expectation that the facilitator of the learning experiences will have a high level of expertise as a *double-loop learner* and skill in engaging in and evaluating others' practice of critical dialogue. The learning concerns and processes for the consultant and for participants are exactly the same because such learning needs to be modelled.

A training curriculum for dilemma management

Teaching people how to manage dilemmas presents a complex adult learning challenge for the facilitator of such learning because of the defensive barriers that are raised by the learners themselves. This manifests as an effort to cover up dilemmas, to resist the unlearning of instinctive skills, and to block the learning of new skills (Cardno 1995; Robinson 1993; Rossmoore 1989). These facets of learning can be viewed as three interrelated and inseparable dimensions of a learning system that must be mastered by those who wish to use double-loop learning organisationally and interpersonally to resolve problems of appraisal practice – particularly the giving and receiving of negative feedback.

Underpinning this learning should be the conviction that norms of effective practice need to be restructured in the light of a theory of effectiveness that offers an alternative to dilemma avoidance. The conscious choice to deal simultaneously with both horns of a dilemma requires the learner to internalise double-loop learning values. It is this choice which ideally is the new norm that guides practice.

Double-loop learning

Single-loop and double-loop learning modes are differentiated by Argyris (1977) on the basis of the values that guide problem-solving attempts. An example of single-loop learning is the ability to learn a new strategy for suppressing conflict in an effort to be effectively governed by values of winning and avoiding unpleasantness. This approach is regularly encountered in research reports of appraisal activity in schools (Cardno 1995, 1999; Robinson 1993; Timperley and Robinson 1998).

In a double-loop learning approach a new learning loop which extends to a re-examination of fundamental values is evident (see Figure 10.2). The value base in double-loop learning focuses upon increasing valid information and internal commitment, and upon a wish to seek and monitor solutions jointly. The instinctive urge to avoid unpleasantness and exert unilateral control which attends single-loop learning and dilemma avoidance must be overcome. A new set of solution strategies is based on quality information and commitment to change that is generated bilaterally.

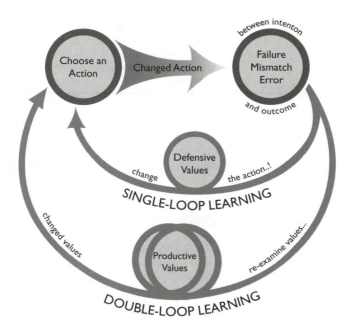

Figure 10.2 Double-loop learning.

In supporting school leaders to deal with dilemmas in performance appraisal contexts in their schools, it is evident that they continue to be challenged by the demands of double-loop learning. However, those who build the capability of other staff as double-loop learners (by including them in school-based training) report the benefits of a core group with common understandings, common skills and a common goal of working towards a culture in which dilemmas are not avoided (see Table 10.1).

Table 10.1 Double-loop learning dimensions in a dilemma management training
curriculum

Dimensions	Competencies to be developed
Dilemma origin factors (problem understanding)	• understanding norms of effective dilemma management • recognition of problem complexity • recognition and articulation of a dilemma • awareness of resistance to innovation
Dilemma maintenance factors (theory understanding)	• understanding typical responses to dilemmas • understanding defensiveness in self and others
Dilemma resolution factors (self-understanding)	• understanding norms of effective theories of action that address dilemmas • evaluating defensive responses in self and others and un-learning skills which are defensive barriers • learning new skills, practising and internalising productive responses • using critical dialogue skills in all challenging encounters

The fundamental training resource is the knowledge base (which is simultaneously theoretical and experiential) about theories of action. Training begins with an introduction of the concept of dilemma management and teaching the theory which enables 'theorising about theories of action' to occur (Cardno 1999; Robinson 1993).

Theories of action: The theory

The differences between espoused theory and theory-in-use (Argyris and Schön 1974) need to be made explicit and the nature of defensive and productive theories-in-use (i.e. theories that govern actions, regardless of what we might espouse) explained. A summary of the key assumptions underlying these two theories might be:

1 Defensive Theory is concerned with the wish to win and to avoid unpleasantness. This leads to strategies based on keeping control, making unilateral decisions, and on protection of self and others.
2 Productive Theory, on the other hand, is concerned with a genuine commitment to change based on freedom of choice. This leads to strategies based on sharing information, seeing difficult issues as a joint responsibility and having continual dialogue.

Diagnosing theories-in-use

Case writing, role-play, video-taping, observation and feedback are all used to construct models of theories-in-use. Data produced helps participants learn because they gain insight into their typical responses and their defensive strategies. These insights enable participants to consider what needs to be changed and to set goals for self-improvement. The consultant helps participants learn how to discover and alter their own theories-in-use and to gain confidence in testing new theories of action in practice. A learning tool to help participants state *what* they think, state *why* they think this way, and to *check* the thinking of others, is used to support a transition from defensive to productive reasoning. It is described in Figure 10.3 as the 'Triple I' approach (Cardno 1998).

INFORMATION
- focus on giving and getting quality information;
- disclose your position or your concerns fully at the outset;
- give and get information that lets you deal with emotions.

ILLUSTRATION
- always illustrate by explaining the basis used for making judgements and by providing examples to illustrate your reasoning and evaluation of a situation;
- seek explanation of others' reasoning and evaluations by asking for illustration.

INQUIRY
- ask relevant questions to seek information, to check others' views and to test your own views;
- do not ask questions that control the response of others;
- ask questions that check your assumptions about the facts and the emotional responses of others.

Figure 10.3 The 'Triple I' approach.

The 'Triple I' approach as a road code

The guidelines in this approach serve to build the skills of critical dialogue which are central to internalising the adoption of a theory-in-use that is embedded in *productive* rather than *defensive* reasoning. In the 'Triple I' approach, participants are consciously attempting to increase the possibility of valid *information* generation, *illustration* of the basis for judgements, and genuine *inquiry* which acknowledges and deals with emotions in interpersonal encounters.

Practising the approach

Each word beginning with the letter 'I' also generates a simple rule that can be memorised to help internalise skills of productive reasoning. Applying the Triple I rules constitutes a form of critical dialogue that is guided by the values of productive reasoning that enable double-loop learning to occur.

Three simple rules for applying the Triple I approach in critical dialogue:

Rule One
STATE YOUR CONCERN
[*inform* – say what you think and feel]

Rule Two
STATE THE REASONS FOR YOUR CONCERN
[*illustrate* – say why you think it and be open about how you feel]

Rule Three
GET REACTIONS
[*inquire* – check what others think and feel and deal with emotions; summarise shared understanding or need for more information; apply Rules again if necessary]

Dilemma management training in action – research with leaders who want to learn

Dilemma management training is a strong aspect of our work in the School of Education at UNITEC Institute of Technology where it is offered in several forms. It is integrated into courses in the formal qualification programmes of *Postgraduate Diploma in School Management* and the *Master of Educational Management*. It is an integral element in executive residential training programmes for secondary school principals, and is also central to school-based action learning consultancy projects where senior management teams are supported in leading change by UNITEC in Schools facilitators.

Since 1997 we have been collecting data through questionnaires and interviews using opportunity and course cohort sampling to capture the views and responses of school leaders who have been introduced to this type of learning. We have been keen to establish initial reactions of learners to the double-loop learning demands of the curriculum. We have also wanted to follow-up their engagement with this learning experience one year or so down the track in order to gauge the extent to which the skills have been applied and to determine the learner's perception of the degree to which the skills have been internalised.

There is little doubt that leaders are inspired and hopeful of being more effective communicators, especially in appraisal contexts, when first introduced to the theory and practice of dilemma management. They are receptive to the pitfalls of avoiding dilemmas and can critically reflect on their own shortcomings. They appear to welcome the potential that the Triple I approach offers as an alternative to conducting dialogues that have hitherto been avoided or that when conducted have compounded defensiveness.

Principals talk about the training

Four of the twenty secondary school principals who attended the UNITEC Institute for Educational Leadership in 2000 commented on what they had learnt and hoped to accomplish as a consequence of this training. Sections of a transcripted interview between the author and these four participants tell this story.

Interviewer: We have proposed the theory and practice of Dilemma Management as a way of dealing with interpersonal issues in appraisal that you may not have confronted openly or effectively in the past. Do you think you have done some relevant learning in these sessions and see this as a useful, alternative approach that you might apply in your school?

Principal A: I think I have. I mean it's given me a lot of confidence to go out and try this, but as I said, I haven't tried it so I don't know how it will be yet. . . . If a teacher is not performing satisfactorily, that's often when you have a dilemma. You've got this problem with the fact of you wanting to relate to this person still because that's one of your biggest stressors as a principal – is not relating well to one of your staff members – and yet you know that on behalf of the school . . . on behalf of the school and students, on behalf of everybody else, you've got a dilemma and that's why I want to use it.

Principal B: I'd like to pick up on that because for me it's caused . . . me to be very reflective on the appraisal process that we have had in our school since it opened . . . and . . . I wasn't particularly effective. But I can see now that I've been doing all the things you described like pussyfooting around and having that large introduction on a more personal note without getting to the core of the business . . . putting the person's needs before the organisation and all those classic things outlined to us. I can't wait to get back now to look at the process documentation and my notes and to use that to be even more reflective and say, 'Where did I go wrong; what can I do next time in terms of seeing this as a dilemma?'

Principal C: I've got a specific case that I'm thinking of and you have given me the push to actually deal with it and he is someone I did not attest and I've provided an action plan and support for him. You know, he has improved an enormous amount in two areas that were weak but not in the third area and the third area is so important I cannot attest him as being competent. So now I feel confident to meet him and to talk just about the third area . . . because before that's why I haven't got him to do anything, make any progress because I've been giving him mixed messages, saying, 'Oh, you're going well, you're trying hard, and I know the kids are difficult and I know the parents are difficult'. Now I can see that all the time I was giving him excuses . . . the whole time. I think that's why it's so hard because our whole culture goes against fronting-up so directly to something that's negative.

Principal A: I think this dilemma management skill actually makes me realise I have permission to do that even though this is just the beginning of learning the skills. The thing I found really interesting is that . . . the . . . 'it's okay to talk about how I'm feeling as well' . . . really surprised me . . . I would never have thought I could be clear about that . . . I would have had a lot of cloud and covered up how I was feeling . . . and now I can see a model.

Principal D: I think this has given us the ability to look at something as a process and consider feelings, emotions involved and know that during the process you can actually say, 'Now let's stop a minute and look at the emotions'. . . . You can acknowledge that somebody is very upset but there is still a need to pursue the issue. So you are working on two levels to get to what you want and also seeing to what they want and you are managing that all the way through the process.

Principal C: That's a formula too, I mean it's easy if you keep in your mind that capital I and the number 3 . . . the triple I and that's why it's a simple process and easy to use.

Principal A: I don't think I know enough about it yet and what I want to do when I get home is to . . . to think again about the single and double loop . . . and to look at where I have gone wrong because I've kept in the single loop, but I need to think how I can move into the double loop.

Interviewer: How could you do that?

Principal D: I like to think that I've got a certain picture in my mind . . . I can think of a thought bubble above my head and if I am talking with you I need to really check out have you got the same picture in your thought bubble because often when you try to examine it . . . we've got two totally different things there.

Principal B: My particular example is . . . is one of a person who only started with me this year and I have hinted there are things we have to work through . . . and I feel much more . . . I use the language, empowered to go back next week and meet with him . . . and I've got an approach, a way of proceeding which is different to what I was planning to do. We talked about Dale Carnegie . . . and how he said, 'Before you deliver criticism or a negative thing, say something positive or say – look, I too have been like this', and try and build that level of empathy before you do deliver the message. Now you say that could be a mixed message . . . and so I've got a bit of unlearning to do in handling this sort of situation, and it became easy when I can say, 'Look – on the one hand I want to stay collegial and keep working with you and on the other hand I have to be a principal and for the sake of students at this school we have to improve what's happening in your classroom'.

In spite of evidence of espousals of interest in the theory and confidence in the potential of dilemma management to help them revisit existing appraisal problems, most of these principals also expressed the need to revisit the theory and reflect before acting. It is conjectured that unless they are motivated to practise the skills soon they may lose both the impetus and recall of the theory base which is fundamental to the intermeshed cognitive and emotional activity that attends the application of Triple I skills in dilemma management.

Responses from participants in postgraduate qualification courses

Eight out of twenty-two students who graduated with the *Postgraduate Diploma in School Management* in 1999 after two years of part-time study, responded to a questionnaire designed to elicit information about:

1   Whether they had encountered appraisal dilemmas recently in their schools.
2   Whether they had applied dilemma management skills learnt on-campus.
3   The extent to which they believed they had internalised these skills.

Encountering dilemmas

Five of the eight respondents indicated that dilemmas had been encountered recently. Descriptions of dilemmas provided by two respondents follow:

> I think I have a classic dilemma as the staff member concerned is the main income earner for her family and the job at the college guarantees both income and housing for her two young boys and husband. On the other hand the school has had concerns about her performance for some time and just recently the Education Review Office commented adversely on her classroom teaching. We should have tried to make her aware of difficulties ages ago.
>
> A teacher within my department appears to be having difficulty with certain aspects of classroom management and as a result has become very negative, with poor interpersonal skills with students making them negative in return. This has adversely affected the classroom atmosphere. In my view it has caused problems with curriculum delivery and discipline and these are recognised by senior management and the house dean. There are both individual and organisational concerns and we have to deal with this. ·

Applying the theory and practice of dilemma management

Six out of eight respondents said that they had applied the learning of theory and skills that occurred in on-campus sessions to situations they met in their schools. Comments from participants are summarised to show (a) which specific skills were used, and (b) what motivated them to apply these skills:

(a) Skills used:

•   Triple I approach
•   rules for productive dialogue
•   critical dialogue checklist

(b) Motivation to apply skills:

- failure of single-loop learning approach
- critical consequences if problem not resolved
- part of role to resolve such problems
- wanting to get to the crux of the problem
- recognising a lot of defensiveness
- wanting more than a quick-fix.

Extent to which skills are internalised

Of the eight respondents only three indicated that they believed they had internalised skills for managing dilemmas and one of the three stated that internalisation had occurred only to a partial degree. Comments from two of these respondents capture this belief as follows:

> I would like to think so, but I must be honest and say that they need to be regularly revised (remembered) because it is easy to slip into a defensive response in the heat of the moment.
>
> I have internalised the Triple I approach which I find most useful in many situations. In my dealings with this staff member I have been honest without pussyfooting around the problems. I know I am often guided by the need to control, with preconceived ideas on what the outcome should be and it is more difficult to change this than I thought which is why I believe I am currently in the process of internalising the skills.

As this small piece of research shows, it is one thing to introduce learners to a curriculum that purports to hold out hope for resolving complex appraisal problems, and quite another thing to expect that this learning, distanced as it is from real situations, will be applied. And even when learners apply the approach, they need practice to maintain contact with theory and practice knowledge that is simultaneously intellectually and intrapersonally challenging. The critical reflection demonstrated in the responses of participants who believe they are internalising the skills does, however, sound a positive note and motivates us to keep teaching these skills and to continually find ways of making a complex and demanding curriculum user-friendly and engaging.

Conclusion

A dilemma management approach has the potential to enable leadership learning that impacts upon complex, recurring problems, and surface those problems which practitioners typically relegate to the 'too hard basket'. This is particularly true of appraisal problems where the focus on professional performance exacerbates defensiveness and the complexity of problems typically results in avoidance.

If leaders are prepared to embark on this learning journey they are inevitably going to be challenged cognitively and emotionally. This is because such learning is both intellectually demanding and at the same time disquieting, revealing as it does that the very skills we are adept at using in some situations backfire on us in others. However, for those who are highly motivated to improve problems of appraisal practice in their schools, and are prepared to persist in mastering a complex dilemma management curriculum and then extending this learning to others, the benefits of internalising productive rather than defensive responses to dilemmas might well outweigh the pain of the learning process in the long run.

References

Argyris, C. (1971) 'The individual and the organisation: Some problems of mutual adjustment', in W.G. Hack, W.J. Gephart, J.B. Heck and J.A. Ramsayer (eds) *Educational Administration: Selected Readings*, pp. 159–78, Boston: Allyn & Unwin.

Argyris, C. (1977) 'Double-loop learning in organisations', *Harvard Business Review*, September–October: 115–25.

Argyris, C. (1985) *Strategy, Change and Defensive Routines*, Boston: Pitman.

Argyris, C. and Schön, D. (1974) *Theory in Practice: Increasing Professional Effectiveness*, San Francisco: Jossey-Bass.

Beer, M. (1987) 'Performance appraisal', in J.W. Lorsh (ed.) *Handbook of Organisational Behaviour*, pp. 286–300, Englewood Cliffs, NJ: Prentice Hall.

Bridges, E.M. (1992) *The Incompetent Teacher*, Lewes: Falmer Press.

Cardno, C. (1995) 'Diversity, dilemmas and defensiveness: Leadership challenges in staff appraisal contexts', *School Organisation* 15(2): 117–31.

Cardno, C. (1998) 'Making a difference by managing dilemmas', *Set – Research Information for Teachers*, New Zealand Council for Educational Research, No. 1, Item 13.

Cardno, C. (1999) 'Problem-based methodology in leadership development: Interventions to improve dilemma management', *New Zealand Journal of Educational Administration* 14: 44–51.

Cardno, C. and Piggot-Irvine, E. (1997) *Effective Performance Appraisal: Integrating Accountability and Development in Staff Appraisal*, Auckland: Longman.

Down, B., Hogan, C. and Chadbourne, R. (1999) 'Making sense of performance management: Official rhetoric and teachers' reality', *Asia-Pacific Journal of Teacher Education* 27(1): 11–24.

McLaughlin, M.W. and Pfeifer, R.S. (1988) 'Teacher evaluation: Organisational change, accountability and improvement', in E.S. Hickcox, S.B. Lawton, K.A. Leithwood and D.F. Musella (eds) pp. 113–40, Toronto: Ontario Institute for Studies in Education Press.

Middlewood, D. (1997) 'Managing appraisal', in T. Bush and D. Middlewood (eds) *Managing People in Education*, pp. 169–85, London: Paul Chapman.

Roberts, G.E. (1998) 'Perspectives on enduring and emerging issues in performance appraisal', *Public Personnel Management* 27(3): 301–20.

Robinson, V. (1993) *Problem-Based Methodology: Research for the Improvement of Practice*, Oxford: Pergamon Press.

Rossmoore, D. (1989) 'Leader/Consultant dilemmas: The primary barrier to satisfying', *Consultation* 8(1): 3–24.

Timperley, H.S. and Robinson, V.J.M. (1998) 'The micropolitics of accountability: The case of staff appraisal', *Educational Policy* 12(1, 2): 162–76.

Chapter 11

Developing standards and assessments for accomplished teaching

A responsibility of the profession

Lawrence Ingvarson

Introduction

There are many good teachers, but methods for recognising their value are generally inadequate. This chapter looks at two approaches to providing experienced teachers with recognition and stronger incentives for evidence of professional development, one in the UK, and the other in the USA. Attention is focused on 'high stakes' teacher evaluation for career advancement, *not annual appraisal nor performance reviews*. The focus in the UK, will be on the 'threshold' assessment of teachers at the top of the existing pay scale, part of the comprehensive government initiated 'performance management' system aimed at reforming the teaching profession in England and Wales. In the USA, the focus will be on 'professional certification'; an emerging system for giving recognition to 'accomplished' teachers provided by an independent professional body, the National Board for Professional Teaching Standards.

These two approaches to assessing teacher performance for career progression will be compared on a number of criteria, particularly their capacity to engage all teachers in effective forms of professional development and assist them to reach their full potential, the fundamental aspiration of any performance management system. Each depends, of course, on credible methods for assessing teacher performance. One, it will be argued, looks backwards and has little chance of achieving its aim; the other points to a possible future and has the potential to change radically the way we think about professional development and methods for assessing teacher performance. It acknowledges the power of professional forms of recognition and demonstrates the commitment teachers are prepared to give to the task of developing their own standards and methods for assessing performance.

Reforms to teachers' career structures and pay systems are unlikely to succeed without the development of credible teaching standards and valid methods for evaluating whether teachers have attained them (Odden and Kelley 1997). How might credibility and validity be best ensured? This chapter will argue that a necessary condition is that these reforms must fully engage teachers and their professional associations. They must lead to the creation of independent structures and institutions with responsibility for these standards and assessments – institutions that will enable the teaching profession and policy makers to talk to each other on equal terms and to exercise their shared responsibility for the quality of teaching and learning in schools.

What teachers know and do is the most important factor affecting the ability of schools to achieve their central educational purposes. However, career structures give less recognition to evidence of professional development than movement into management and administration. Investment in effective teacher education and professional development is the best way to improve the quality of student learning outcomes (Darling-Hammond 2000), yet pay systems offer few incentives for teachers to provide evidence that they have developed professionally. Pay systems typically imply that teachers have got as good as they are ever going to get after about eight or nine years, when they reach the top of the salary scale, though any teacher at this stage knows they still have much to learn. They imply there is little for them to get better at, even though research indicates that teachers reach a key transition point after ten years or so when most are ready to move into greater experimentation and innovation, given opportunities and support for professional development (Huberman 1999).

Origins of teaching reforms in the UK and the USA

Many countries are shifting their reform efforts to focus on teacher policy and strategies that relate more directly to the promotion of quality teaching and learning. Recognition that teacher knowledge and skill is the most important influence on student learning has led to increased emphasis on the development of policies and strategies that aim to attract, prepare and retain good teachers and promote their continuing professional development toward high professional statements (Darling-Hammond 2000). Common to these strategies are plans to restructure career paths and pay systems so that they place greater value on teachers' work and give greater recognition to evidence of professional development.

The Secretary of State for Education in England and Wales released a Green Paper late in 1998 called *Teachers: Meeting the Challenge of Change* (Secretary of State for Education and Employment, 1998). It foreshadowed a wide range of reforms designed to 'accord the teaching profession an entirely new status'. The Green Paper sets out the government's vision for 'a modernised teaching profession'.

> Teachers deserve rewards for good performance, better career prospects, (and) opportunities to keep their skills and subject matter knowledge up to date. ... We propose two pay ranges for classroom teachers, with a performance threshold giving access to a new, higher range for high performing teachers with a track record of consistently strong performance. Crossing this threshold would be a significant career step. Above the threshold, teachers would continue to focus on classroom teaching but would be expected to take

responsibility for making a wider contribution to raising standards in their school.

(Secretary of State for Education in England and Wales 1998: 32)

The Green Paper introduces a new career structure to recruit, retain and reward good teachers. Teachers at the top of the incremental salary scale who demonstrate high and sustained levels of achievement and commitment will be able to cross the 'threshold' (top of the incremental salary scale) to gain a 10 per cent pay increase and access to three further pay steps on the new extended pay scale. Only eighteen months after the Green Paper was published, over 200,000 teachers applied to be assessed by their headteachers against a brief draft set of standards that teachers received, three months before their application forms were due.

In similar vein, the USA has had a series of major national reports since the early 1980s expressing concern, among other things, about the capacity of the profession to compete with other occupations for quality graduates and to retain good teachers in the classroom (A Nation at Risk 1982; Carnegie Forum on Education and the Economy 1986; National Commission on Teaching and America's Future 1996). One of the most significant recommendations of the Carnegie Forum was that a National Board for Professional Teaching Standards (NBPTS) be established.

The NBPTS was founded in 1987 with a broad base of support from state governors, teacher unions and school board leaders, administrators, college and university officials, business executives, foundations and concerned citizens. It is a non-profit, non-partisan organisation governed by a 63-member board of directors, the majority of whom are teachers. The National Board has a three-part mission:

- to establish high and rigorous standards for what accomplished teachers should know and be able to do;
- to develop and operate a national voluntary system to assess and certify teachers who meet these standards; and
- to advance related educational reforms for the purpose of improving student learning in American schools.

Although the aims of the National Board sound similar to those expressed in the Green Paper, in practice it provides a striking contrast to the methods used to implement the UK reforms. The long-term aims of the NBPTS are to build a national certification system operated by teachers for teachers in all schools. Certification aims to provide an independent and credible professional assessment of teacher performance against the Board's standards. The NBPTS is building its certification system only as quickly as it can complete the necessary research to ensure its feasibility, acceptability and rigour. The Board spent six years and $50m before it invited the first candidates to apply for certification: 10,000 teachers applied for certification in 2000.

As the Board's certification gains credibility, and as the professional development benefits of the process become apparent, states and local education authorities are gradually introducing methods for giving recognition and incentives for teachers who become National Board Certified Teachers. Most areas now give some form of recognition, which may range from a salary increase (12 per cent in North Carolina; 15 per cent in Los Angeles) to accepting certification as a means by which teachers may meet state requirements for licence renewal purposes.

The NBPTS is a private organisation (government did not set it up) but teachers dominate its policy making and its operations. Approximately 50 per cent of its funding over the past thirteen years has come from untied federal government grants. The rest has come from a wide variety of bodies such as the Carnegie Foundation, and the National Science Foundation. In 1997 President Clinton pledged to support the NBPTS in its goal of certifying 105,000 teachers by 2005 with grants amounting to nearly $20m per year.

Teaching standards and teacher evaluation: Whose responsibility?

A tension between political and professional responsibility arises in any attempt to establish systems for teacher evaluation and accountability, as with most professions. Where does legitimate authority rest for teacher evaluation and teacher accountability? On what conceptual foundation should teaching standards be based? Who has the authority, or the expertise, to develop standards for what teachers should know and be able to do? How should procedures for assessing teacher performance be developed and validated? Who should apply those procedures and how should they be trained?

The research literature is awash with reports of failed teacher evaluation schemes for purposes such as merit pay (Murnane and Cohen 1986), career ladders (Rosenholtz and Smylie 1987), or career advancement (Smylie and Smart 1990). Many schemes fail because of insufficient awareness of the complexity of the task. Developing professionally credible standards and reliable methods for assessing teacher performance is not easy. Many schemes fail because they are conceptually flawed and because insufficient research and development has been conducted to ensure a legally defensible and professionally credible evaluation system before implementation (Bacharach et al. 1990; Conley 1994). Few things undermine teacher morale as quickly as an invalid teacher evaluation system. Industrial rather than professional priorities and timelines may drive their implementation, as with the advanced skills teacher concept in Australia in the early 1990s (Ingvarson and Chadbourne 1997). Above all, schemes often fail to enlist teacher ownership through their involvement in the development of standards and assessment procedures. They fail to build mechanisms whereby responsibility for the teacher evaluation system is shared with the profession.

Answers to the above questions become particularly pointed where responsibility for 'performance management' is devolved to local school managers who are expected to follow 'guidelines' determined centrally by government, or government agencies with little training. Comparability from school to school may be low and governments find they may not mandate what matters in so far as teachers' practice and commitment is concerned. The temptation is to go for even more regulatory control. A long history of research indicates that teachers' work does not lend itself to remote bureaucratic control (Lortie 1975) which has consequences that make teaching even less attractive to the innovative and able people it needs (McNeil 1986). Changing practice is primarily a problem of teacher learning, not one of management or restructuring organisations, as Peterson *et al.* (1996) found. Managerial models for appraisal and teacher accountability often prove counterproductive, or descend into mere annual routines and rituals (Darling-Hammond 1986). Teachers identify more with the values and images of good practice of their professional associations than they do with the charters of self-managing schools (Chadbourne and Ingvarson 1998).

Many teacher evaluation schemes also fail because they are conceptually flawed. At the heart of many performance management schemes lies a mismatch between teachers' work and the means used to evaluate it. The criteria often underestimate what teachers are trying to achieve. Indicators of performance may belittle the sophistication of what good teachers know and do. Teachers are held accountable for student test scores instead of the quality of learning opportunities they provide. Standards for practice are not owned and valued by the profession.

Two purposes for teacher evaluation: Performance management and professional certification

Two main purposes for teacher evaluation can be distinguished. The first is to safeguard the educational interests and welfare of students and ensure that their teachers are able to fulfil their contractual duties. This purpose is based on the undeniable requirement that teachers be publicly accountable. Standards for this purpose are mainly generic and common to all teachers. The second purpose emphasises the complementary need to ensure that teachers continually review and improve their practices in the light of contemporary research and profession-defined standards. Responsibility for developing standards for high quality practice in most professions usually rests with professional bodies.

These two purposes are similar to the distinction Natriello (1990) makes between teacher evaluation designed to control or influence the performance of teachers *within* their current positions and teacher evaluation for the purposes of making decisions about *movement* from one position to another, such as promotion in a career structure.

Can these two purposes best be met within the one system of teacher evaluation, or do they point to the need for two separate systems (Ingvarson 1994)? The UK Green Paper reform, for example, establishes a performance management system that combines these two purposes and places responsibility for teacher evaluation policy in the hands of government and implementation in the hands of school managers. Annual appraisals of teachers are to be conducted by senior school managers based on teachers' individual job descriptions and agreed objectives. Assessment of a teacher at the performance threshold is to be conducted by his or her headteacher and reviewed by an external assessor drawn from a pool of 'nationally trained experts'.

In contrast, the NBPTS operates independently of employing authorities. Professional standards, by definition, are not employer or school specific. Appraisal or performance management on the other hand is the responsibility of school managers within local school districts, or part of state requirements for renewal of state licences to teach, and is distinct from the certification role that the NBPTS plays.

As an independent professional body, the NBPTS awards certification, not employers, although employing authorities, unions and other stakeholders are active partners in the development and operation of the Board's certification system. Board certification provides an endorsement that a teacher has attained performance standards set by the profession. Certification belongs to the individual. It is portable – it is not tied to a particular position, or job, or role within any specific organisation, nor is it an academic qualification, or an accumulation of academic credits. Specially trained peers from outside their school system assess the evidence that teachers provide for Board certification, for example, portfolio entries, although workplace colleagues and managers may be called upon to validate evidence provided by candidates. They cannot assess teachers known personally to them.

Though the two purposes for teacher evaluation outlined above overlap, they help to distinguish two spheres of responsibility – one quite properly that of government, the other perhaps best delegated to the profession. While the first purpose reflects teacher accountability to management and to the public, the second points to the need for the development of strong normative structures for accomplished teaching with which teachers identify strongly. The rest of this chapter concentrates on the latter purpose, providing recognition to teachers for evidence of professional development.

The UK and the US approaches will be compared on the following criteria:

- Methods used for developing *standards* for accomplished practice.
- Methods used for *assessing* whether teachers have attained those standards.
- The extent to which each is likely to lead to build a more effective *infrastructure for professional learning*, related to improve student learning outcomes.

Defining standards: What should teachers get better at?

Fair assessment of teacher performance relies upon valid and clear standards. Standards aim to define teachers' work and what is to be assessed. There are two aspects to validity here. The first concerns the process by which the standards are defined and who is involved, or *procedural* validity. The second refers to whether teachers who meet the standards are more likely to provide higher quality learning opportunities to learn than are those who do not. In measurement terms, standards aim to define the domain of what is to be assessed. In other words they should also have *content* validity. Content validity also relates to the match between the assessment tasks and the construct of interest – in the case of this chapter, accomplished teaching at the threshold in the UK, or standards for National Board certification in the USA.

Several texts on educational measurement describe these validity procedures, including Messick (1992) who introduces the concept of consequential validity. Valid standards and assessment should, for example, promote professional development; standards should provide teachers with a vision of highly accomplished practice. Assessment tasks themselves should be a vehicle for learning.

The procedures used to develop standards for threshold assessments in the UK and National Board certification can be compared using these criteria. While it is not possible to go into depth here, some observations can still be made. The NBPTS provides detailed evidence of the procedures and the research it undertakes to ensure the validity of each set of standards (Moss, forthcoming). In the case of the threshold assessment used in 2000, it is difficult to find evidence that those involved gave attention to the procedural or content validity of their standards before implementation.

Hattie (forthcoming) draws on the work of the National Commission of Certifying Agencies in the USA to identify criteria for assessing *procedural validity* when specifying a set of standards for any profession. The process by which a set of standards is developed will be a critical issue, not only for the validity of the subsequent operationalisation of assessment procedures, but also for their legal defensibility. In summary, these criteria are designed to ensure:

- the integrity and independence of the body responsible for developing the standards;
- that the standards developing body is composed primarily of those who are already highly accomplished practitioners;
- that the diversity of perspectives in the profession is represented;
- that the process of defining the standards is developed on a sound scientific basis and that the process of developing the standards be formally documented;
- that a wide sampling of agreement is sought for the standards from the major professional groups regarding the appropriateness and level of standards.

This summary does not do justice to Hattie's paper, but it suffices as a means of discussing the balance between political and professional engagement in the development of the UK and USA standards.

Standards for the threshold assessment in England appeared early in 1999, shortly after the Green Paper, as a two-page annex to a 'Technical Consultation

Document on Pay and Performance Management' issued for consultation by the Secretary of State for School Standards. The only information provided about their development in the Consultation Document is that the threshold standards build on Qualified Teacher Status and Induction teacher standards developed some years before by the government's Teacher Training Agency – not a professional body.

Before the NBPTS was underway, many teacher associations in the US were already demonstrating their ability to write convincing and challenging teacher standards. The first, and one of the best, was produced by the National Council for the Teaching of Mathematics in the USA (NCTM 1991), based on a clear vision of quality learning in mathematics, and what teachers need to know and be able to do to implement that vision. National subject associations in Australia for mathematics, science and English teachers are doing the same (Ingvarson 1999a). Teachers develop a powerful sense of ownership for their own standards.

In 1999 the Department for Education and Employment in England decided to fund a major project to develop a framework describing effective teaching – teaching standards in effect – with a mind to using the findings to support the green paper reforms at a later date. Instead of enlisting existing national teacher/ subject associations it commissioned a private consulting firm, Hay McBer, to undertake the task, missing perhaps a major opportunity to promote the development of the profession. Hay McBer produced a major report in June 2000, *A Model of Teacher Effectiveness*, based on its findings (DfEE 2000b).

The approach used by Hay McBer is *circa* 1970s process-product research on teacher effectiveness, which seeks to find correlates between generic teacher behaviours and student outcomes. It does not reflect the major paradigm shift that has taken place over the past fifteen years in research on teaching, based on extensive evidence that what expert teachers know and do is fundamentally subject and level specific (Berliner 1992; Shulman 1987).

Consequently, the Hay McBer research does not reflect well what highly accomplished teachers know about how to help students learn what they are teaching. Its criteria do not identify what effective English teachers know about how to help students write better, or what effective science teachers know about how to probe a student's initial beliefs about a concept in science, and how to use that knowledge to anticipate and deal with possible misconceptions. Generic characteristics of effective teaching lend themselves to the development of observational checklists that managers who do not know much about the field of teaching they are assessing can use.

In contrast, the NBPTS is developing advanced standards in more than thirty *certification fields*, working with teacher associations, educational researchers and unions. The National Board's certification fields are structured around student developmental levels (for example, early childhood, primary, early adolescence, adolescence and young adulthood) as well as by subject area. Standards have already been developed in twenty-one fields and a typical set of National Board standards is thirty to forty pages long. The Board's standards for each certification field are embedded in particular subject areas and teaching levels, consistent with recent research on the domain-specific nature of expertise. They might describe what accomplished teachers of science know and do to engage their students in scientific inquiry, or what English teachers know about learning to write. They acknowledge that what an accomplished teacher of art knows about how to help students progress in that field is different from what an accomplished early primary teacher knows about how to promote development in numeracy, and NBPTS standards aim to reflect that knowledge (Brophy 1991).

When the Board decides to develop standards for a particular certification field such as high school science, or generalist primary teaching, it takes the following steps. It appoints a standards committee, the majority of whom must be distinguished teachers currently practising in that field. Teachers usually chair the committees. Other committee members include experts in child development, teacher education and the relevant academic discipline. Committee appointments last three years, the period it usually takes to complete the cycle of developing the standards.

The committees are charged to develop standards that identify what accomplished teachers in that field know and do. They do this within a framework of core principles for accomplished teaching developed by the Board:

- Teachers are committed to students and their learning.
- Teachers know the subjects they teach and how to teach those subjects to students.
- Teachers are responsible for managing and monitoring student learning.
- Teachers think systematically about their practice and learn from experience.
- Teachers are members of learning communities.

While these principles are 'generic', the challenging task for committee members is to work through what they mean for particular curriculum areas and levels of schooling. Committee members are asked, for example, to develop standards that reflect their holistic nature of teaching; describe how the standards come to life in different settings; identify the knowledge, skills and dispositions that support a teacher's performance at a high level; and show how a teacher's professional judgement is reflected in observable actions.

The NBPTS reviews the draft standards before a public review process. It works closely with professional teaching associations, who support the Board's efforts, to establish advanced standards of knowledge and practice in their respective fields. Many teachers from these organisations serve as Board members and standards committee members.

The Board's standards are not competitive standards for 'super' or 'elite' teachers. They represent the profession's conception of standards *that most teachers should be able to attain* over the first ten to twenty years, given appropriate opportunities for continuing professional learning.

The NBPTS case is an illustration of how the development of standards can provide an excellent opportunity to place greater responsibility for the professional development agenda in the hands of teachers, with beneficial consequences for all. That opportunity has yet to be taken up by policy makers responsible for the Green Paper reforms in the UK.

How are teachers assessed against the standards?

There is a striking contrast between the methods developed for the threshold assessment in England and those developed by the National Board for certification. Once again there are fundamental differences in the role that the teachers play at all stages of the assessment process and the degree of attention given to research issues before implementation.

Assessment at the threshold in the UK

In the case of the threshold assessment, teachers and their organisations appear to have played no role in the development of the methods for assessing teacher performance. Nor are they involved in carrying out the assessments. The assessments appear to have been implemented before a trial period and without any research into their validity or feasibility. There is a long history of research on teacher evaluation (Millman and Darling-Hammond 1990), but little evidence that this has been drawn on. There is also considerable research on the need for training to control bias (Scriven 1994), and problems with cronyism in the micropolitics of school life (Blasé 1990). In the opinion of many headteachers, the one brief day of training they receive is unlikely to equip them sufficiently to carry out these evaluations as well as they would wish.

Similarly, there is little evidence of research into fundamental issues such as the reliability of the methods used to assess or *score* teacher performance or the comparability of assessments from headteacher to headteacher. It is one thing to write a list of standards, which include statements such as that teachers should demonstrate that they consistently and effectively plan lessons and sequences of lessons to meet pupils' individual learning needs, and quite another to establish clear guidelines as to what counts as meeting that standard. Little attention seems to have been given to *setting* standards – how good is good enough to meet the standard? – and ensuring there is similar interpretation of evidence from school to school.

The method used for assessing teacher performance at the threshold is almost breathtakingly crude. Teachers are asked to complete a form that they submit to their headteacher. The form contains pages with boxes for teachers to fill in for each standard. In relation to the standard above, for example, it is suggested that teachers summarise evidence in a box less than two inches deep, that they consistently and effectively:

- use their knowledge of pupils' learning needs to plan lessons and sequences of lessons, to target individuals and groups effectively and to ensure good year-on-year progression;
- communicate learning objectives clearly to pupils;

- make effective use of homework and other opportunities for learning outside the classroom.

As sources of evidence, teachers are told they can 'use feedback from classroom observation, evaluation of performance through a school's monitoring system or from OFSTED inspections'. Other sources could be teaching materials, record books, pupils' work and marking of homework. How headteachers are to ensure some reliability in their own assessments, let alone with other heads, in interpreting this type of unstructured evidence is not clear. There is also a risk of unfairness here as teachers will make different interpretations of how much and what type of evidence to present.

One headteacher wrote to the TES (30 June 2000) describing the heavy workload that threshold assessments caused, but concluded 'my thanks will be seeing my good teachers rewarded – like most people in the profession, they are a great bunch!' This attitude may be commendable, but there is plenty of research evidence to suggest that it is unwise to put principals in this role of making evaluations about the quality of teaching of their own staff when they have to live with the consequences. My prediction is that the threshold pass rate will be around 90 per cent, as it turned out to be for the Advanced Skills Teacher in Australia some years ago. Consequence? The assessment gains no respect, there is no recognition and the salary progression quickly becomes automatic, which was what the teacher unions aimed for anyway.

Assessment for National Board certification

All teachers applying for Board certification undertake two forms of assessment, a portfolio and an assessment centre. They prepare evidence of their teaching in a portfolio containing six 'entries' of three types. Two entries are based primarily on *student work samples*, two are based on videotape clips of class discussion and the last two are based on documentation of professional accomplishments outside the classroom. Each entry is like a whole 'piece' of a teacher's work. Some titles give some idea of the holistic nature of the entries: *Teaching a Major Idea Over Time; Making Real World Connections: Probing Student Understanding*. Each entry takes about twenty to thirty hours to prepare and is about twelve pages long. Teachers are provided with detailed guidelines on how their entry will be scored.

As an example, one of the portfolio entries for high school English teachers, *Analysing Student Writing*, asks them to analyse a piece of writing from each of three students, in the context of the student as a developing writer and their approach to teaching writing in the class. Teachers are advised to collect samples of work over time from a larger number of students and to select later those they will use in the actual portfolio entry. Candidates must include the prompt or assignment that occasioned the writing, all the drafts, other student work that shows the writing process that the student used, peer or teacher conference notes, and any written feedback the teacher provided.

Teachers are provided with a clear structure for the portfolio and guidelines for preparing their entry. For example, for *Analysing Student Writing*, candidates are asked to describe the context of the class, and write a *commentary* on the students' writing addressing the following questions (the full guidelines are much more detailed):

Part 1: Analysis of individual students (no more than three pages per student)

Instructional context

- What was the teaching sequence that led to the piece of student writing?
- What promoted this piece of writing?
- What were your teaching goals?

The student

- What about the student (background, skills and interests) helps explain this piece of writing?

The student's writing

- What do you see as the special, defining characteristics of the writing?
- What does it suggest about the student's development and accomplishment as a writer?
- How did you assess this writing?
- How did you present assessment feedback back to the student?

Planning

In light of this student writing, what did you do next to build on what the student accomplished?

Part 2: Reflective essay (two pages)

How do these three students' writings, considered together, and the teaching context that shaped them, demonstrate your goals and approaches to the teaching of writing and the challenges you face as a teacher of writing? Use the three students' work you have submitted to illustrate your discussion.

The next two entries are based primarily on *videotape clips*. Candidates are advised to make many videotapes of different classes, from which they can select one later for their entry, and to involve other teachers and students in making and analysing them. One entry asks teachers to demonstrate the strategies they used for *small-group teaching* (the other focuses on whole class discussion). They are asked to present a twenty-minute videotape (uninterrupted and unedited) in which students work purposefully in small groups and a ten-page written commentary about their teaching recorded on that tape. The focus of this performance assessment is on the development of students' ability to engage with the teacher and with each other in meaningful discourse as they work in small groups on an important topic in language arts and on their integration of teaching. Teachers are provided with detailed guidelines about the questions they should address in their written commentary, similar to those above for the student writing entry.

The final two entries ask teachers to document their accomplishments in areas outside the classroom. The first focused on contributions to *professional community* over the past five years, such as leadership in curriculum and professional development within their school, and wider contributions to educational policy and practices through work in professional organisations and other settings. The second entry asked for descriptions and documentation of those activities and achievements that illustrated commitment to the *families and communities of their students*. Teachers are asked to provide evidence of the significance and impact of their accomplishments and letters of verification must come from someone who is personally knowledgeable about the achievements they are describing.

The assessment centre

One of the National Board's guiding principles from its inception has been that highly accomplished teachers should have a rich understanding of the subjects they teach and appreciate how knowledge in their subject is created, organised, linked to other disciplines and applied in real world settings. Evidence of this type of subject specific pedagogical knowledge can be achieved in part through portfolio entries. However, the Board believes supplementary methods are needed, so teachers attend an 'assessment centre' for one full day on any day that suits them over a six-week period near the end of the school year. The day usually consists of four ninety-minute sessions. Candidates are asked to respond to four specific prompts, some of which are based on stimulus materials sent to candidates well in advance of the assessment centre date. Here is one example.

> **Teaching and Writing**: Candidates are sent three professional articles about teaching and learning writing. They are told to read the articles in preparation for an exercise in which they will be asked to use information from the article as a basis for talking about teaching writing. At the assessment centre, a written scenario is presented. Candidates are asked to construct an argument on a topic presented by the scenario, using the stimulus articles as a support.

Comment: It is expected that teachers will take most of a school year to complete their portfolios. The 'pass rate' is around 40 per cent. Teachers who miss out can reapply and 'bank' portfolio entries on which they did well enough to meet the Board's standards.

It has taken many years to develop assessment methods like these. Teams of teachers are involved at all stages of the development and trailing process. The National Board has involved many national figures in educational measurement in research on the validity, reliability and generalisability of the assessment methods. It is important to note that many promising ideas for assessment tasks have been tried and found wanting. The portfolio entries may sound simple, but they take a lot of research and development before they are ready for wider use. Teachers must see them as 'authentic' teaching tasks – tasks they regard as a normal part of their work. Each task provides evidence of multiple standards. They must link back clearly to the standards, and assessors must be able to score them reliably.

These assessments call for assessors who have deep knowledge of the relevant teaching field. School managers may have been successful teachers, but they are unlikely to have the expertise to assess across all the certification fields, not to mention the many potential sources of bias that may come in when assessing their own staff.

In 2000, nearly 10,000 teachers applied for Board certification. Hundreds of teachers are assembled each summer at several centres across the USA and paid to carry out the assessments. Most have never been assessors before, but after four days' training they reach high levels of reliability in their assessments. They cannot assess teachers known to them already. Teachers are trained to assess only one portfolio entry or one assessment centre exercise. Assessments are constantly monitored to check on reliability. Two teachers working independently assess each entry and exercise. This means that, across the six entries and four exercises, twenty teachers may be involved in the assessment of one teacher's evidence. After two to three weeks examining the work of many candidates it is understandable that these teacher–assessors come to appreciate this as one of the most valuable professional development experiences they have ever had.

One of the cardinal rules for reliability is that assessment should involve multiple assessors and multiple forms of evidence. It is unlikely that the threshold assessment in England will meet this criterion, even with the use of external assessors to verify through sampling that a headteacher has applied the performance threshold standards correctly (DfEE 2000a).

While the National Board has conducted many research studies on the reliability of its assessments, reliability alone does not guarantee validity – that the process is effective at identifying teachers who actually are highly accomplished. This is a very difficult criterion against which to validate the Board's assessments. The NBPTS has commissioned several research studies to investigate this question. One provides independent confirmation that successful candidates differed significantly from those who did not gain certification in terms of the quality of their classroom teaching practices.

In contrast, no research of this kind has been reported as yet for the threshold assessment in England. Applicants for the threshold assessment in England are asked to provide evidence for one of the standards that, as a result of their teaching, 'their pupils achieve well relative to the pupil's prior achievement, making progress as good or better than similar pupils nationally. This evidence should be shown in marks or grades in any relevant national test or examinations, or school based assessment for pupils where national tests are not taken.' This value-added approach sounds reasonable, but it places a great deal of faith in the validity of the national tests, as measures of what the teachers are teaching, and without mechanisms for isolating teacher effects from a range of other factors affecting student test scores.

It remains to be seen whether research in the UK will provide evidence to confirm interpretations of teacher effectiveness based on these test scores. But this does point to another difference between the Board and the threshold assessments. The Board's portfolio entries ask teachers to offer evidence that they can provide high quality *conditions* for learning, consistent with current research and professional judgement and with professional models of accountability, as set out in the standards. Portfolios provide direct evidence of student work and classroom activity – the 'outcomes' of the conditions for learning established by the teacher – whereas the threshold assessment attempts to hold teachers accountable for standardised 'outputs'. More research will be needed before we have a better understanding of which is a more valid basis for teacher assessment, which is fairer and which has more consequential validity.

Linking the assessment process to professional development and improved student learning

As mentioned earlier, both the teacher reforms in England and Board certification in the USA aim to provide stronger incentives and recognition for professional development. Each reform can, therefore, be examined in terms of its potential to engage most teachers in more effective methods of professional development, as well as effects on self-esteem and professional relationships in the schools. Each reform can also be analysed in terms of its capacity to place greater responsibility for the professional development system in the hands of teachers and their organisations.

There is considerable evidence that teachers who have been through the NBPTS certification system regard it as one of the most powerful professional development experiences they have ever had (Tracz *et al.* 1995). The certification process has the effect of engaging many teachers in forms of professional learning that are consistent with research on the characteristics of effective professional development (Little 1993; Wilson 1999; Ball and Cohen 1999). Teachers regularly claim that they have become better teachers *as a result* of the certification process (Ingvarson 1999b; Wolf and Taylor, forthcoming).

One reason appears to be that each portfolio entry must contain evidence of what the students are doing (video), or evidence from student work samples – evidence which can be directly linked to what the teacher is doing, together with analysis and reflection by the teacher on that evidence. Teachers must necessarily engage in close analysis of, and reflection on, their teaching and its effects on students' learning, tied to concrete examples of student work. Candidates often join networks of other candidates or form their own to help them do this. They often make many videos for their portfolios and use other teachers and students to help them with their analysis, a process strongly encouraged by the NBPTS. The standards provide significant reference points for this process, which is completely consistent with the idea of schools as professional learning communities.

According to Berliner (1992), opportunities for reflected-upon classroom experience with colleagues help to explain the differences between novices and expert teachers. The research on teacher change indicates that this kind of inter-action with colleagues about the details of student learning and de-privatisation of practice is one of the defining characteristics of good professional development.

It is too early for any research to have been done on the effects of undertaking the threshold assessment. But it is possible to say that nature of the process in which teachers engage is very different. Teachers are not asked to provide 'whole' examples of their work as teachers are for NBPTS portfolios, nor are they asked to provide analysis and reflection on actual 'cases' of teaching such as videos or student work. It seems unlikely that the threshold process will engage teachers in similar kinds of analyses to those for National Board candidates. Avenues for collegial analysis and reflection seem unlikely to develop as well. Teachers can provide evidence for the threshold assessment such as 'schemes of work, lesson plans, feedback from observation (by a school manager or OFSTED inspector) but these tend to be isolated and unrelated pieces of information. Teachers are advised, 'Don't say "I make sure my teaching is appropriate to each child's needs". Do say "Feedback from observation/OFSTED praised the way . . .".' This advice does not seem to place much value on self-analysis and reflection. Unlike the Board's assessment tasks, the threshold form provides little structure or guidance for analysis and reflection on teaching, or about how the evidence teachers provide will be 'scored'.

I have just worked with a group of teachers at Monash University who have completed NBPTS portfolios together over several months and, despite the work involved, there is no doubt they enjoyed the experience. It is hard to imagine that teachers would enjoy filling in the forms for the threshold assessment. The Board's approach appeals to teachers' professionalism and imagination – 'show us an example of how you engage your students in scientific inquiry'; the other seems to threaten, and deaden – show us your 'books marked in line with school policy'.

Conclusion

This chapter has compared two strategies for reforming the teaching profession, one from the UK and one from the USA. The focus was on the capacity of these reforms to strengthen professional responsibility and engage all teachers in effective forms of professional development.

In England, the 1998 Green Paper *Teachers: Meeting the Challenge of Change* 'sets out the *Government's* vision for a modernised teaching profession' (author's emphasis). The Minister's aim is to 'strengthen school leadership, to provide incentives for excellence, to engender a strong culture of professional development, to offer better support to teachers, to focus on teaching in the classroom, and to improve the image, morale and status of the profession'.

This could have been a vision to which the profession was invited to contribute, for example, by engagement in developing standards and assessments, but that was not the direction in which the government chose to proceed. Policy makers in the UK have not brought the profession along with it in these reforms, nor capitalised on the many opportunities they provide to enhance the responsibility the profession undertakes for the development of standards and assessment of teacher performance. Professional involvement in its operation has been minimal. As the Green Paper indicates, the threshold is part of a unified system for the management of teacher performance, not a system for professional development and recognition. Managers manage teacher performance and teachers teach. The threshold reform treats assessment *as an event not a process for learning*. As a consequence perhaps, the performance assessment process for the threshold in its current form does not look as if it will stand up well to scrutiny against standards for the evaluation of systems for evaluating teachers (e.g. Joint Committee on Standards for Educational Evaluation, 1988).

The need for a better balance between political and professional authority is not recognised in the Green Paper reforms. In fact there is little evidence in official documents that teaching standards and assessments might even be considered to be an area where the profession could have expertise. While the Hay McBer model emphasises that effective teachers 'create trust', provide 'challenge and support', and build 'confidence' and 'respect for others', these standards do not appear to have been applied by the government to the way it works with the teaching profession in England. As good teachers develop, they slowly learn how to 'let go' control. Maybe governments have to learn to do the same, if they are to promote the capacity and commitment in the teaching profession on which the success of their reforms will depend.

The National Board for Professional Teaching Standards in the US plays a more limited role in reform. It has one core function – to provide a national voluntary system to assess and certify teachers who reach high standards. Its job is to do this in the most credible way possible. But, as the Board's certification gains respect, indications are that the effects of this function will be far reaching.

In this system, the profession builds its own infrastructure for defining teaching standards, promoting development towards those standards and providing recognition for those who reach them. The aim of a standards-based professional development system like the NBPTS (Ingvarson 1998) is to build a system for which teachers, individually and collectively, feel responsible. The system is complementary to, not a replacement for, the in-service education that employers should provide to support the implementation of changes and reforms they have initiated.

Professional certification is a broad reform strategy for the collective advancement of the profession, one which does not rely primarily on government action or the imperfect working of the market (Sykes, forthcoming). The NBPTS was forged from the mutual interests of teacher organisations, politicians and other stakeholders in quality teaching, who found they were readily able to build a common vision for the teaching profession. Although they had their differences in other arenas, when they came together in the arena that the NBPTS provided to talk only about good teaching and how to promote it, those differences faded into the background. The discussion had been moved outside the industrial arena. To attend a meeting of the NBPTS is to witness something of a miracle for eyes accustomed to Australian industrial relations. Yet industrial relations between unions and employers in the US have been as fraught as in Australia, or the UK, perhaps more so (Kerchner et al. 1997). What is clearer now is the necessary relationship between the development of teaching as a profession and the development of more effective systems for teacher evaluation and professional development based on profession-defined standards. Getting this relationship right seems to be of far more significance than refining systems for performance review!

References

Bacharach, S.G., Conley, S.C. and Shedd, J.B. (1990) 'Evaluating teachers for career rewards and merit pay', in J. Millman and L. Darling-Hammond (eds) *The New Handbook of Teacher Evaluation* (pp. 133–46), Newbury Park, CA: Sage Publications.

Ball, D.L. and Cohen, D.K. (1999) 'Developing practice, developing practitioners: Toward a practice-based theory of professional education', in L. Darling-Hammond and G. Sykes (eds) *Teaching as the Learning Profession: Handbook of Policy and Practice*, San Francisco: Jossey-Bass.

Berliner, D.C. (1992) 'The nature of expertise in teaching', in F.K. Oser, A. Dick and J.-L. Patry (eds) *Effective and Responsible Teaching: The New Synthesis* (pp. 227–48), San Francisco: Jossey-Bass.

Blasé, J. (1990) *The Politics of Life in Schools: Power, Conflict and Cooperation*, Newbury Park, CA: Sage Publications.

Brophy, J. (ed.) (1991) *Advances in Research on Teaching, Volume 2. Teachers' Knowledge of Subject Matter as it Relates to their Teaching Practice*, Greenwich, CT: JAI Press.

Carnegie Forum on Education and the Economy (1986) *A Nation Prepared: Teachers for the 21st Century*, Washington, DC: Carnegie Forum on Education and the Economy.

Chadbourne, R. and Ingvarson, L.D. (1998) 'Some effects of the Professional Recognition Program in Victoria's schools of the future', *Australian Educational Researcher* 25(20): 61–95.

Conley, S.C. (1994) 'Teacher pay systems', in L.C. Ingvarson and R. Chadbourne (eds), *Valuing Teachers' Work* (pp. 46–69), Melbourne: Australian Council for Educational Research.

Darling-Hammond, L. (1986) 'A proposal for evaluation in the teaching profession', *The Elementary School Journal* 86(4): 531–51.

Darling-Hammond, L. (2000) 'Teacher quality and student achievement: A review of state policy evidence', *Educational Policy Analysis Archives* 8(1): 430–41. (http://epaa.asu.edu/epaa/v8nl/)

Department for Education and Employment (2000a). *Teachers: Meeting the Challenge of Change. Technical Consultation Document on Pay and Performance Management*, London: Department for Education and Employment. (www.dfee.gov.uk/teachers)

Department for Education and Employment (2000b) *A Model of Teacher Effectiveness. Report by Hay McBer to the Department for Education and Employment*, London: Department for Education and Employment.

Hattie, J. (forthcoming) 'Validating the specification of standards for teaching: Application to the National Board for Professional Teaching Standards', in L.C. Ingvarson (ed.) (forthcoming) *Assessing Teachers for Professional Certification: The National Board for Professional Teaching Standards*, Amsterdam: Elsevier.

Huberman, M. (1999) 'Professional careers and professional development: Some intersections', in T. Guskey and M. Huberman (eds) *Professional Development in Education: New Paradigms and Practices* (pp. 193–224), New York: Teachers College Press.

Ingvarson, L.C. (1994) 'Setting standards for teaching: An agenda for the profession', in F. Crowther, B. Caldwell, J. Chapman, G. Lakomski and D. Ogilvie (eds) *The Workplace in Education: Australian Perspectives*, Australian Council for Educational Administration 1994 Yearbook, Rydalmere, NSW: Edward Arnold.

Ingvarson, L.C. (1998) 'Professional development as the pursuit of professional standards: The standards-based professional development system', *Teaching and Teacher Education* 14(1): 127–40.

Ingvarson, L.C. (1999a) 'Science teachers are developing their own standards', *Australian Science Teachers Journal* 45(4): 27–34.

Ingvarson, L.C. (1999b) 'The power of professional certification', *Unicorn* 25(2): 52–70.

Ingvarson, L.C. (ed.) (forthcoming) *Assessing Teachers for Professional Certification: The National Board for Professional Teaching Standards*, Amsterdam: Elsevier.

Ingvarson, L.C. and Chadbourne, R. (1997) 'Reforming teachers' pay systems. The advanced skills teacher in Australia', *Journal of Personnel Evaluation in Education* 11(1): 7–30.

Joint Committee on Standards for Educational Evaluation (1988) *The Personnel Evaluation Standards: How to Assess Systems for Evaluating Educators*, Newbury Park, CA: Sage Publications.

Kerchner, C.T., Koppich, J.E. and Weeres, J.G. (1997) *United Mind Workers: Unions and Teaching in the Knowledge Society*, San Francisco: Jossey-Bass.

Little, J.W. (1993) 'Teachers' professional development in a climate of educational reform', *Educational Evaluation and Policy Analysis* 15(2): 129–51.

Lortie, D. (1975) *Schoolteacher: A Sociological Study*, Chicago: University of Chicago Press.

Millman, J. and Darling-Hammond, L. (1990) *The New Handbook of Teacher Evaluation*, Beverly Hills, CA: Sage Publications.

McNeil, L. (1986) *Contradictions of Control: School Structure and School Knowledge*, New York: Routledge & Kegan Paul.

Messick, S. (1992) 'Validity', in R.L. Linn (ed.) *Educational Measurement* (3rd edition, pp. 13–103), New York: Macmillan.

Moss, P.A. (forthcoming) 'A critical review of the validity research agenda of the National Board for Professional Teaching Standards', in L.C. Ingvarson (ed.) (forthcoming) *Assessing Teachers for Professional Certification: The National Board for Professional Teaching Standards*, Amsterdam: Elsevier.

Murnane, R. and Cohen, D.K. (1986) 'Merit pay and the evaluation problem', *Harvard Educational Review* 56(1): 1–17.

National Board for Professional Teaching Standards (1989) *Toward High and Rigorous Standards for the Teaching Profession*, Detroit: NBPTS.

National Commission on Excellence in Education (1983) *A Nation at Risk: The Imperative of Educational Reform*, Washington, DC: US Department of Education.

National Commission on Teaching and America's Future (1996) *What Matters Most: Teaching for America's Future*, New York: National Commission on Teaching and America's Future.

National Council of Teachers of Mathematics (1991) *Professional Standards for the Teaching of Mathematics*, Reston, VA: NCTM.

Natriello, G. (1990) 'Intended and unintended consequences: Purposes and effects of teacher evaluation', in J. Millman and L. Darling-Hammond (eds) *The New Handbook of Teacher Evaluation* (pp. 35–45) Beverly Hills, CA: Sage Publications.

Odden, A. and Kelley, C. (1997) *Paying Teachers for What They Know and Do: New and Smarter Compensation Strategies to Improve Schools*, Thousand Oaks, CA: Corwin Press.

Peterson, P.L., McCarthy, S.J. and Elmore, R. (1996) 'Learning from school restructuring', *American Educational Research Journal* 3(1): 1999–154.

Rosenholtz, S. and Smylie, M.A. (1987) 'Teacher compensation and career ladders', *Elementary School Journal* 85(2): 149–66.

Secretary of State for Education in England and Wales (1998) *Teachers: Meeting the Challenge of Change*, London: Department for Education and Employment.

Scriven, M. (1994) 'Using the duties-based approach to teacher evaluation', in L.C. Ingvarson and R. Chadbourne (eds) *Valuing Teachers' Work: New Directions in Teacher Appraisal*, Melbourne: Australian Council for Educational Research.

Shulman, L. (1987) 'Knowledge and teaching: Foundations of the new reform', *Harvard Education Review* 57(1): 1–22.

Smylie, M.A. and Smart, J.C. (1990) 'Teacher support for career advancement initiatives: Program characteristics and effects on work', *Educational Evaluation and Policy Analysis* 12(2): 139–55.

Sykes, G. (forthcoming) 'Educational reform and the National Board for Professional Teaching Standards', in L.C. Ingvarson (ed.) (forthcoming) *Assessing Teachers for Professional Certification: The National Board for Professional Teaching Standards*, Amsterdam: Elsevier.

Tracz, S. and associates (1995) 'Improvement in teaching skills: perspectives from National Board for Professional Teaching Standards field test network candidates'. Paper presented at the Annual Meeting of the American Educational Research Association, 18–22 April, San Fransisco.

Wilson, S. (1999) 'Teacher learning and the acquisition of professional knowledge: An examination of research on contemporary professional development', in A. Iran-Nejad and D.P Pearson (eds) *Review of Research in Education*, Volume 24, Washington DC: American Educational Research Association.

Wolf, K. and Taylor, G. (forthcoming) 'Effects of National Board for Professional Teaching Standards Certification on teachers' perspectives and practices', in L.C. Ingvarson (ed.) (forthcoming) *Assessing Teachers for Professional Certification: The National Board for Professional Teaching Standards*, Amsterdam: Elsevier.

Chapter 12

The future of managing teacher performance and its appraisal

David Middlewood

Forecasting the future is a dangerous venture under any circumstances; given the turbulence and controversial nature of the topic of appraising the performance of professionals in education, forecasting the future there may seem downright foolhardy. Nevertheless, given that effective leaders and managers are those that have a strategic view and given the range of practices presented in this book, it may be helpful to suggest some aspects of development in this field and try to draw out their implications for these leaders and managers in education.

Teacher performance appraisal in the context of education

Taking into account the wide range of contexts for performance appraisal described in previous chapters, it seems certain that a continuum of practice in the field will continue to exist, even though specific contexts will inevitably change. In South Africa, for example, as the new Republic develops into a mature democracy, the way its teachers are appraised may move through a sequence such as in Figure 12.1.

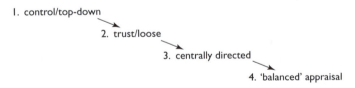

Figure 12.1 Possible sequence of appraisal models.

Alternatively, learning from experience elsewhere and from the apartheid period, it may omit phase 3 and build its appropriate system directly out of its attempts in the immediate post-apartheid era.

Although a continuum of practice is likely to continue (similar to that suggested in Chapter 1), the position on the continuum for any particular nation is likely to vary over time. The optimistic view would be that, in a number of developing countries, sufficient experience will have been gained for them to have developed systems of teacher performance management and appraisal which will achieve some key purposes of education. For this to happen, I believe two important recognitions need to have occurred which significantly affect the context within which this management takes place.

First, the societies in these countries will have grown through (I am tempted to say 'grown out of'!) the political belief that good education is the answer to everything, and consequently poor education is the cause of all society's ills. In the last parts of the 1990s and the early part of the new century, there are encouraging signs of this realisation (neatly summarised by Mortimore 1997: 484):

> . . . education is able to *change* certain societies in other parts of the world. In Singapore, Taiwan, and parts of the Indian subcontinent it is clearly doing this. The question of whether such change is possible in the industrially advanced Western societies is not yet clear. My own view is that school effectiveness provides an opportunity for this to happen. I do not believe, however, that it should be thought of as a panacea.

> The challenge is to ensure that these changes make it more rather than less likely that schools – in whatever form they exist in the future – can better compensate for the worst ills of society.

> (Ibid.)

If education can be placed in a more realistic perspective in relation to society's 'good', and remaining vitally important in this, then the proper perspective will be given to educational processes and less over-concentration, even obsession, with the individual educationalist, i.e. the teacher.

This movement away from over-concern with assessment of the individual is the second recognition referred to. At the time of writing this chapter, the national media in the United Kingdom – and thereby the government – is preoccupied with a series of 'scandals' concerning the incompetence of highly paid specialist practitioners in the medical professions. Legislative reactions to these revelations are to result in, rightly, tighter control of medical consultants, regular assessment of the competence. Although these improvements in individual practice are clearly desirable and necessary, they will not contribute significantly, I suggest, to an improvement in the general state of health and medicine in the United Kingdom – compared with, for example, a reduction in public dependence upon the use of antibiotics.

What I am arguing is that the improvement of education, as health, is dependent for its effectiveness upon much more than the individual competence and skills of its individual practitioners, critically important though these are. Therefore the assessment or measurement of educational success and improvement needs to look beyond the assessment of these individuals. A collection of highly skilled individual teachers does not in itself make a good school, any more than a collection of highly skilled medical practitioners guarantees a healthy nation. The focus upon individual teachers can and does in my view work against those aspects of a school which give it its effectiveness, e.g. leadership and management, shared values, consistency in approach to external relations and a collaborative culture.

In this context, performance appraisal must be seen as an integral part of a move to improve education, not just individuals:

> appraisal can be a powerful force for continuing professional development and consequent school improvement. . . . But this will not happen unless . . . such appraisal is seen as an integral part of the move to improve education.
> (Hellawell 1997: 38)

Without the signals that this is the case, performance appraisal will always be at risk of being an 'add-on'. When it is an 'add-on', as the UK experience of the first introduction of teacher appraisal showed, it is doomed to lose importance when other priorities press in on busy schools and teachers. As various writers (Middlewood 1997a; Cardno and Piggott-Irvine 1997), have pointed out, only when appraisal is managed as part of an overall approach to managing people performance can it become effective. It has to be seen to be central to improvement for this effectiveness to occur, central to the improvement both of the teachers' work and to the improvement of the school or college. As discussed in Chapter 1, it is the task of the manager of appraisal and performance to ensure that these two are inextricably linked. The extent to which this linkage occurs effectively is inevitably affected by the wider, especially national, systems within which the schools and teachers operate and these, as mentioned briefly in Chapter 1, are themselves influenced by a number of factors. Some of these factors are likely to remain constant, others can be seen as emerging now as significant because of trends that we can discern.

Constant factors affecting schemes of performance management and appraisal which managers have to take account of include:

Political imperatives

As discussed in Chapter 1, the concept of performance and appraisal in education will inevitably always be significantly influenced by the attitude that national government has at any one time towards education and its professionals. This attitude may be influenced by the economic context, by a need to demonstrate to taxpayers and voters a particular stance that the government is taking, the relative current importance of education and, occasionally, a 'knee-jerk' policy reaction to a public demand following occurrences. Whatever the reason, the more closely a government influences a national framework, the more certain it is that the model of performance and appraisal will be 'top-down', because of the need to demonstrate control. The less government influence there is, the more likely it is that a 'softer' model will emerge, with a greater focus on the professionals' needs (see Figure 12.2). This is likely to be applicable to other public services, not merely education.

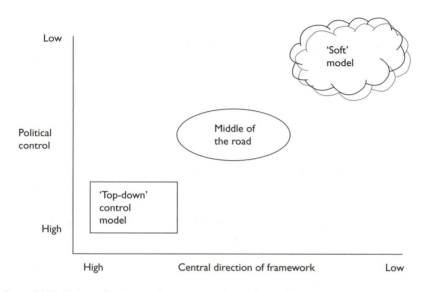

Figure 12.2 Models of performance appraisal in public services.

Previous established practice

As with much practice in education a major factor for leaders and managers of schools in implementing change is the nature of the practice that already exists and existed previously. This may be part of a national or individual school culture – 'the way we have done it here'. The school manager's task, especially when new, is often to influence that culture and make it more appropriate (Bush 1998), but sometimes the context in an individual school is profoundly influenced by a wider context of custom and habit in the profession nationally. Two examples are briefly considered.

Slovenia became an independent country in 1991 and introduced a system of teacher promotion in 1992, which depended upon a formal type of teacher appraisal for a higher salary to be gained. Erculj (2000: 1) describes how head-teachers had long been expected to observe teachers' lessons, but that even after a 1996 Act defined one of their tasks as 'attendance in the classroom in order to evaluate teachers' work' many have not done this. The National Leadership School of Slovenia, established in 1995, incorporated management of teacher performance into the requirements for acquiring headship licence, but the appraisal aspect of this management remains loose and haphazard. Performance for promotion is based on:

- length of service in education;
- days of in-service trainings (as credits);
- additional professional work;
- performance 'at work'.

Whereas the first three of these are carefully calculated, and checked by the National College, the last is not assessed in any systematic way. Erculj's (2000) view of what she terms the 'Headteacher's Burden?' is that change cannot be expected at school level unless national clarification as to evaluative and developmental appraisal is made and headteachers are given full training and support. The implication is that it is easier as in current practice to focus on the quantifiable aspects of performance.

In Greece the 'centralised bureaucratised and authoritarian system of control over education' (Ifanti 1995: 277) has meant a civil-servant status for teachers and little official devolution to regional and local level. In reality, headteachers, who are officially responsible for 'supervising the teaching staff', operate their own ways of managing teachers' performance, and appraisal at a local level falls into disuse, whatever the official documentation states. Greece, in fact, provides a clear example of how the performance of teachers and its appraisal slips far down a government agenda because of more pressing education priorities, and because of an established culture of perceptions of teaching as a 'job for life' profession, inertia becomes a natural state. Attempts therefore by the Greek Ministry (1997) to standardise teacher appraisal and introduce a clear process needed only opposition from the teaching unions to ensure that for over three years no attempt whatsoever has been made to implement the 1997 regulations.

These 1997 regulations made it clear that teachers' performance was to be monitored and appraised by school councils (i.e. headteachers plus local representatives of subject specialist associations). Whilst some of the elements of effective performance are recognisable as ones used elsewhere (e.g. keeping subject knowledge up-to-date, encouraging pupil participation, etc.), opposition is almost guaranteed because:

- good practice in certain areas is unspecified (the unions pointed this out with particular regard to record-keeping);
- in a profession where teachers do not see themselves as having professional entitlements which are taken for granted elsewhere (e.g. cover being provided if a colleague is on maternity leave or absent through sickness), it is difficult to envisage teachers acknowledging the right of others to assess them closely, until that situation is improved.

One headteacher in Crete, for example, described that if a teacher is absent and no one takes his or her place, 'the children have no classes – they go home. This therefore encourages a culture in which virtually all teachers send their own children to private extra classes, and many of them take on extra jobs outside their teaching hours. Many run private schools for the extra income.'

Of course, established practice in managing teacher performance is also affected by the status of teachers in a society. In Greece, it is clearly not high. In the UK, government statements about the need to raise the status of teachers have occurred at the turn of the century in a context of teacher shortages and recruitment problems, accompanied by a stress on pay increases tied ostensibly to improved performance or productivity. However, in some societies, the status of teachers is quite different because of religious and cultural traditions which place a high value on learning and education. Reynolds and Farrell (1996: 54–7), in examining a number of studies, list 'the high status of teachers in the Pacific Rim societies' as one of the key factors in the superior educational achievement of students in East Asia, whilst Lewis (1995) notes the prestige of teaching in Japan as high relative to other professions. National schemes (or the absence of them) for managing and assessing performance in these cases reflect a reluctance to impose unnecessary bureaucracy on high status employees or a satisfaction with the way this high status is achieved and maintained.

Extent of links with pay, promotion and career structure

Career patterns and structures, including the nature of contracts and security of tenure, inevitably affect the way performance is managed. In Japan, mentioned above, requirements to rotate to demographically different schools during their careers (e.g. in Tokyo in each of the city's three geographic regions, which roughly correspond to major socio-economic divisions (Lewis 1995), and to teach different grades and age groups) almost certainly ensures a 'weeding out' of unsuitable teachers. Performance management as such focuses on *advice* from 'master teachers' or visiting supervisors but not formal assessment.

In a number of countries mentioned in this volume, teachers' career structures are formalised (New Zealand and the UK, Israel and Singapore for a considerable period, for example) in the sense that progression to a next stage depends upon some form of assessment.

This clearly has implications for pay since an increased salary will accompany a step up the career ladder, but the issue of performance related pay (PRP) is far more contentious. Bassey (1999) refers to extensive reviews of PRP in the USA, showing that there was little to encourage the belief that performance related pay can effectively improve teacher performance.

Others, such as Tomlinson (1992, 1999), have argued that relating pay to performance can be seen as an integral part of the practice of performance manage-ment, and indeed that if a culture is to exist within which performance management will flourish, then demonstrating that there are rewards for improved performance is central. Bassey (1999) is among those who believes that PRP works essentially against the collegial approach of the most effective schools, but above all that if a government, such as the UK, considers introducing PRP then research should be undertaken. At present, he argues, such an introduction is a gamble.

The essential argument here is about motivation. Whereas for Tomlinson (1999: 10): 'It is important for the motivation of highly effective teachers not to reward equally those who are contributing significantly less . . .' those who take the opposite view believe that the essential team elements at the heart of an effective school will be destroyed by rewards differentiation. It is possible of course for rewards to be applied to teams, not individuals. Even for those who advocate team performance appraisal (e.g. Draper 2000), the implications of PRP for this are as yet unclear.

If the above are likely to be constantly affecting the way teacher performance is managed and appraised, there are at the beginning of the twenty-first century other factors which also appear likely to affect it.

Increased emphasis on learning

The most significant change to affect the way performance in teaching can be managed and assessed is that which sees the new century as 'the century of learning' (Holland 1998), in the sense that the needs of the individual learner are seen as paramount and therefore ways of ensuring that meeting these needs is central becomes the key focus of educational leadership and management. Factors involved include:

- the increasing influence of the use of ICT;
- the increasing understanding through research of how the human brain works;
- understanding of the importance of learning styles;
- recognition of different kinds of intelligence and ability;
- acceptance of 'emotional intelligence' as important;
- realisation of many different factors (e.g. environmental) which can affect the learning effectiveness of the individual;
- awareness that learning occurs outside of school and all through life.

All these underline the emphasis that is increasingly placed on the need for effective schools to become learning schools or learning organisations, as opposed to the concept of schools in western societies up to at least the 1980s which would now be characterised as teaching organisations.

There are obviously huge implications for teachers and the nature of teaching in all this: the role and function of the teacher changes from transmitter of knowledge to manager of learning; but as Law and Glover (2000: 166) point out: 'Leading and managing learning is not, however, that simple. Teachers may be adept at creating and "managing" learning opportunities, but they cannot directly "lead" or "manage" others' learning'.

They quote Perrott (1982: 17): 'The best the teacher can do is induce students to engage in activities deemed instrumental in the covert psychological processes he hopes to affect . . . opportunities for slippage are enormous.'

If the emphasis is increasingly on the *indirect* impact that a teacher has upon learning, and teaching is essentially about creating opportunities for learning, how can 'good' teaching be fairly and accurately assessed? What about the teacher who creates endless opportunities for learning which, if taken, would result in effective learning outcomes, but whose students do not take them and the outcomes therefore are weak? The answer presumably lies in the good 'manager of learning' being able to motivate the learners to want to take these opportunities and certainly the ability to motivate is commonly recognised as one of the attributes of an effective teacher. This ability however does not lend itself easily to measurement.

Moreover, as schooling is re-organised to recognise many of the factors affecting individual learning, more learning situations away from the physical presence of the teacher seem certain to be seen as the norm (e.g. work at home and on line). Traditional modes of assessment involving observation will be irrelevant in these contexts.

Underpinning the whole of this growing emphasis on learning is of course the stress upon *learning as a process*. A new learning paradigm of Law and Glover (2000: 164) includes:

- focusing on 'learning how to learn';
- learning is a journey;
- inner experience valued;
- teacher learns too – from pupils;
- concern with individual potential and overcoming limitations.

It is impossible to assess the achievement of the person who has 'managed' the learner in this if the criteria for assessment is focused simply upon outcomes, i.e. on what was found at the end of the journey, not the journey itself.

Leadership more than management

John West-Burnham has dealt fully with this issue in an earlier chapter on the appraisal of school leaders in the UK. Its implications for appraising the performance of leaders at all levels, however, should be considered. Since leadership has certain invisible and individualistic elements compared with management, just as learning does compared with teaching, the appraisal of the performance of, for example, subject leaders in schools must have some of the same problems as that of school leaders. If a subject leader or head of a team of staff is responsible for the performance of that team, to what extent can his/her own performance be assessed as weaker because one member of the team has 'failed'? Has the leader let the team down, let the individual down or has the individual let the leader or team down? Obviously, situations are rarely as simple as these questions make them appear, but it does raise the whole issue of whether appraising team performance is viable, or whether it is preferable to individual appraisal. I will return to team performance appraisal later.

Closer integration with management practice in business and industry

As writers such as Bush (1999) have described, management in education drew heavily in its early days as a recognised discipline on theory and practice outside of education, especially from business and industry. Although education management has become a discipline in its own right, western governments have continued to draw on expertise from business and industry, assuming that education could benefit from this. Clearly in such matters as financial management, external relations, strategic planning, organisation theory, there may be much to be gained from such expertise. However, in the central purpose of schools – learning and teaching – there is no real equivalent. Nevertheless, this does not prevent government agencies from continuing to press the educational world ever closer to adopting perceived best practice from worlds outside education. In the field of performance management and its appraisal, this is likely to continue as governments continue to link education with economic performance (see Chapter 1). Valuable lessons may clearly be learned from sectors outside of education, as long as they are carefully adapted to the special circumstances in schools.

A review of performance management in business and industry in the UK (IiE 2000) raised some points of interest to schools such as:

- The term 'appraisal' is rarely used now because it implies looking back, whereas the emphasis in performance management is on the future.
- The introduction of any scheme must not be rushed and the process must be constantly fine-tuned by individual organisations.
- As far as pay is concerned, the emphasis is on performance-linked *progression* rather than performance related pay.
- The critical importance of individual organisational cultures.

For the purposes of this book, research was carried out in two non-educational sectors in the UK, accountancy (a professional activity privately operated) and local government (specifically, environmental services). An example of each is given here.

Whilst there is an established performance appraisal format in the accountancy profession, taking the form of an Annual Performance Review (APR), a number of firms, especially more recently established ones, appear to have become dissatisfied with this. Led by seniors who felt the APR approach which they themselves experienced to be seriously flawed, they have adopted new forms of appraisal which reflect the competitiveness between accountancy practices today. The APR system in their eyes is both inadequate, largely form-filling, and in any case, as quoted by one senior partner: 'The important parts of appraisal – the other side of the form – were never shown to you anyway. These would contain the real praise or criticism.'

One such firm, Harris Foster of Northampton, has adopted an approach centred on individual goal-setting within a team context. It operates through a weekly meeting with each member of the practice. The overall goals for the practice have been agreed by the senior staff, and each individual team member is allotted a number of specific goals for her or him to achieve within a specified period. The number of goals and the period are likely to be similar for each person, but the individual has the opportunity to negotiate amendments at the meeting; for example reducing the numbers of goals if one or more is known to be more difficult or requiring more time than the managers realised. The goals will involve a range from simple to complex. Within the agreed set of goals, the individual is free to determine priorities, allocate time. As long as the needs of the client are met to the appropriate standard of client satisfaction then the performance is deemed effective.

The system, according to the senior partner, achieves three things. First, and it must always be first, it meets the needs of clients – on whom the business depends. Second, it enables the effective performance of individuals to be accurately appraised, as there is a measurement which is both current and also enables progress over time to be seen. Third, it allows individual development to be considered, through the opportunity to negotiate what is achievable.

In local government services, operated in the UK through county, district and borough councils, systems for managing performance and its appraisal are well established, especially since local authorities operate in terms of having to follow national strategies and contribute towards national targets. Since local government operates a service, as with education, there are clear parallels. However, 'service delivery' targets in the field of environmental services can be quite specific by the time these are turned into specific targets for individual personnel. The practice of applying PRP varies from council to council, but in analysing its applicability to managing performance effectively, officers were clear that significant subjectivity remained when annual pay was discussed.

In one environmental service, for example, certain performance areas are not only specified but *weighted* individually. Thus 'specific projects' might have a weighting of 30 (of 100), whilst 'public relations' had one of 10. Performance in each of six differently weighted areas is graded on achievement from 5 (significantly exceeding target) to 1 (not approaching target). When the multiplication takes place, the idea is of course that achievement in what the organisation decrees are the most significant areas is the most rewardable. Nevertheless, the relationship between employee and manager remains crucial – as it should – leaving question marks over what happens when that relationship breaks down. As Longenecker and Ludwig (1995) found, ratings can be subject to manipulation and, as one environmental officer said, as far as PRP is concerned:

> One is just not going to jeopardise an employee's life in terms of their financial commitments even when their performance is only satisfactory. Targets therefore are negotiated which is as it should be anyway. But PRP doesn't

help with individuals – it muddies the waters because the targets may have to be scaled down to what is reasonable for the person's capability. That's fair in many ways, but replicated throughout an organisation it could have dangers.

Whether either of the two examples above could have implications for managing teacher performance in schools is something managers may wish to consider. For example, the weighting of different areas of a teacher's work has never been seriously addressed, except in managing recruitment and selection (Bell 1988; Middlewood 1997b) and would vary from country to country. In the UK and similar situations, where the teacher's role extends outside of the classroom into pastoral welfare, parental links, etc, such a procedure might be worth considering since the role of a Head of Year in a secondary school, for example, would have a higher weighting for pastoral work than a head of subject. It might also draw attention in a practical way to the importance of tutorial work of classroom teachers.

Central issues for managing effective performance and its appraisal

Given the variety of factors influencing teacher performance and its appraisal, its effective management depends upon the manager being aware of the ones in her or his particular situation and acting accordingly. This action will be underpinned by key principles, several of which have been indicated throughout the chapters in this book. Before considering these, I suggest that there are key questions that will remain central to any form of performance and appraisal which has to be managed.

Who is to appraise whom?

Whilst practice varies from country to country (headteachers, line mangers, external inspectors or supervisors) the issue itself is absolutely crucial. In some countries assessment is carried out by panels or committee, e.g. South Africa (Chapter 7) and China (Washington 1991), but this process is for cultural or political reasons and is unlikely to be followed on a widespread basis because of resource implications. Unless it is part of an established way of working, as in China, it would prove cumbersome to operate. What the manager needs to consider – allowing for any imposed regulations – may be that, since some form of dialogue between appraiser and appraisee remains at the heart of performance management and appraisal, it will work more effectively when:

- a positive relationship exists between the two, i.e. when trust exists that there will be no manipulation or hidden agenda, when appraisal for example is perceived as something that is done *with* you, not *to* you;

- the teacher believes that the manager/appraiser has a good understanding of what the teacher's specific job entails;
- the teacher believes that the appraiser has the capability to deliver on any issues identified which require resources;
- the teacher believes the appraiser understands any inhibiting factors within the school (Poster and Poster 1993).

What data should be collected and how?

Data should be both qualitative and quantitative. The latter will become easier to access because of increasingly sophisticated ICT; however, this also brings the danger of collecting too much data with consequent complications of appraisal. The qualitative data will become increasingly important so that the focus for the manager is on the source of the data, i.e. from whom will data be collected. Whomever this is, the significant issue is to ensure the collection process is open and transparent to the teacher. It is surely impossible, in the context of an increased emphasis on individual learning, for any form of appraisal of teacher performance not to include feedback from the students or pupils, as the people most affected by that performance. How that feedback is managed to the satisfaction of both the professional and the young person or child is a key task for the manager.

What linkage is there between performance appraisal and pay and promotion?

As more countries adopt career structures for the teaching profession which make publicly *clear* the rewards of moving on to a next stage, that part of the process is *clear* for managers. However, with these rewards being known, the pressure on managers of performance increase because of the limits on such rewards. Not everyone can go forward. There will be therefore intense scrutiny to ensure equity of treatment in the process. I have argued previously (Middlewood 1997a) that ensuring that everyone is seen to be treated equally is crucial to effective appraisal. (Also, see Edwards in Chapter 5). Without this openness to scrutiny, referred to by various writers in this volume, the ethos of trust within which effective performance management operates can never be created. Nationally imposed linkages in terms of rewards for reaching a certain stage will be clear but, as schools become more and more autonomous and managed according to individual circumstances, so the likelihood of special schemes in terms of rewards increases. Even more important here will be the need for managers to make such schemes open and transparent with criteria known to everyone.

Managing teacher performance and its appraisal – effective practice

Education, as with other services, is being monitored as never before and is likely to remain under considerable scrutiny for the foreseeable future. However, as responsibility for managing individual schools is devolved more and more, leaders and managers of those schools will surely need to balance reasonable external demands for organisational accountability with the understanding that effective management of people in the school is the key to effective individual and team performance. In this context, as rigorous self-evaluation of schools replaces for many schools the sometimes 'sledgehammer' (and expensive) approach of external inspection, so the management and assessment of individuals and teams will increasingly recognise the importance of self-review, negotiation, reflection and feedback. These are key to effective professional performance and make it likely that so-called 360 degree feedback will eventually become the norm in the most effective schools. What might the manager of teacher performance be aiming for and doing now to achieve those aims?

(1) Develop a culture of trust (See Chapter 9 for details) because only in such a context will the best performance be drawn from all staff. Good school leaders will have a strategic view, a vision, of what kind of school they wish theirs to be in the future. It may even be that that vision is one of a school with such a culture that no appraisal is needed at all, as Deming argued. In terms of national requirements, this may be some way off!

Within an ethos of trust, the sense of ownership that everyone feels about management processes and innovations is central. This ownership extends from the leaders to staff performing the most humble of tasks. Wilson's (1999) research into New Zealand principals' perceptions of their own appraisal scheme found that in considering the current instrument as inappropriate for both accountability and their development, they above all wished to remain 'in control of' the process.

(2) Whatever the plans from national level, 'reinvent' them at school level to meet the needs of the individual school. Ensure that everything is located in what you as a manager see as good employer practice and ensure that in line with agreed and challenging school goals, you are enabling each individual and team to see clearly 'what's in it for them', so that they can understand that the school is offering its staff as much as it asks from them (Sweetman 2000).

(3) Show respect for individuals by being open about what is asked, how the scheme works *but* also emphasising confidentiality where that is relevant. There are some aspects of human existence which may affect performance – which are not the business of employers/managers, unless the teacher employee wishes them to be.

(4) Ensure equity of treatment (see above)

(5) In the new context of a greater emphasis on learning, be continually aware of the changing nature of what being a teacher means. This will be constantly shifting. Some at least of the forecasts of Dalin and Rust (1996: 145):

'The distinction between student and teacher will become blurred.'
'Teachers and students will engage in mutual learning activities, in activities such as co-operative learning.'
'The teaching profession will consist of many people who function as full-time professionals and be active their entire working life.'
'They will be expected to stimulate the curiosity of each child . . .'

are almost certain to become a reality. In this context, managers must ensure that their understanding of teacher performance and therefore of its appraisal must focus on process as much as, and probably more than, outcome. Ways must be found to acknowledge the teacher who raises student self-esteem and motivation and leaves that student stimulated to learn more, including beyond schooling. Data for appraising performance must be qualitative as much as, probably even more than, quantitative.

An example might be of the growing emphasis on emotional intelligence in reviewing leadership and management. If such 'competences' as:

- trustworthiness
- conscientiousness
- conflict management
- empathy

are to be seen as key to effectiveness, they must necessarily be part of any leader's or manager's performance appraisal. Only the use of qualitative data will make this possible.

(6) Develop the use of 360 degree feedback. The manager who begins to address the issue of collecting qualitative data (above) from an increasing range of relevant sources may be on the way to this process. Its 'power for genuinely evaluating individual performance and supporting development' (Tomlinson 2000) is likely to be recognised as feedback from students and parents becomes more widely accepted. It also has considerable possibilities of influencing aspects of teacher attitude more strongly than judgement from a line manager where comments on a teacher's classroom attitude may simply cause stress by being taken as personal criticism of personality. The ethos of trust within which teachers can accept such feedback from students and parents as positive may not come quickly in some areas, but this kind of feedback *will* come in effective schools.

(7) Apply team appraisal. Given the many changes referred to in this book, a movement to a much greater emphasis on appraising the performance of teams of teachers rather than individuals seems inevitable. Collaborative cultures where teachers develop powerful professional relationships have been recognised as features of effective and improving schools and Reynolds and Farrell (1996) concluded that collaborative working was a very important contributor to the high educational achievements in countries of the Pacific rim.

Team performance appraisal can be integrated more easily into the management of the school, can permeate the school more easily and of course can be less expensive in terms of time. Individual teachers can be motivated and less threatened (Chapter 9) if, for example, personal 'results' fall below expectations. However, individual personal action or development plans can be developed from this process which fits comfortably with the notion of individual teachers' professional career portfolios (Draper 2000), a concept likely to spread in various countries. Whether the practice would move to the point where regular meetings set regular team and individual goals (such as in the accountancy practice mentioned earlier) is impossible to say at present. It would require as a minimum some restructuring of schools as organisations – seen as essential and desirable of course by many in order for them to be able to meet the needs of the twenty-first century.

These seven suggestions do not offer a 'recipe' for effective management of performance and its appraisal. However, in the world of education and of globalisation, the effective manager will be aware of the need to manage both the immediate situation in her or his school and the envisaged long-term situation. If the latter is not addressed, events will quickly take the decision for that manager.

References

Bassey, M. (1999) 'Performance related pay for teachers; research is needed', *Professional Development Today* 2(3): 15–28.

Bell, L. (1988) *Management Skills in Primary Schools*, London: Routledge.

Bush, T. (1998) 'Organisational culture and strategic management', in D. Middlewood and J. Lumby (eds) *Strategic Management in Schools and Colleges*, London: Paul Chapman.

Bush T. (1999) 'Introduction: Setting the scene', in T. Bush, L. Bell, R. Bolam, R. Glatter and P. Ribbins (eds) *Educational Management: Redefining Theory, Policy and Practice*, London: Paul Chapman.

Cardno, C. and Piggot-Irvine, E. (1997) *Effective Performance Appraisal*, Auckland: Addison Wesley Longman.

Dalin, P. and Rust, V. (1996) *Towards Schooling for the Twenty-First Century*, London: Cassell.

Draper, I. (2000) 'From appraisal to performance management', in *Professional Development Today* 3(2): 11–21.

Erculj, J. (2000) *Appraisal in Slovenia – The Headteachers' Burden?* Paper specially commissioned for this volume (unpublished).

Hellawell, D. (1997) 'Appraisal for primary heads', *Professional Development Today* 1(1): 29–40.

Holland, G. (1998) 'Learning in the twenty first century', *New Childhood* 13(1): 4–5.

Ifanti, A. (1995) 'Policy making, politics and administration in education in Greece', *Educational Management and Administration* 23(4): 217–78.

Industry in Education (2000) *Milestone or Millstone? Performance Management in Schools: Reflections on the experiences of industry*, Radlett: IiE.

Law, S. and Glover, D. (2000) *Educational Leadership and Learning*, Buckingham: Open University Press.

Lewis, C. (1995) *Educating, Hearts and Minds: Reflections on Japanese Pre-School and Elementary Education*, New York: Cambridge University Press.

Longenecker, G. and Ludwig, D. (1995) 'Ethical dilemmas in performance appraisal revisited', in J. Holloway, J. Lewis and G. Mallory *Performance Measurement and Evaluation*, London: Sage.

Middlewood, D. (1997a) 'Managing appraisal', in T. Bush and D. Middlewood (eds) *Managing People in Education*, London: Paul Chapman.

Middlewood, D. (1997b) 'Managing recruitment and selection', in T. Bush and D. Middlewood (eds) *Managing People in Education*, London: Paul Chapman.

Ministry of Education (Greece) (1997) *Regulations for Teacher Employment*, Athens. (Translated into English by A. Sarris and S. Sarris).

Mortimore, P. (1997) 'Can effective schools compensate for society?', in A. Halsey, H. Lauder, P. Brown and A. Wells (eds) *Education: Culture, Economy, Society*, Oxford: Oxford University Press.

Perrott, E. (1982) *Effective Teaching*, London: Longman.

Poster, C. and Poster, D. (1993) *Teacher Appraisal: Training and Implementation*, London: Routledge.

Reynolds, D. and Farrell, S. (1996) *Worlds Apart: A Review of International Surveys of Educational Achievement Including England*, London: HMSO.

Sweetman, J. (2000) *Curriculum-Confidential 10*, Westley, Suffolk: Courseware Publications.

Tomlinson, H. (1992) *Performance Related Pay in Education*, London: Routledge.

Tomlinson, H. (1999) 'Performance management and performance measurement', *Professional Development Today* 3(1): 7–12.

Tomlinson, H. (2000) '360 degree feedback – how does it work?', *Professional Development Today* 3(2): 93–8.

Washington, K. (1991) 'School administration in China: A look at the principal's role', *International Journal of Educational Management* 2: 4–5.

Wilson, R. (1999) 'Investigation into the appraisal process of principals of New Zealand schools', unpublished MBA dissertation, University of Leicester.

Index